Funding Public Schools

STUDIES IN GOVERNMENT
AND PUBLIC POLICY

Funding Public Schools

Politics and Policies

Kenneth K. Wong

 University Press of Kansas

Published by the University Press of Kansas (Lawrence, Kansas 66049),
which was organized by the Kansas Board of Regents and is operated and
funded by Emporia State University, Fort Hays State University, Kansas State
University, Pittsburg State University, the University of Kansas, and Wichita
State University

Library of Congress Cataloging-in-Publication Data

Wong, Kenneth K., 1955–
    Funding public schools : politics and policies / Kenneth K. Wong.
      p. cm. — (Studies in government and public policy)
    Includes bibliographical references (p.   ) and index.
    ISBN 0-7006-0987-3 (cloth : alk. paper). — ISBN 0-7006-0988-1
(pbk. : alk. paper)
     1. Education—United States—Finance. 2. Politics and education—
United States. 3. Education and state—United States. I. Title.
II. Series.
LB2825.W56   1999
379.73—dc21   99-30548

British Library Cataloguing in Publication Data is available

Printed in the United States of America

10 9 8 7 6 5 4 3 2 1

To Ellen

Contents

Preface

This book examines the role of politics in funding our public schools. In arguing that politics matters in allocating school resources, I aim to fill a conceptual imbalance in the current literature. For too long, the field of school finance has been dominated by two analytical traditions: one focuses on cost efficiency; the other highlights the spending disparity between wealthy and poor districts. In my view, both of these perspectives are narrowly conceived.

Primarily concerned about cost efficiency, economic and other policy analysts, who focus on the school's production function, generally conclude that dollars do not significantly contribute to better student performance. Yet in almost all these studies, the analysts do not differentiate the sources of school revenues, thereby failing to specify the effects of different kinds of resources allocated at different levels of government. Knowing that dollars do not always produce higher test scores does not tell us which governmental programs at what level of the multilayered school policy organization are the least effective.

At the same time, attorneys and advocates of funding reform, seeing school finance as a constitutional rights issue, provide extensive evidence of the spending gap between the haves and the have-nots. This literature, which is based almost entirely on interdistrict differences in individual states, suggests a strong correlation between local taxable wealth and school spending. From this perspective, unequal spending reduces schooling quality and undermines equal educational opportunity in poor communities. This kind of evaluation offers the basis for litigation that challenges the constitutionality of the educational finance systems in dozens of states. Although this research accurately relates school quality to its most immediate cause, that is, the district's revenue-raising capacity, most analysts in this tradition have paid little attention to the way political constraints can dampen the high expectations for reform. Institutional stalemate and the lack of political will to act often explain legislative deadlock in reducing funding inequity.

In short, the two dominant perspectives tend to narrow the research agenda to the relationship between school spending and educational quality, including student outcomes. These studies have largely overlooked the importance of broader political and institutional forces that shape resource allocation. To develop a more complete understanding of the promises and the limits of educational reform efforts, we need to recognize the role of politics in the structural context of federalism and the policymaking process at each level of government.

In this book, I define how politics has sustained various types of decision rules that affect the allocation of resources at the federal, state, and local levels. Although these rules have been remarkably stable over the past twenty to thirty years, they have often worked at cross-purposes. Over time, layers of allocative practices have contributed to policy fragmentation that constrains teaching and learning in schools with the greatest needs. Findings from this book provide an empirical basis for policymakers to redesign strategies to use resources more effectively toward the goal of raising academic standards.

This research project would not have been completed had I not received generous support from various sources. I formulated the project's initial ideas on state politics in funding education during 1989–1990 when I was awarded a Spencer postdoctoral fellowship by the National Academy of Education. The fellowship enabled me to take a one-year leave of absence from teaching and gave me the time to gather original data from a sample of states, districts, and schools. This research on state politics received further support from the Spencer Foundation, the Benton Center in the Department of Education at the University of Chicago, the Institute for Poverty Research at the University of Wisconsin, Madison, and the small grant program in the Division of Social Sciences at the University of Chicago. Further, my research on local educational politics and reform policy was supported by the Social Science Research Council and the Culpeper Foundation. The Joyce Foundation generously provided two major grants for my study of school reform in Chicago. Finally, I am grateful to the National Center on Education in the Inner Cities and the mid-Atlantic region's Laboratory for Student Success at Temple University for their continuing interest in my research on the design and implementation of federal policy, particularly the Title I (compensatory education) program.

Over the course of conducting this study, I was fortunate to have the opportunity to interact with and learn from a group of first-rate interdisciplinary colleagues in the Department of Education at the University of Chicago. At Chicago, I would particularly like to thank Robert Dreeben and Terry N. Clark for providing extensive comments on draft chapters of the book. Their insights on organizational politics and political culture have challenged me to reassess my earlier arguments. I also benefited from numerous conversations with Dan Lortie, Paul Peterson, Gary Orfield, Herbert Walberg, Margaret Wang, Philip Jackson, Charles Bidwell, Tom James, Jim Cibulka, Robert Crowson, Clarence Stone, Richard Venezky, Laurence Lynn, Robert Michael, J. Mark Hansen, Warren Chapman, the late J. David Greenstone, and the late Robert Jewell. Mike Kirst, Linda Darling-Hammond, and Arthur Wise also provided helpful comments. Given the fairly extensive data collection efforts, this research would not have been fully implemented without my many hardworking graduate student assistants. I would like to thank my cross-disciplinary team of current and former assistants, particularly Dorothea Anagnostopolous, Pushpam Jain, Susan Flinspach, Gail Sunderman, Jaek Yung Lee, William McKersie, Fausto Ramos Gomez, Stacey Rutledge, Mark Moulton, and Jason Ur. They responded to every one of my deadlines without a word of complaint. Finally, I greatly appreciate the efforts by Fred Woodward and his staff at the University Press of Kansas.

Over the years, my family has been a constant and unwavering source of support for not only this book project but also the many professional challenges I faced. I am deeply grateful to my wife, Michelle, for her many years of cheerful encouragement. When I was tempted to give up on this project on more than one occasion, Michelle persuaded me to stay on. Drawing on her experience with the legislative process and her insights into financial management, Michelle challenged me to reflect on my basic analytical assumptions. Finally, my daily conversations with our daughter, Ellen, have kept me in touch with the reality of school life. Her fifth-grader's insights into how school "really" works often challenge my intellectual tendency to fit everything neatly into conceptual boxes. Through her spirited depictions of the many facets of school life, Ellen has enriched my understanding of the human dimensions of educational issues.

Funding Public Schools

1
Politics of Allocating Resources in Schools

In the 1997 state of the union message that marked the beginning of his second term, President Bill Clinton announced that his priority for the next four years was "to ensure that all Americans have the best education in the world." He asked Congress and the American people to work together to meet several goals: "every eight-year-old must be able to log on to the Internet, every eighteen-year-old must be able to go to college, and every adult American must be able to keep on learning for a lifetime." Framing educational improvement as a national crusade, President Clinton envisioned a nation in the twenty-first century in which every student would have the opportunity to learn new skills, develop academic competence, and go to college.

Clinton's national educational crusade is the culmination of fifteen years of local, state, and federal efforts to improve student performance in public schools. Beginning with the 1983 publication of the federal report *A Nation at Risk,* improving the overall performance of all students became the lead issue in educational reform. The report, endorsed by the Reagan administration, issued a national warning that "the educational foundations of our society are presently being eroded by a rising tide of mediocrity that threatens our very future as a nation and a people."[1] In response, the federal government, states, and districts sharpened their focus on student performance, developed curricular standards, and strengthened professional development. Improvement in student performance was clearly on the national agenda when President George Bush convened the first educational summit with governors from all fifty states. As a former governor who advocated educational reform, Clinton pushed forward legislation on eight national educational goals during his first year in office.

To be sure, the political rhetoric about maintaining the best education in the world is ahead of policy details. A major challenge is to allocate resources

1

more effectively to produce better student performance. This is, however, not an easy task. According to a 1997 report on the status of educational improvement in the fifty states, resource allocation was identified as a key area in which substantial reform is generally lacking.[2] If the ambitious goal of educational excellence is to succeed, resource allocation has to be given undivided attention by policymakers. Although the level of resources dominates the agenda of many reformers, equally important is how resources are used, an issue that ought to receive great attention in an era of governmental budget constraints. School reformers need to reexamine the guiding principles that shape the use of educational resources. Although the notion of improving school performance is widely accepted by political leaders and the general public, the way we allocate resources to schools has remained basically unchanged for the last twenty to thirty years. This remarkable stability in allocative practices calls for a more systematic examination of the details of the rules and the politics that sustain these practices.

This book focuses on the key decision rules that govern resource allocation in public elementary and secondary schools.[3] This study is guided by several policy questions. What are the decision rules for distributing resources in public education? How do these rules come about? What role does politics play in maintaining the dominant rules of the allocative game? Are there policy differences among the federal, state, and local governments? In what ways do these policies operate at cross-purposes? What are their effects on equal educational opportunities? Are they aligned in ways to promote better student outcomes? To address these issues, I conducted an extensive examination of the allocative politics at each level of the government over the past twenty to thirty years. I employed a variety of research strategies, including empirical analysis of funding trends, comparative case studies of policymaking in political institutions, in-depth interviews with policymakers and practitioners, observation of classroom activities, and synthesis of documentary sources on resource allocation.

In this introductory chapter, I briefly review the contributions made by economic and political studies of resource allocation in education and, based on a synthesis of this rich literature, develop a typology of five major allocative rules in public education:

1. Social targeting that originates from the federal government
2. Various institutional forces that shift greater fiscal responsibility to the state
3. State-level attempts to even up spending in poor districts
4. Social equity at the state level
5. Pressure on local school boards to assign an equal number of students to each teacher

These themes provide the structure for the rest of the book.

THE NEED FOR REFORM: EFFICIENCY AND FUNCTIONAL PERSPECTIVES

This study aims to sort out the ways allocative decisions are shaped by political circumstances and governance arrangements in our complex, multilayered educational policy system. In differentiating the roles of the federal, state, and local governments, I specify the connection between politics and policy decisions, thus filling a gap in the understanding of resource allocation in public education. In the current literature, two approaches to understanding resource allocation are dominant. Both argue for a need to alter existing arrangements to attain greater efficiency and better outcomes. Yet neither places proper emphasis on the politics of allocation. Whereas the "efficiency perspective" depicts schools as lacking fiscal discipline, the "functional perspective" identifies organizational slack and functional duplication among all three levels of government as the key problems. Clearly, there is a need to reconsider the proper role of government in providing educational services. In this section, I briefly discuss the strengths and limitations of these two approaches. I then build on these analytical lenses to propose a typology for understanding allocative politics in education.

Enhancing Cost Efficiency in Schools

After the publication of *A Nation at Risk* in 1983, dozens of national commissions issued reports that pointed to employers' frustration with workers who had not been properly trained by the public schools. Parents, too, felt that their children were not getting the education they needed and deserved. Concerned about the nation's poor academic ranking internationally, national policymakers and various professional associations focused on raising standards in key subject areas, enhancing the knowledge base in teaching, and strengthening professional development. It was in this context of public discontent with education that a group of well-known economists gathered to develop an economic agenda for educational reform in the early 1990s. In addition to panel organizers Eric Hanushek and Dean Jamison, panel members were Charles Benson, Richard Freeman, Henry Levin, Rebecca Maynard, Richard Murnane, Steven Rivkin, Richard Sabot, Lewis Solmon, Anita Summers, Finis Welch, and Barbara Wolfe. The Hanushek report, as it is commonly referred to, filled several gaps in the education policy literature. It made a cogent argument about school reform from the perspective of economic science. As the report pointed out, "Economic ideas have been notably, and most unfortunately, absent from plans for reform."[4] These economists argued that the benefits produced do not match the long-term increases in spending. While cost per pupil in real dollar terms has grown almost 3.5 percent annually, student performance has not shown any significant progress in the past three decades.[5] Hanushek wrote, "Little systematic relationship has been found between school resources and student performance."[6] In illuminating the imbalance between escalating costs and performance outcomes, the report not only directed its concern at inefficiency but also offered an alternative system, one that monitors and rewards efforts that produce better student performance. Finally, the arguments were grounded in a rich literature on educational reform, resource allocation, and school finance from the past thirty years.

This economic perspective could not have been more timely, as policymakers and the public are keenly concerned about controlling costs. It also has the advantage of not being the first major study to advocate replacing the current system with school choice and other performance-driven systems; *Politics, Markets, and America's Schools* heightened the debate about the search for solutions to the nation's educational problems.[7] The Hanushek report conveyed a sense of urgency about the need for school reform, yet it did not overlook the many challenges involved in putting together an alternative system.

To reverse the trend of "throwing money at schools" (to use Hanushek's term), the report urged educators to adopt three fundamental economic principles. The order of the principles is revealing. At the top of the list is cost efficiency; that is, educational programs must be assessed in terms of costs and benefits. Costly programs that produce limited academic gains would be eliminated. Examples of programs that ought to be critically reassessed include smaller class size, higher overall salary levels for teachers without consideration of supply and demand in particular subject areas, and teacher education programs. But the central argument goes beyond simply cutting programs. Hanushek is critical of the dominant practice in the current system, which does not pay sufficient attention to cost efficiency. As the report observed, "Schools historically have been averse to evaluating programs and to analyzing the cost-effectiveness of different policies."[8]

The second principle is to reward actions that improve student performance. This can occur in two ways. The less effective option is to alter the performance incentives for teachers and administrators without restructuring the existing administrative structure. Examples include privatization of schools or services, charter schools, merit pay, and school-based management. The more effective way is to rely on consumer choice in rewarding and punishing service suppliers in a marketlike system. Examples range from magnet schools and interdistrict choice among public schools to tuition tax credits and vouchers that involve the nonpublic sector. Effective implementation of this principle, however, depends on whether clear goals and measures of progress toward goals can be fully developed. Unfortunately, as the report recognized, "Nobody knows what incentives work effectively in the varied settings of the nation's schools."[9] Evidence of a workable assessment-reward framework is virtually absent at present. Despite the many uncertainties, the Hanushek report cited with confidence the potential merits of a performance assessment system that measures the value-added contributions of teachers and schools. This conviction is understandable, as the new reward system depends on a well-functioning monitoring and assessment system.

Third on the list is continuous organizational learning and adaptation. The challenge is to put in place a system that is performance and incentive driven, which would alter existing functions and authority among key players in public education. According to the Hanushek report, teachers entering the new systems would sign on to contractual terms that entail "fewer tenure guarantees, more risks, and greater flexibility and rewards."[10] State governments would depart from their traditional regulatory role. They would define performance standards and encourage schools and districts to experiment with new incentive systems. In carrying out responsibilities to promote equality of opportunity, the federal government would incorporate performance evaluation and incentives into existing programs. Schools districts would enjoy autonomy from state regulations in setting their curricula and developing their management priorities. At the district level, business would be more directly involved in defining the academic skills needed for employment. And the list goes on and on.

The report's contributions notwithstanding, let me briefly mention three shortcomings. First, in challenging educators to focus on cost efficiency and test performance, it conveys the message that school dollars have purchased few measurable benefits for children. Hanushek's key argument is that additional money is not the solution. As he summarizes, "Reform will come more assuredly from an improved decision process that focuses attention on student performance than from further attempts to overwhelm the problems of schools with resources."[11] In my view, this misconception is based on a narrow definition of school accountability that relies on aggregate measures of spending and test scores. If one broadens the concept of efficiency to include societal needs and to differentiate the functions performed by various levels of the system, as I have done in this book, school dollars are actually employed to combat various forms of inequity that have an impact on student performance. For example, the federal government has directed most of its education spending to counter the inequity that arises from class, linguistic, cultural, and racial cleavages; the states have tried to equalize funding disparity among districts; and districts and schools at the local level have ensured that a comparable number of students (regardless of social and political differences) is assigned to each teacher. Indeed, funding for education is critical to produce the societal good of equal schooling opportunity, particularly in the current era of major sociodemographic changes. In other words, dollars spent can be seen as the amount of effort made to improve educational opportunity for all.

Further, missing in the Hanushek report is any mention of the complicated political forces that operate in our school system. To be practical, reform plans must come to terms with the political reality, an issue that is not systematically considered by most economists. Indeed, teaching and learning are substantively shaped by decisions about resource allocation made at various policy levels beyond the reach of educators. For example, collective bargaining agreements between school boards and unions define work rules, salaries, and other rewards and incentives for school employees. In many districts, the mayor selects the school board members, who prioritize resource allocation. Partisan contention in the state capital often determines the level of state funding and allocation for specific programs. Politics permeates the educational system, and thus the distribution of school resources. The challenge for reformers, then, is to maintain a political coalition that supports new initiatives.

Finally, the efficiency perspective does not focus on policies to strengthen the professional skills of the 2.5 million teachers, as well as those of principals and administrators, so that they could be more effective in producing learners in the classroom. Even if an incentive system is put in place, the question remains, Can teachers provide effective instruction systemwide? To address this fundamental issue, one must carefully consider the interplay among the nature of the teaching profession, the knowledge base in teaching, and various combinations of curricular and instructional organization. In sum, the Hanushek report was a major step toward educational reform. However, a more complete understanding of productivity and efficiency needs to incorporate broader political and social forces, in addition to economic ones.

Reallocating Functional Responsibility

The "functional" argument for reform is grounded in our federalist structure. All three levels of the government play a part in public education. The U.S. constitutional framework enables the states to exercise authority over public education. The state government defines the role of the local school board, establishes standards in delivering services, institutes teacher certification provisions, and restricts the taxing and spending practices of districts. State authority, however, does not preclude federal and local influence over educational issues. For example, educational funding comes from all three governmental sources. As Table 1.1 shows, a student in public schools was allocated, on average, $5,988 in constant dollars in 1995. The rate of growth seems to have slowed in recent years. Increases in per pupil spending were 49 percent and 73 percent in the 1950s and 1960s, respectively; spending grew by 20 percent in the 1970s and about 35 percent during the 1980s. In the early 1990s, there was only a modest increase in per student spending. In 1995, local sources made up 46.4 percent of the total funding, and states provided 46.8 percent. The federal government remained a distant fiscal partner. These fiscal patterns are summarized in Figure 1.1.

Although the federal government has been reluctant to be involved in regular school programs, it has been the primary promoter of equal educational opportunity since the Great Society era.[12] While districts are bound by a state-defined school code in providing services to children, local school boards develop the curriculum, negotiate union contracts, and draw up student attendance zones. Consequently, the structural division of control has created many systems of public education. There are clearly fifty state systems, each of which is embedded in the particular constitutional framework and political culture of the state. Within each

Table 1.1. Per Pupil Expenditures and Sources of Revenue in Public Schools,
1951–52 to 1994–95

| | PER PUPIL CURRENT EXPENDITURE | | | SOURCE OF REVENUE | | |
	Unadjusted Dollars	Constant 1995 Dollars	% Increase over Previous Period	Federal (%)	State (%)	Local (%)
1951–52	246	1,408	—	3.5	38.6	57.9
1961–62	419	2,097	49	4.3	38.7	56.9
1971–72	990	3,617	73	8.9	38.3	52.8
1981–82	2,726	4,356	20	7.4	47.6	45.0
1991–92	5,421	5,900	35	6.6	46.4	47.0
1994–95	5,988	5,988	2	6.8	46.8	46.4

Source: Tables 158 and 169 in *Digest of Education Statistics,* National Center for Education Statistics, www.nces.ed.gov, November 1998.

state, there are also wide variations in the resource base available to schools at the local level.

This seemingly high degree of overlap calls for institutional alternatives to the division of functions between the federal government and the states. Two options have been proposed in light of anticipated budgetary constraints. One proposal for the redesign of federalism comes from Alice Rivlin, former director of the Economics Studies Program at the Brookings Institution. Seeing the growing federal deficit as a threat to the long-term economic well-being of American citizens, Rivlin recommended dividing the job between the federal and state governments.[13] Her plan would reduce the size of the federal government by devolving to the states virtually all the functions that constitute human capital investment and infrastructural improvement. States would assume responsibility in elemen-

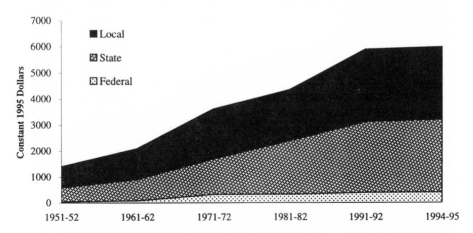

Figure 1.1. Per pupil expenditures in public schools by revenue source. (Tables 158 and 169 in *Digest of Education Statistics,* National Center for Education Statistics, www.nces.ed.gov, November 1998)

tary and secondary education, job training, economic and community development, housing, highways and transportation, social services, and pollution control programs. These programs, according to Rivlin, would enable the states to
"take charge of accomplishing a productivity agenda of reforms designed to revitalize the economy and raise incomes."[14] The devolution would allow the federal
government to balance the budget. Equally important, the smaller federal government would focus on the most costly redistributive services. It would be in
charge of the nation's health financing system, with the objectives of containing
costs and providing universal health coverage. Social Security would remain a
federal responsibility. Aid to Families with Dependent Children (AFDC) would
continue as a joint state-federal function. In Rivlin's view, states have both the
administrative capacity and the financial base to take over additional functions,
while the federal government is burdened with a growing deficit. Consequently,
the federal role has to be selectively redistributive. In other words, states would
have complete authority over educational priorities, ranging from special education to regular instructional services.

Its sound economic rationale notwithstanding, Rivlin's proposal to divide the
job has several shortcomings. First, by making the states responsible for promoting
economic growth, the federal government escalates interstate competition over
capital, labor, and other resources. In the long run, the economic gap between states
may worsen. Since educational resources are heavily dependent on state and local
revenues, states that are less economically competitive are likely to lag behind in
their support for schools. Second, states pursuing a pro-growth strategy are likely
to leave behind those who are hard (and costly) to train, particularly in times of a
slack labor market. Consequently, equal educational opportunities may be undermined. Third, competition over the allocation of state resources will intensify as
interest groups target the state capital. Under these circumstances, disadvantaged
groups are likely to be the losers.

A second proposal comes from Paul Peterson, a political scientist at Harvard,
who argues that different levels of the government should focus on those functions they are good at.[15] Although this division would not eradicate social inequality, attempts to alter existing functional allocation in our federalism would exact
a price that the American public ought not to pay. Specifically, Peterson points
out that the national government should "continue to assume increasing responsibility for financing and setting the standards for redistributive policy."[16] Health
care, welfare assistance, and Social Security are prime examples of federal redistributive functions. However, there is a limit to the federal role. Peterson argues
strongly against federal intervention in big-city problems beyond what federal
programs can offer at the current budget level. Instead, big cities are expected to
become fiscally disciplined and should not "expect another level of government
to do the job for them."[17] To regain fiscal solvency and to improve service quality, cities are urged to enhance cost efficiency by involving the private sector in
delivering education and other services. From Peterson's perspective, problems

in our declining urban schools will be solved neither by allocating more federal dollars nor by shifting responsibilities to another level of government. Rather, alternative schooling arrangements, such as choice in the private sector, offer the most promising solution.

Clearly, Peterson's focus on cost efficiency as a way to solve seemingly intractable urban problems is consistent with the new reality of fiscal constraint. In the current climate of public skepticism about governmental effectiveness, middle-class voters are not likely to support programs that allocate additional dollars to address urban problems. A halt to expansion of the federal grants-in-aid system may force cities and their schools to look for innovative ways to improve service quality. However, federal disengagement from urban problems tends to widen the economic and political gap between cities and their suburbs. Indeed, cities may become more isolated economically as well as politically. In the long run, if federal disengagement is carried to its logical conclusion, many old industrialized cities will be abandoned by businesses and by their most productive taxpaying residents. Under these circumstances, it would be impossible to enhance the organizational capacity of such existing institutions as schools and neighborhoods.

A DIFFERENTIATED PERSPECTIVE ON ALLOCATIONAL POLITICS

A synthesis of both the efficiency and the functional perspectives is useful in analyzing the politics of allocation in education. Building on these perspectives, this study aims to specify the types of allocative decisions, identify their political origins, and assess their impacts on issues related to equity and excellence. From the efficiency approach, one recognizes how incentives and sanctions can shape organizational performance. From the functional view, one appreciates the benefits and the costs associated with the division of governmental roles in our federal system. Particularly important in education is the role of the states and how their funds are distributed. Building on these perspectives, I specify the relationship between decision rules and the political structure and I identify five major types of decision rules that have been sustained by political forces over the last twenty to thirty years. Together, these rules govern the way resources are allocated in our educational policy system. They shape our thinking and guide our practices at all levels of government. First I define each of these decision rules, and then I discuss the political nature of the policy challenge for school reformers trying to promote better performance for all students.

1. Social Targeting at the Federal Level

Many governmental resources are distributed to ameliorate social inequality. Social inequality is often associated with racial and income stratification, as well as linguistic and cultural differences in many big-city school systems. Since 1970, the

racial composition of large school systems has changed significantly. Between 1971 and 1986, the white, non-Hispanic enrollment in nineteen large central-city school systems fell from 44 to 22 percent. Hispanic enrollment doubled from 12 to 24 percent, and black enrollment increased from 43 to 48 percent.[18] In Chicago, for example, only 12 percent of elementary students were white in 1990. Further, there is a high concentration of poor children in central-city school systems. By 1990, one-third of the children in the nation's big cities fell below the poverty level. Poverty figures were 47 percent in Detroit, 43 percent in Atlanta, 38 percent in Milwaukee, 34 percent in Chicago, and 31 percent in Minneapolis.[19] Clearly, children from poor and minority backgrounds constitute a major challenge to urban schools. As Figure 1.2 shows, when compared with the nation as a whole, the seventy-five largest cities have more poor children, more minority children, and more children who live in extremely impoverished neighborhoods.

To promote equal opportunity, the federal government has played an active role in providing supplemental services to disadvantaged students, a major focus of chapter 2. Through its grants-in-aid system, the federal government has financed compensatory education, special education, the free and reduced-price school lunch program, and bilingual instruction. In the 1990s, about six out of every ten federal dollars were directed at social equity. Chapter 2 examines the politics and implementation of federal legislation to promote socially redistributive policy in

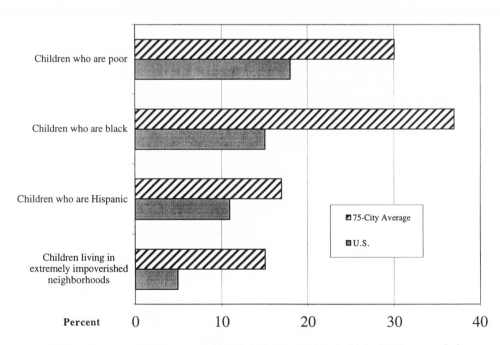

Figure 1.2. Poverty and race among children in U.S. cities and in the United States as a whole. (Compiled from data reported in *Education Week* 17, no. 17, January 8, 1998, p. 62)

education. Three aspects of the allocative process can be distinguished. First, the national legislative process decides on policy objectives and appropriates funds to states and localities. Second, the implementation process occurs when states and localities adapt national policy objectives to their own circumstances. Third, at the school and classroom level, federal resources provide supplemental instruction for at-risk students. Given our decentralized educational system, the federal government faces the challenge of a widening gap between inner-city schools and their suburban counterparts. My analysis suggests that the federal government can play a more active role in strengthening the organizational capacity of schools in low-income neighborhoods.

2. Increased State Fiscal Responsibility

Over the last thirty years, state governments have assumed a major role in financing public education. Equally significant is the trend of local governments substantially reducing their contributions to public schools. In 1964, 39 percent of school revenues came from the states, and 56 percent came from local sources. Two decades later, the state share exceeded the local share. Since the early 1980s, the state has maintained a dominant role in financing education. The trend toward greater state responsibility has been driven by court rulings to address funding inequity, taxpayers' dissatisfaction with the local property tax burden, and interest-group politics.

To be sure, there are variations among states in terms of their fiscal role. Chapter 3 looks at the importance of state aid and examines interstate variation over time. At issue is whether there is an empirical basis for the widely accepted view that state governments have shifted from a "parity" status (providing less than 50 percent) to a "dominating" role (providing more than 50 percent) in school financing. If such a trend were true, interstate variation in the level of support would be expected to diminish over time. Based on a state-by-state analysis covering 1959 to 1996, I classified all fifty states into several distinct fiscal patterns. During the thirty-eight-year period, only fourteen states (including Iowa and California) actually followed the parity to dominance path. Ten states (including Hawaii and Washington) had a dominating role even before the late 1950s and maintained it. Four states shifted from dominance to parity during this period. The remaining twenty-two states (including New Hampshire and New York) virtually always stayed below the 50 percent support level, thereby maintaining a parity status over the years. These patterns are associated with several political differences among states.

3. Leveling-Up Spending in Poor Districts

In states across the nation, there are interdistrict differences in fiscal capacity caused by the disparity in taxable wealth. Earlier works showed that a district with high assessed valuation was able to tax at a lower rate and yet produce a high level of per student spending.[20] Using 1959–60 funding data on classroom units in all fifty states, Wise found that "seventeen states have ratios between high and low expenditure classroom units [within state] exceeding 4 to 1, seven of these having ratios of at least 6 to 1."[21] Thirty years later, some analysts found that interdistrict spending disparity had worsened. According to Kozol, "[A]ny high school class of 30 children in Chicago [in 1989] received approximately $90,000 less each year than would have been spent on them if they were pupils of a school such as New Trier High [in the northern suburbs]."[22] Similarly, in Texas, the richest 10 percent of districts taxed at 47 cents for each $100 of assessed worth but spent over $7,000 per student; the poorest 10 percent of districts had "an average tax rate more than 50 percent higher but spent less than $3,000 for each student."[23] These disparities suggest not only a spending gap but also an uneven burden on property taxpayers across districts.

As chapter 4 shows, many of the funding reform initiatives in the last two decades have been directed at reducing interdistrict spending disparity. Based on an analysis of detailed financial reports of a representative sample of eighteen states between 1972 and 1988–1990, I calculated that states used 78 percent of their total school aid to address interdistrict inequities in the late 1980s and early 1990s. Less than 8 percent of state aid was specifically targeted for the socially disadvantaged. In other words, what has emerged from the fifty-state system of educational policy is a two-tiered strategy for addressing educational equity. The primary purpose of state funding is to address interdistrict inequities in fiscal capacity, and the secondary function is to address social inequities. Chapter 4 specifies the political and institutional factors that have facilitated the states' efforts to equalize fiscal capacity among districts, and limitations of the states' leveling-up strategy are examined. Indeed, based on my analysis of 1994 data on district spending state by state, the most affluent 5 percent of districts spent an average of 54 percent more per student than the poorest 5 percent of districts.

4. Social Equity at the State Level

The secondary functions of state school aid can be seen as a form of social targeting to counter the educational deficits of at-risk children. Chapter 5 examines the politics and the development of the states' social equity strategies and the classroom impact of these decision rules.

From a broader perspective, legislative efforts to equalize school resources have implications for policy research. It is important to examine the link between state fiscal strategies and classroom activities. After all, a key policy question is whether state spending has purchased more instructional services in the classroom. Currently, there are few systematic studies about the instructional effects of state aid on the school and the classroom. Research is needed to examine whether differences in state reform strategies have contributed to variations in instructional organization in the classroom. Indeed, the current debate on school finance equity generates not only a challenge to policymakers but also a new set of empirical questions for the research community.

In light of these concerns, chapter 5 examines the ways in which state funding of special-needs programs (that is, social strategy) has an impact on the organization of classroom instruction in four selected states and their major urban districts. "Categorical" programs were studied because their funding structure allows state dollars to be traced from the statehouse all the way down to the classroom. Specifically, state compensatory and bilingual education programs are designed to meet the special needs of economically and academically disadvantaged elementary school students. How well these special-needs programs are funded by the states and whether their funds are targeted help determine the organization of the instruction they provide. Using case studies of urban elementary schools in Michigan, Illinois, Oklahoma, and New Mexico, I examined the different circumstances that link funding and targeting to classroom instruction. In general, I found that programs whose funding is high and targeted tend to be structurally distinct; for example, classes are self-contained, and program participants have limited contact with their peers in the regular classroom. Programs whose funding is either low and targeted or high and untargeted tend to have transitional arrangements in which disadvantaged students are pulled out of regular classes for special instruction. Finally, untargeted programs with low funding tend to be structurally diffuse. For example, aides may tutor small groups of disadvantaged students in the regular classroom. In short, variations in state social strategies produce different schooling opportunities for the disadvantaged at the classroom level.

5. Allocation of Teachers without Regard for Student Needs

There is no doubt that the teaching staff is the most valuable resource under the control of local school boards. Teachers in the regular classrooms are substantially supported by local property tax revenues. In many districts, the cost for instructional personnel accounts for 70 percent of the total school budget. Pressured by the teachers union and in accordance with the professional norm of "fairness," school boards have developed allocative rules that assign a comparable number of students to each teacher without paying close attention to either the socioeconomic backgrounds of the students or the teachers' experience and salary level. These seemingly "universalistic" practices regarding teacher-to-pupil ratio, however, may result in uneven instructional quality for students. In their study of first-grade reading in several schools in Chicago, Barr and Dreeben found significant instructional variation among teachers. They argued that student learning is closely connected to curricular coverage, the amount of instructional time, and the match between instruction and the ability levels of groups.[24] Teachers with effective instructional skills are not evenly distributed throughout the district. Experienced and qualified teachers often find the work environment in inner-city schools unattractive.[25] Because new teachers in urban districts are often assigned to the most depressed neighborhood schools, their retention rates average only around 50 percent over the first five years of teaching.[26] Further, Oakes and others have documented extensive racial and class differentiation in the tracking system.[27] These and other limitations in the local allocative rules are the subject of chapter 6.

Institutional Effects of Rule Layering

Having laid out the five allocative practices that are in operation simultaneously, it is important to consider their institutional effects. Schools are substantially shaped by different decision rules that originate from the federal, state, and local levels. Decision rules are marked by a distinct set of political and social circumstances at the time of adoption. When they are first designed, decision rules serve important policy and political purposes. Social targeting, for example, broadens educational opportunity for the disadvantaged. An increase in state funding responsibility is intended to reduce the tax burden of property taxpayers in resource-poor districts. Decision rules are seldom seriously reexamined in terms of their impact on the aims of schooling.

As the goals of public education change, there is a need to rethink the relationship among various decision rules. Given current concerns about outcome-based accountability for all students (including the disadvantaged), the five types of rules may have to be redesigned to reduce institutional fragmentation, enhance systemwide accountability, and improve achievement outcomes for all.

The pervasiveness of multiple allocative practices suggests that our resources in public schools are used in a fragmentary manner. Policy fragmentation results from two structural sources. First, our federal system creates barriers to policy coordination, because many decisions are made by different levels of government. Local control has been cherished since the nation's founding era, although constitutional authority for education is vested in the states. Second, within each level of government, various institutions and organized interests shape allocative rules in public education. Often, allocative rules are designed by one level of government to address specific political demands and social needs in a given era. These rules may conflict with decisions made at other times and at other levels of government.

Instead of overcoming structural separation, each of the decision rules has taken up a distinct purpose in the educational domain. Conflict over resource distribution and management seems inevitable. For example, as chapter 2 points out, federal programs for the special-needs population are likely to be tempered at the district level, where the needs of the disadvantaged are seldom given a high fiscal priority. There are institutional conflicts over resource control issues. At the state level, there is increasing gubernatorial involvement in educational reform. The courts may call for equalization of interdistrict spending, but state legislatures and governors can block any attempt to revamp the funding system. Efforts to improve urban education are often hindered by long-term mistrust between cities and suburbs.

The politics of resource allocation over the last thirty years can be characterized as a process of "layering," adding more guidelines and more social responsibilities on the school's core instructional function. With the passage of time, layers of decision rules become institutionalized and remain the driving forces in today's educational enterprise. Allocative rules, once adopted, are seldom reassessed. Rule termination almost never occurs. Consequently, today's allocative rules are grounded in policy decisions made some twenty or thirty years ago. At issue is whether these existing decision rules can accommodate the recent demands for better student performance. Are educational systems so accustomed to regulatory compliance that they lack the capacity to meet new standards of academic accountability? Is there a mismatch between the rules embedded in the concerns of the 1960s and the policy goals of the 1990s? Can such a mismatch be better managed? For example, while a district's allocative routines stipulate a fixed and comparable number of students for each teacher (a policy that has been supported by the teachers unions since the 1960s), this same rule may hinder innovative strategies that require variable class size. In short, a systematic examination of the existing allocative practices will provide the knowledge base for school reformers to redesign decision rules to improve student learning. In light of these concerns, the concluding chapter of this book explores four alternatives for resource governance in public education.

UNDERSTANDING THE POLITICS OF ALLOCATIVE REFORM

Whereas there is an abundance of ideas on how to restructure school systems, I see a lack of systematic understanding of the proper role of politics in shaping educational reform policy. To improve schools' accountability to meet higher academic standards, reformers have proposed strategies such as site-level management,[28] parent empowerment[29] and choice,[30] higher curricular standards, and professional development.[31] These and other reform initiatives have had mixed results. More important, much of the current literature has overlooked the pervasiveness of the broader governance structure and the extent to which it can either enable or constrain teaching and learning. In adopting an institutional-political approach, this book sharpens the focus on the role of political institutions in educational policymaking. Our understanding of the politics of school reform needs to go beyond the schoolhouse and the district's central office.

Various institutional actors create and constrain the conditions for educational policy and practices. First, federalism enables the states to develop their own policy character. In decisions on educational resources, state governments adopt a unique two-tiered allocative strategy over time. States are primarily concerned about interdistrict fiscal disparity and pay secondary attention to social inequities. Although the federal government allocates most of its resources for social targeting, it has not devoted much attention to interdistrict disparity. Local school boards, too, have their own guiding principle on the use of their most valuable resources— namely, allocating a comparable number of students to each teacher.

Second, variation in allocative rules among the three levels of government leads to institutional tension. On the one hand, there is a certain degree of functional division among the three levels of government. On the other hand, different decision rules often result in institutional conflict and policy incoherence. Funding criteria adopted at one level may not comprehend other conditions affecting resource allocation at another level. For example, federal programs often take into consideration the special-needs population without regard for the district's overall fiscal capacity. Consequently, federal funds are channeled to affluent districts even when their local taxes can provide supplemental services for the disadvantaged. At the same time, state aid to poor districts may overlook the needs of the disadvantaged, as it is allocated according to the tax burden of the property owners. Clearly, there is a need to improve policy coherence within the federalist framework.

Third, political and economic institutions exercise significant influence over educational policy at each level of government. To begin with, differences between state and local institutions and national institutions must be recognized. Through a synthesis of the state and local politics and policy literature, this study specifies how the politics of federalism has contributed to the division of equity functions in education. The differentiated state role is readily defined by the states' development of their own political and economic institutions in recent decades. Because governmental institutions play a central role in school finance, a political-institutional perspective can provide an enriched understanding of allocative policy.

Fourth, to the extent possible, I attempt to document the impacts of allocative decisions on schooling opportunities for students, particularly those from disadvantaged backgrounds. The question "Does money matter?" has polarized the academic community.[32] To be sure, this is a critical policy question, yet it is difficult to address. As Murnane pointed out, "In some districts [increasing expenditures will help], but in others it will not help unless strategies are devised to change the way people interact."[33] In my view, learning and instruction are nested in a multilayered policy organization, where decisions on resource allocation made at the higher level (state, district) can constrain or facilitate productive activities at the lower level. For example, teacher contracts made through collective bargaining at the district level may define the pool of potential applicants to the system, thereby affecting teaching quality at the classroom level. Likewise, the length of the school day, the schedule of sessions, and the assignment of teachers and students are all decisions made above the classroom level, but they have a tremendous impact on instruction and learning inside the classroom.[34] In other words, an examination of the linkage between funding and learning must take into account the organizational properties of the public school system.

Through an analysis of programs for special-needs children, chapter 5 maps the empirical linkages between "macro" policy set in the statehouse and "micro" practices in schools and classrooms. State-funded programs for at-risk children are likely to involve a different set of allocative practices. Often, they have a well-defined set of educational goals, an eligible group of students, and, in some cases, a distinct curriculum. Two state-funded programs—compensatory and bilingual programs—were selected for study. Chapter 5 examines the relationship between supplemental state resources and instructional organization for at-risk students, including the use of ability grouping, the allocation of instructional time, and curricular coordination between the special programs and the rest of the school program. These issues are examined by means of case studies from several states with different funding strategies. Overall, two key lessons emerge from these case analyses. First, additional dollars do contribute to the schooling opportunities of disadvantaged students. Second, the ways schools use their resources have a direct bearing on student learning.

Fifth, this study takes up a challenge that confronts analysts in the politics of education. As policymakers look for coherence in school services and formulate more comprehensive solutions to chronic social problems, policy analysts have to become increasingly multidisciplinary in conducting their research. The politics of education can be strengthened by adopting perspectives and tools from various disciplines. In this book, the economic concepts of human capital investment, incentives, and rational expectation are applied. From sociology, the nature and functions of bureaucracy, school organization, the process of producing learners, social capital, and the urban underclass are considered. The importance of contextualizing the findings, as historians do, is exemplified. As in political science, attention is paid to the governance structure, the political process, interest groups, and the distribution of power. Taken as a whole, this book represents the latest trend in the politics of educational research, with researchers moving from a single-focus analysis to one that encompasses multiple orientations.[35] In short, these five points of departure from the current literature provide a useful step toward a more comprehensive understanding of the structure and the process of school governance and educational equity.

2
Politics of Social Targeting at the Federal Level

In public education, the federal government has clearly focused on social redistribution by promoting racial integration, protecting the educational rights of the handicapped, funding compensatory education, and assisting those with limited English proficiency.[1] These programs are seen as allocating resources to address inequities that arise primarily from class, status, and racial differences.[2]

The literature on federalism has looked for structural sources to explain why social redistribution is more likely to come from the national government. The federal government enjoys a broader revenue base in which taxes are raised primarily on the ability-to-pay principle and represents a constituency with heterogeneous demands.[3] In other words, it has both the fiscal capacity and the political resources (often facilitated by interest groups) to respond to social needs. In contrast, localities are more limited in their ability to address social needs because their most active voters come mostly from the middle class, they compete with one another for investment in an open system in which businesses and labor can move freely, and they have a restricted tax base (namely, reliance on land values as a major source of income). Compared with local governments, states are somewhat more likely to provide redistributive services because they enjoy a broader tax base, they command a larger pool of resources, and they encompass a larger geographical boundary that tends to reduce the threat of resident out-migration.

Over the years, the federal government has spent billions of dollars in social redistributive programs; virtually all of them are categorical (or single purpose) in nature. In fiscal year 1997, the federal government allocated $7.7 billion to compensatory education, $4 billion to special education, and $262 million to bilingual education projects. Title I, or the compensatory education program, provides services to 5 million disadvantaged pupils in prekindergarten through grade twelve. Since the beginning of the Title I program in 1965, the federal government has disbursed over $100 billion to needy schools.

To be sure, federal funding for educational programs has fluctuated over time. Between 1970 and 1980, federal aid to special-needs programs showed persistent growth in real dollar term, as Table 2.1 shows. However, federal redistributive support declined during the Reagan years. In constant dollars, federal funding for major redistributive programs dropped by almost 11 percent between 1980 and 1985. Although major categorical programs began to receive new levels of federal support during the Bush administration, federal funding in 1990 fell short of the 1980 level. Because total federal spending in elementary and secondary education experienced major declines during the Reagan years, the portion of federal funds that went to redistributive categorical programs remained significant. During the Reagan and Bush years, six out of ten federal dollars for education were allocated for redistributive purposes (see Table 2.1).

By 1992, the last year of the Bush administration, federal spending for special-needs programs clearly exceeded that of the previous administrations. The Clinton administration went further, reaching an unprecedented level of over $14 billion in real dollars for redistributive educational programs. Overall, the last year of the Bush administration and the first two years of the Clinton administration showed strong support for public education, as well as equity. By 1994, 62.4 percent of federal education dollars was spent on major special-needs programs. Head Start, for example, saw a jump from $1,570 million to $2,232 million in constant dollars in only two years (1992 and 1994). As the nation approaches the twenty-first century, the federal role in addressing equal educational opportunity remains strong.

AN INSTITUTIONAL PERSPECTIVE ON ALLOCATING FEDERAL RESOURCES

Given the importance of the federal role, researchers have examined the politics surrounding the allocation of federal aid. For analytical purposes, I identify three distinct yet interrelated aspects in the allocation of federal resources: policy legislation, implementation, and impact on schools. These aspects can be differentiated in terms of their key actors, the institution from which resource allocation takes place, and the politics that emerges.

Federal programs involve resource allocation at three different levels of the policymaking system, each of which focuses on a distinct set of policy issues and politics. First, the national legislative process, in which both the president and Congress are prominent, determines national policy objectives and appropriates federal funds to states and localities to implement federal programs. National educational policy is clearly embedded in the political dynamics between the legislative and executive branches. Second, in receiving federal aid, state and local

Table 2.1. Federal Expenditures for Elementary and Secondary Education, Selected Fiscal Years, 1970–1994

	1970	1975	1980	1985	1990	1992*	1994*
Special-Needs Programs (millions of 1983 dollars)							
Compensatory education	3,446.6	3,484.5	3,893.7	3,903.9	3,443.5	4,391.2	4,630.0
Special education (P.L. 94-142)	203.6	281.0	998.5	944.6	1,238.3	1,599.5	2,418.1
Head Start	838.4	750.9	893.0	997.6	1,109.0	1,569.9	2,231.9
Child nutrition programs	769.9	2,699.8	4,103.2	3,400.7	3,812.5	4,368.5	4,855.9
Bilingual education	54.8	172.3	205.9	146.2	144.7	141.4	172.7
Native American education	n.a.	74.4	113.5	76.4	53.2	48.9	55.1
Desegregation assistance	27.3	349.1	369.9	n.a.	n.a.	n.a.	n.a.
Subtotal	5,340.6	7,812.0	10,577.7	9,469.4	9,801.2	12,119.4	14,363.7
Percent changes in special-needs programs over previous period	—	46.3	35.4	-10.5	3.5	23.7	18.5
Federal Spending for Elementary and Secondary Education							
Total (millions of 1983 dollars)	15,007.5	19,737.4	19,473.7	15,684.4	16,488.2	19,911.9	23,027.9
Percent change over previous period	—	31.5	-1.3	-19.5	5.1	20.8	15.6
Special-needs programs as percent of federal spending (millions of 1983 dollars)	35.6	39.6	54.3	60.4	59.4	60.9	62.4

Sources: U.S. Department of Education, National Center for Education Statistics, *Digest of Education Statistics* (Washington, D.C.: U.S. Government Printing Office, 1994). Data on desegregation assistance come from information on emergency school aid, as reported in U.S. Department of Education, National Center for Education Statistics, *Digest of Education Statistics* (Washington, D.C.: U.S. Government Printing Office, 1979 and 1982).
Note: The desegregation assistance program was consolidated in the Education Consolidation and Improvement Act Chapter 2 block grant in 1981.
n.a., Not available.
*Percentage change over the preceding two years.

educational agencies play a pivotal role in carrying out national policy objectives. Policy implementation in our federal system is far from straightforward. Instead, intergovernmental politics defines the use of federal aid at the state and district levels. Whether local administrative agencies are in compliance with federal fiscal regulations is an important topic. At issue is whether federal resources target the intended beneficiaries. Third, at the school and classroom levels, federal resources are likely to shape curricular and instructional organization. Policy analysts are paying particular attention to curricular fragmentation and discrete grouping between special-needs students and their peers in the regular classroom.

The linking of policy formation to implementation at the district and school levels reflects a growing interest among policymakers in documenting the impacts of federal programs. Over the years, researchers and policymakers have developed an increasingly comprehensive and realistic understanding of the role of federal categorical programs in addressing educational inequities. There has been a gradual shift of attention from the national level to the instructional setting at the micro level. During the mid and late 1960s, in the initial period of federal categorical involvement, much attention was focused on the allocative formula that disbursed federal aid on a state-by-state and county-by-county basis according to a count of students living in poverty. During the 1970s, the federal government became more concerned about implementation—whether local agencies were in compliance with federal targeting guidelines. By the late 1980s, the federal government paid greater attention to the categorical impact on classroom organization and student learning.

A broadened scope of inquiry notwithstanding, researchers are not always in agreement on matters of resource allocation. This disagreement is clearly due in part to the fact that analytical perspectives are often time bound and context specific. As I discuss later in this chapter, congressional and presidential involvement in education legislation reversed itself between the 1960s and the 1980s. On policy implementation, the earlier view on conflictual federal–local relations has gradually been replaced by the perspective of intergovernmental accommodation. On resource allocation within the school, the earlier concern with administrative compliance is now overshadowed by serious debate that centers on fragmentation and integration between special-needs programs and the regular core curriculum.

This chapter examines politics and policy in the process of legislating and implementing federal programs for the disadvantaged. The next two sections review the changing legislative politics in the federal role of promoting social targeting in education. The following section specifies the political and institutional factors that have facilitated administrative compliance from districts and states. Then I discuss recent federal efforts to promote learning among disadvantaged students. The concluding section briefly explores ways to reduce policy mismatch between decision rules and educational needs.

SOCIAL TARGETING AS A NATIONAL CONCERN

To understand how social targeting became a major decision rule in the nation's capital, two bodies of literature are particularly useful. One focuses on presidential leadership, and the other looks at the legislative process. Based on a synthesis of these studies of national institutions, I identified the factors responsible for keeping social targeting a part of federal educational policy over the past thirty years.

Presidential Activism

Numerous studies have focused on the dynamics of presidential leadership and congressional power in shaping educational policy.[4] A good example is the passage of the compensatory education program as Title I of the 1965 Elementary and Secondary Education Act (ESEA). This legislation significantly expanded federal involvement in public education. It offered an opportunity for analysts to appreciate how groups and actors with different interests and priorities could form legislative coalitions to overcome institutional obstacles. For years, the national education bill was deadlocked by budgetary considerations, concerns over federal aid to segregated schools and to parochial schools, and issues of local autonomy. These barriers were reinforced by the authority structure of Congress—the committee system, which allowed a powerful few to effectively kill a bill behind closed doors, and the seniority system, which preserved the privileges of committee chairs at the expense of voting rights of the rank and file.[5]

Institutional barriers were finally overcome in 1965. The legislative victory was the result of a combination of political factors. Congressional leaders overcame the "separation of church and state" issue by agreeing to provide aid directly to students instead of to schools. There was a clear public mandate in support of a more "activist" federal government following passage of the 1964 Civil Rights Act. The 1964 election produced a new cohort of liberal lawmakers who formed the rank and file of an emerging liberal majority in Congress. But above all, the legislative success was due to presidential leadership. President Lyndon Johnson was fully behind the bill and saw compensatory education as a major strategy in his newly declared War on Poverty.

Institutional Safeguards

The role of the president and Congress was reversed, for the most part, during the 1970s and 1980s. Whereas studies had identified congressional obstacles during the 1950s and early 1960s to the executive branch's activist agenda, analysts in the 1970s and 1980s found congressional safeguards against an administration that wanted to cut back on school and other social programs. The role reversal was in large part facilitated by divided governance when the Republican Party virtually secured its hold on the presidency and the Democratic Party dominated Congress throughout the 1970s and the 1980s.[6] In other words, Republican administrations made numerous attempts to contain the federal social role. Yet even when the president claimed public mandates to reduce federal involvement in domestic programs, as was the case in Nixon's first term and during the Reagan years, the Democratic-controlled Congress was able to exercise enormous restraints.[7]

A closer look at the institutional safeguards suggests that they come from diverse sources. First, legislative restraints are rooted in the division of labor in Congress, incumbency power, and seniority privileges. For example, congressional members who supported the passage of ESEA in 1965 subsequently held leadership positions with long tenure in the 1970s and 1980s.

Second, the educational bureaucracy has come to identify with its clients' interests and has become an advocate for special-needs programs.[8] A dramatic example was the conflict in the Justice Department between the career legal professionals and the politically appointed attorney general over school desegregation policy during the first year of the Nixon administration. In response to the administration's abandonment of using the fund cut-off mechanism to promote racial integration in public schools in August 1969, nine out of ten attorneys in the Civil Rights Division protested the White House strategy.[9]

Third, over time, federal programs are preserved by a fairly stable bipartisan coalition that consists of top bureaucrats, key members of Congress, and prominent interest groups.[10] Major educational programs for the needy have received bipartisan support in part due to growing public concerns about human capital investment. Indeed, public support for both the Head Start program for preschoolers and compensatory education has broadened over the years. Just as important is the territorial impact of federal categorical grants. In 1990 the federal Chapter 1 program provided supplemental resources to 64 percent of all the schools in the nation.[11] Clearly, big districts are not the only beneficiaries of compensatory education funds. Indeed, over 20 percent of federal aid goes to districts with fewer than 2,500 students. Districts with enrollments between 2,500 and 25,000 receive almost 45 percent of the funds. Because there are Chapter 1 programs in every congressional district, partisan conflict has generally been limited during the appropriations process.[12]

Finally, judicial decisions cumulate in a legal framework that legitimates the national government's involvement in educational inequities. Although the Supreme Court rejected federal involvement in school finance in the 1973 *San Antonio* case, it justified national leadership in racial desegregation, civil rights, gender equity, and equal educational opportunities. Even in the presence of opposition from the Nixon White House, the Supreme Court actively pursued desegregation in the South during the late 1960s and early 1970s. Consequently, between

1968 and 1972, the degree of racial segregation in southern schools declined sharply—the percentage of blacks attending schools with more than 90 percent minority enrollment decreased from 78 to 25 percent.[13] However, with a prevailing conservative mood during the Reagan years, the Supreme Court seemed ready to curtail its role as a social agent.

Institutional safeguards have reinforced social targeting. Even during the federal fiscal retrenchment of the 1980s, the socially redistributive character of federal grants to states and localities was largely preserved. During fiscal year 1984, in the midst of the Reagan retrenchment, the appropriations process in Congress ensured that over half the 142 federal formula grants were targeted at those who fell below the poverty line. Another 13 percent was channeled to other special-needs groups. These grants totaled $85 billion and amounted to 87 percent of all federal transfers to state and local governments. In education, training, and employment-related services, over 80 percent of the federal funds went to special-needs groups.[14] Overall, only one-third of these formula-based grants went to activities that were not socially targeted—mostly infrastructural investment projects, research and development activities, and general administration.

Due to opposition from Congress and various interest groups, the Reagan administration also failed to deliver its campaign promise of dismantling the U.S. Department of Education, which would have substantially reduced the federal role in educational equity. Instead, compensatory education received even more funds in the 1980s than it had in the 1970s: its focus on low-achieving students living in impoverished communities was retained, its administration remained in the hands of state and local program professionals, and its allocative practices were not replaced by a voucher arrangement.[15] By the early 1990s, the largest federal educational program, Chapter 1, continued to target resources in districts with the greatest needs. Districts with the highest concentration of children in poverty (where at least 21 percent of the enrollment is poor) received 45 percent of the Chapter 1 funds, even though they enrolled only one-fourth of the nation's public school students. Conversely, districts with the lowest concentration of poor students (where less than 7.2 percent of the students are poor) received only 11 percent of Chapter 1 aid, although they educated 27 percent of the nation's public school students.[16]

The Reagan administration also made several failed attempts to promote a nationwide voucher policy for Chapter 1 participants. The administration tried three times to convert the federal compensatory categorical program into a voucher program. The most serious proposal was the Equity Choice Act (H.R. 3821) in November 1985, also known as TEACH. This bill would have allowed Chapter 1 students, at their parents' request, to attend any school in the district. No funding increase was proposed for the Chapter 1 conversion. None of the Reagan proposals were seriously considered by Congress, particularly after the 1986 election, when the Republican Party lost its six-year control of the Senate.

POLITICAL CONFLICT OVER THE FEDERAL LEGISLATIVE AGENDA

Since the election of Ronald Reagan in 1980, partisan conflict over social targeting has become highly visible. In this section, I discuss the Republican efforts to reduce federal "rule layering," as well as to reduce the overall federal commitment to social targeting. However, many of these attempts were met with strong resistance from the Democrats. Although there were some alterations to the federal decision rules, by and large, social targeting remained the dominant guiding principle in allocating federal resources to schools.

Impact of the New Federalism

Although the federal role in social targeting remained largely unchanged, the Reagan administration succeeded in terminating several smaller categorical programs, reducing funding levels in others, and consolidating various categorical programs into broadly defined block grants.[17] Indeed, when institutional safeguards are weak, programs can actually be eliminated.

Termination of the Emergency School Aid Act (ESAA) Title VI for desegregation programs is a good example of how a federal policy failed to receive either bureaucratic advocacy or bipartisan support. By eliminating ESAA, the Reagan administration substantially trimmed federal fiscal support for racial integration. It took four years for the federal government to enact another categorical program on racial desegregation. The Magnet Schools Assistance Program, which started in 1985, became the only major program that supports racial integration in urban districts. Funding for this highly competitive grant program remained around $75 million during the Reagan years but increased to $114 million for fiscal year 1989. These grants are not specifically for big urban districts, however. According to a General Accounting Office (GAO) study, four of the eleven largest school districts in the South and the West applied for the grant in 1985, but only one received funding. In 1987, eight of these districts applied for the grant, and only three received funding.[18]

Another major impact of the Reagan administration was decentralization of decision making on federal aid.[19] When states are given allocative decisions, they are less likely to focus on redistributive issues. At the state and local level, "policy generalists" and their constituencies tend to dominate the decision-making process. Generalists include elected officials (e.g., state legislators) as well as top appointees in education agencies. A good example of how federal dollars can be diverted from redistributive needs is the block grant program created under Chapter 2 of the Education Consolidation and Improvement Act. The block grant program consolidated twenty-eight categorical programs (including the ESAA desegregation program) and shifted allocative authority to the states. State control weakened the redistributive focus of the antecedent programs. Orland and Tillander's fifty-state analysis of the allocation of block grant funds found that seventeen of the twenty-six largest urban districts received less revenue than they had in the immediate pre–block grant year.[20] Virtually all the losers had received a significant amount of ESAA funds before the consolidation. More important, 80 percent of the states distributed most of the federal aid without regard to any special-needs criteria. Only two states targeted the block grant at districts with high-needs factors. In other words, devolution of federal aid resulted in less governmental support for educational equity.

Efficiency in the Absence of Federal Leadership

From a broader perspective, Reagan's New Federalism can be viewed as an attempt to improve efficiency without active federal involvement. In sharp contrast to the Kennedy-Johnson years, Reagan focused primarily on efficiency and excellence. The shift toward efficiency occurred in a global context of public distrust of the New Deal–like social welfare state. No doubt, to deliver categorical services, the school bureaucracy had grown steadily throughout the 1960s and 1970s. By the early 1980s, many policymakers began to see the educational bureaucracy as interfering excessively with instructional and curricular activities at the school and classroom levels.

The public's growing distrust of the school bureaucracy can be related to the perceived decline in student performance (as measured by SAT scores and other standardized tests) since the early 1970s. Equally important is the broader climate of rapid political and economic changes that swept both the West and the East within the last decade. The practice of Reaganomics in the United States, the repeated electoral endorsement of Thatcherism in the United Kingdom, and the rise in popular support for conservative coalitions in other industrialized countries during the 1980s called into question the tradition of the social welfare state and its ever-expanding administrative agencies. The disintegration of the former Soviet Union, the introduction of a market economy in the former Soviet-dominated Eastern Europe, and the extensive deregulation in Latin American countries raised new hopes that market-oriented initiatives could be effective in solving social and economic problems.

Within this political context, the public school system became a target of antibureaucratic sentiments. Increasingly, policymakers, businesses, and parents blamed the central bureaucracy for the decade-long decline in student performance. At the same time, demographic trends and economic restructuring heightened public concerns about the future performance of public schools. Will high school graduates acquire adequate skills to compete with their peers in other countries in the global economy? Does the projected labor shortage mean that employers will have to hire less skilled workers in the future? Can the new workforce perform well in a technologically complex world? These concerns were further fueled by publication of *A Nation at Risk,* as well as by numerous other reports that documented the decline of public education in the United States. No doubt, the public was uncertain that the bureaucratized school organization could be effective in meeting these challenges. Subsequently, the efficiency debate encouraged various efforts to decentralize the school system—site-based management, parent empowerment, school choice, and dismantling of the central bureaucracy.

Overall, the Reagan impact was uneven among policy domains. Although Congress succeeded in preserving most of the major educational programs, the Reagan administration was able to reduce federal support in low-income housing and other social policy areas. Consequently, the federal grants-in-aid program in the late 1980s returned to the level of the early 1960s, in terms of the percentage of gross national product (GNP).

Efficiency under Federal Leadership

Since 1993, the Clinton administration has assumed greater responsibility for improving governmental performance. Like Reagan, Clinton has focused on productivity in a period of budgetary constraint. Unlike Reagan, Clinton has clarified the federal role. Instead of deferring responsibility to states and marketlike forces, the Clinton administration specified areas where federal leadership should be exerted and areas where a partnership between the federal government and other entities would be constructive.

The Clinton administration has undertaken several initiatives to enhance policy coherence and accountability. First, seeing a linkage between preschool services and instructional programs in the lower grades, the administration strongly supports early childhood intervention strategies. Second, federal leadership is directed at setting new national standards and designing a national examination system in five core areas: English, mathematics, social studies, science, and foreign languages. Third, new standards are being developed for teachers and other professions, as well as for the school organization itself (labeled service delivery standards).

Finally, efforts are being made to address organizational fragmentation and intergovernmental contention. One major attempt to streamline the federal bureaucracy was outlined by the 1993 report of the Commission on National Performance Review, chaired by Vice President Al Gore. The report called for trimming the overall federal workforce by 12 percent. It suggested the elimination of almost one-sixth of the 230 programs administered under the Department of Education. To reduce duplication, the Gore report recommended extensive program consolidation both within the Education Department and between Education and other entities, such as the Labor Department. It also recommended the creation of flexible block grants for state agencies. Program consolidation gained support in the 1995–96 Congress as Republicans held the majority in both houses for the first time in forty years.

Another effort toward greater accountability was the redesigning of the federal compensatory education program (Title I, formerly Chapter 1). The administration's legislative proposal, which was enacted as the Improving America's Schools Act of 1994, was directed at the overall quality of the schools that poor children attend. It raised the standards for low-achieving students and encouraged instruction and curriculum that teach students critical thinking skills. The legislation was clearly consistent with earlier reviews of Title I. As the 1992 report of the Commission on Chapter 1 argued, the federal program should be substantially improved with a new accountability framework that aimed at "producing good schools, not simply good programs."[21] Instead of mandating schools to meet accounting standards, the commission recommended that schools be accountable for student progress in learning. In return, poor schools would be given one-fifth of the federal grant for staff development, curricular enrichment, and organizational improvement. Such a restructuring would reduce the "categorical" nature of Title I, thereby enhancing programmatic coordination among federal, state, and local staff in poor schools. If the largest federal program could be restructured in ways that produced better schools in poor neighborhoods, the Clinton administration could rightfully claim that equity and efficiency can be pursued simultaneously.

A Year of Institutional Rivalry

Rather than bringing bipartisan support for federal education programs, 1995 was punctuated by institutional conflict in the nation's capital. It was an unusual year of political change. The 1994 midterm elections produced the first Republican majority in Congress in forty years. The new congressional leadership attempted to shrink the federal role in social programs and to shift programmatic authority to state and local governments. Policy conflict was heightened by two sets of political processes. First, reorganization of the House of Representatives under the Republican leadership weakened bipartisan support for educational programs in the short run. Second, the adversarial relations between the president and the new Congress became particularly salient. These two political changes produced what I call the politics of deinstitutionalization in the short term.

Deinstitutionalization in Congress

The process of deinstitutionalization can be seen in a comparison of the membership of two crucial education-related committees in the House and Senate in 1993, the first year of the Clinton administration, and in 1995, the first year of the Republican era in Congress. I focus on committees because they are key decision-making components in the division of legislative labor. Committees comprise lawmakers who are most devoted to particular policy areas. Committee members set the legislative agenda, write the bills, mobilize political support for legislative proposals, debate the merits of initiatives, and kill hundreds of proposals by not reporting them to the floor for further action.

Table 2.2. Decline in Institutional Memory, U.S. Congress, 1993–1995

	AVERAGE NO. OF YEARS IN CONGRESS AMONG MEMBERS OF THE MAJORITY PARTY		
	1993 (Democratic Majority)	1995 (Republican Majority)	Percent Change
House Committees			
Education and Labor (now Economic and Educational Opportunities)	7.22	4.96	−31.3
Appropriations Subcommittee: Labor, Health, and Human Services	16.56	5.88	−64.5
Senate Committees			
Labor and Human Resources	12.9	4.1	−68.2
Appropriations Subcommittee: Labor, Health, and Human Services	15.88	10.88	−31.5

Sources: Based on information reported in Congressional Quarterly, *Players, Politics, and Turf of the 103rd Congress* (Washington, D.C.: Congressional Quarterly, 1993) and Congressional Quarterly, *Players, Politics, and Turf of the 104th Congress* (Washington, D.C.: Congressional Quarterly, 1995).

Institutional memory and legislative knowledge declined significantly between the two years under study (see Table 2.2). In the House, the average number of years of legislative experience for committee members of the majority party in the Education and Labor Committee was 7.2 in 1993. This dropped to 5 years in 1995, which constituted a decline of 31.3 percent from the previous session. In the House Appropriations Subcommittee on Labor, Health, and Human Services, there was a decline of 64.5 percent, from an average of 16.6 years to an average of only 5.9 years. Similar patterns are seen in the Senate committees. In 1993, Democratic members of the Senate Labor and Human Resources Committee had an average of 12.9 years of legislative experience. In 1995, the Republican average dropped to only 4.1 years, a decline of 68.2 percent. Between the 1993 and the 1995 sessions, legislative experience of members of the majority party in the Senate Appropriations Subcommittee on Labor, Health, and Human Services declined by 31.5 percent, or from 15.9 years to 10.9 years on average. These changes are likely to reduce the importance of seniority, weaken the contribution of policy expertise, and enhance the currency of party loyalty in the legislative process. As one report observed, the Republican takeover in the House "brought in a large class of junior Republicans who are hungry for action on their agenda and are skeptical of giving power to [committee] chairmen."[22] Among the first reforms that restructured the internal operation of the House was a six-year term limit for committee chairs.

Conservative control over the educational agenda contrasted sharply with the longtime liberal dominance of the House Education and Labor Committee. According to Sroufe, the committee under Democratic control was "easily the most liberal in Congress. It include[d] strong representation from radical minorities and women, and ha[d] close ties with both the Black Caucus and the Hispanic Caucus. Issues of equity . . . have seldom been absent from the committee."[23] Soon after the Republican takeover, the House moved to weaken the institutional practices that gave special attention to various targeted populations. For example, the new leadership eliminated three standing committees that had long served Democratic constituencies: the Committees on the District of Columbia, Merchant Marine and Fisheries, and Post Office and Civil Service. The fiscal year 1996 spending bill for the District of Columbia failed to pass in the House because of partisan conflict over the Republican voucher proposal that would have authorized $5 million for a program to allow 1,500 poor children to enroll in private schools.[24]

Further, the leadership style of new House Speaker Newt Gingrich tended to undermine long-term institutional practices in decision making. After all, Gingrich had gained power under the most unusual political circumstances when his predecessor, Democrat Tom Foley, became the first House Speaker to be defeated since 1860. For one thing, the new Speaker conceptualized social and governmental issues in polarizing terms. Naming his core political caucus the Conservative Opportunity Society was "a semantic counterpoise to the three words Gingrich strove to discredit: Liberal Welfare State."[25] He depicted the government as the major cause of poverty, the bureaucracy as the major source of waste of taxpayers dollars, and the private sector as the only real solution to social inequality. Further, he circumscribed the seniority practice to make sure that his first-term allies gained greater representation in crucial committees. For example, freshman lawmakers got nine of ten open seats on the Commerce Committee, seven of eleven on Appropriations, and three of ten on the powerful Ways and Means.[26] At the same time, Gingrich handpicked three "activist conservativists," sidestepping seniority consideration, to lead three major committees. His direct involvement in drafting the federal budget also placed enormous constraints on the programmatic jurisdiction of committees. To make sure that his legislative agenda was followed, the Speaker created task forces to come up with legislative proposals instead of relying on committee support. Consequently, he was able to secure House approval on nine of the ten items in his "Contract with America."

Rivalry between Two Branches

The heightened political confrontation between Congress and the president became highly visible during 1995. The 1994 election was the only midterm election in U.S. history when a first-term elected president's party lost the majority in both houses of Congress.[27] Whereas the first two years of the Clinton administration saw major legislative accomplishments (such as the Goals 2000 legislation), the next two years brought a significant loss of political capacity to govern. The acrimonious relationship between the two branches was seen in the impasse on the fiscal year 1996 budget to keep federal agencies in operation.

The congressional response to the administration's budgetary requests between 1993 (Democratic control) and 1995 (Republican control) dramatically highlights the gap in educational policy between the Clinton administration and the new Republican majority. As Table 2.3 shows, the Republicans in 1995 wanted to reduce the level of federal funding in every major educational program, as well as reduce the overall budget for the Department of Education. Significant disagreements occurred over major redistributive programs. For example, the House proposed a 19 percent cut in compensatory education, a 66 percent reduction in bilingual programs, and a 7 percent cut in special education. The cuts proposed by the Senate were less drastic. In contrast, the 1993 Democratic Congress had been generally supportive of the administration's budgetary requests for those redistributive programs.

In the end, the highly visible partisan conflict over federal educational programs witnessed in 1995 was more of an exception than the rule. By 1996, the Republican leadership had abandoned its quest to eliminate federal involvement in education. From a broader perspective, federal support for social targeting in education remains unchanged, despite partisan shifts in the executive and legislative branches. Whether there will be another major effort aimed at eliminating federal programs remains to be seen.

IMPLEMENTATION PROCESS: CONFLICT AND ACCOMMODATION TO FEDERAL RULE LAYERING

As federal dollars are disbursed, policy analysts focus on how federal redistributive resources are actually used in school districts. Implementation studies, as they are often labeled, offer two distinct perspectives on the administrative effectiveness of federally funded programs. In particular, studies focus on whether federal resources are targeted to the intended beneficiaries. In other words, a key research question is whether district and state agencies comply with federal auditing and administrative requirements. Based on a synthesis of the literature, I argue that our understanding of policy implementation in the intergovernmental system has shifted from a conflictual to an accommodative perspective. In other words, over the last thirty years, districts and schools have adapted to "rule layering" in federal programs.

Intergovernmental Conflict

The first set of evaluation studies (or first-generation studies) came out in the 1970s and covered a wide range of policy topics—from compensatory education and busing programs to achieve integration to job training and employment

Table 2.3. Differences between Congress and President Clinton in the Federal Education Budget, 1993 and 1995 (in Thousands of Dollars)

Major Educational Programs	Clinton Request	House Bill	Percent Difference from Clinton Request	Senate Bill	Percent Difference from Clinton Request	Percent Difference from House Bill
1993 (Democratic Congress)						
Training and employment services	$6,867,218	$5,083,762	-25.97	$4,958,623	-27.79	-2.46
Head Start	$5,051,477	$4,169,806	-17.45	$4,296,796	-14.94	3.05
Compensatory education	$7,110,155	$6,871,147	-3.36	$6,971,620	-1.95	1.46
Education reform	$585,000	$133,750	-77.14	$166,000	-71.62	24.11
Bilingual, immigrant education	$232,251	$242,789	4.54	$232,251	0.00	-4.34
Special education	$3,124,921	$3,039,442	-2.74	$3,134,734	0.31	3.14
Vocational, adult education	$1,447,566	$1,474,243	1.84	$1,483,433	2.48	0.62
Education research	$352,579	$277,244	-21.37	$301,398	-14.52	8.71
Total, Education Department	$30,921,629	$28,627,320	-7.42	$28,755,410	-7.01	0.45
1995 (Republican Congress)						
Training and employment services	$5,464,484	$3,180,441	-41.80	$3,427,305	-37.28	7.76
Head Start	$3,934,728	$3,397,429	-13.66	$3,401,675	-13.55	0.12
Compensatory education	$7,441,292	$6,014,499	-19.17	$6,517,166	-12.42	8.36
School improvement	$1,554,331	$892,000	-42.61	$1,157,653	-25.52	29.78
Bilingual, immigrant education	$300,000	$103,000	-65.67	$172,959	-42.35	67.92
Special education	$3,342,126	$3,092,491	-7.47	$3,245,447	-2.89	4.95
Vocational, adult education	$1,668,575	$1,162,788	-30.31	$1,273,627	-23.67	9.53
Education research	$433,064	$250,238	-42.22	$322,601	-25.51	28.92
Total, Education Department	$28,220,106	$23,213,105	-17.74	$24,747,105	-12.31	6.61

Sources: Based on information reported in Congressional Quarterly, Where the Money Goes (Washington, D.C.: Congressional Quarterly, 1993) and Congressional Quarterly Weekly Report, September 23, 1995.

programs in economically depressed communities. They were highly critical of how federal programs operated. In reviewing the complex intergovernmental administrative structure of such programs, analysts often found confusion, conflict, and failure to meet national social objectives.[28] In other words, federal resources set aside for socially redistributive goals seldom got into the hands of the intended beneficiaries.

These early studies no doubt raised important political and policy issues—whether federal regulations are the best way to achieve national social objectives, and whether the federal government can overcome obstacles at the subnational level to improve services for the intended beneficiaries. At the same time, these studies had several methodological shortcomings. They were predominantly single case studies, often focused on the first couple of years of programs (conceivably the period of greatest implementation problems), and did not distinguish between programs that addressed social inequity and those that did not.

Toward Accommodation

More recent (or second-generation) implementation studies tended to overcome the methodological shortcomings of first-generation studies. First, these studies differentiated socially redistributive objectives from other purposes in federal programs. Having made explicit the differences in national purposes, the second-generation studies considered intergovernmental conflict as a function of social redistribution goals.[29] Second, even when they conducted a single case study, the second-generation researchers adopted a longitudinal view. Policy analysts often collected information from multiple years of the implementation process, thereby enabling them to denote cycles of political compromise and programmatic accommodation within the complex intergovernmental system. The third methodological characteristic of the second-generation studies was the use of comparative cases involving multiple schools, districts, or states. Researchers were able to specify the sources of local compliance and resistance by taking into consideration any variation in the local context.

Programs that address the disadvantaged often require local governments to reformulate the way services are delivered. Because revenues in these programs come mostly from Congress, the federal government tends to impose numerous and complicated standards on local schools. These regulations are intended to make certain that disadvantaged pupils directly benefit from federal dollars. In compensatory education, for example, local districts are required to use federal funds in schools with the highest concentration of poor students, to spend as many local dollars on those schools as on any other school in the district, and to commit at least the same level of local resources as was provided in previous years. In special education, the federal provisions (P.L. 94-142) give service recipients an official policymaking voice in the service delivery system. The individualized education plan (IEP) provision is designed to allow as much parental participation as possible in evaluation and placement decisions for handicapped students. During the 1970s and early 1980s, the compensatory education program required advisory councils composed of parents of children participating in the program.

As expected, there is often local opposition to federal targeting of special-needs populations. In a comparative study of four major federal education programs in four districts, Peterson, Rabe, and Wong found that local districts were tempted, to a greater or lesser extent, to divert funds from these redistributive programs to other purposes.[30] Compensatory education funds, for example, were used for general operating purposes that tended to benefit the entire school population. Implementation difficulties were also found in special education. However, programs such as vocational education and ESEA Title IVB that were not primarily redistributive in focus showed minimal conflict or even cooperation among levels of government.

With the passage of time, a tendency toward increasing intergovernmental accommodation seems to have emerged in social redistributive policy. The compensatory education program, for example, has evolved through three distinct phases.[31] Originally it was little more than general federal school aid, with virtually no stipulations attached to the use of funds. Extensive local misuse of these resources prompted the federal government to write tighter regulations. Notably, a study conducted by the NAACP Legal Defense Fund during the early years found that federal funds were being used for "general school purposes; to initiate system-wide programs; to buy books and supplies for all school children in the system; to pay general overhead and operating expenses; [and] to meet new teacher contracts which call for higher salaries."[32] Consequently, throughout the 1970s, the program acquired an exceedingly well-defined set of rules and guidelines that many state and local officials had difficulty putting in place. Intergovernmental conflict seemed to have abated by the late 1970s and early 1980s, when federal, state, and local administrators worked out their differences.

This transformation from institutional conflict to accommodation was facilitated by several factors. At the district and school levels, a new professional cadre more in accord with program objectives was recruited to administer special programs, and local officials became more sensitive to federal expectations. At the federal level, policymakers began to realize that detailed regulations, tight audits, and comprehensive evaluations were mixed blessings. With the state agency serving as an active mediator, appropriate changes and adjustments were made. Over time, administrators developed program identifications that transcended governmental boundaries, and a commitment to a coordinated effort gradually emerged.

The pace of moving toward federal-local cooperation in the management of special programs is not uniform. There are significant variations among districts.[33] I found that local reform in redistributive services depends on the district's fiscal condition, political culture, and policymaking autonomy of program professionals. More severe and prolonged conflict is likely to be found in districts with a weak fiscal capacity and a program apparatus that is subject to strong political (machine-style) influence. A combination of these fiscal and political circumstances hinders local reform toward redistributive goals. In Baltimore, a 1978 federal audit faulted the local administration for supplanting almost $15 million. Since the city's mayoral office had direct access to the Title I account, it was likely that federal funds had been used for patronage employment. During fiscal year 1976, for example, the district used federal funds to hire employees whose duties were "handling requisitions for repair of equipment, preparing reports on a state-funded driver education program, coordinating printing for the entire district, and budgeting control on personnel position and payroll authorization for the entire system."[34]

At the other end of the continuum are districts with a strong fiscal capacity, autonomous program professionals, and, most of all, teacher commitment to policy objectives.[35] In these circumstances, one expects to find rapid transformation from the conflictual to the accommodative phase in special-needs programs. This institutional process of adaptation (e.g., targeting resources to those eligible) is a necessary condition for instructional and academic improvement in disadvantaged schools.

ALLOCATION OF FEDERAL RESOURCES TO PROMOTE CLASSROOM LEARNING

Moving beyond Administrative Compliance

As fiscal accountability becomes more manageable, improvements in teaching and learning for disadvantaged students emerge at the top of the policy agenda. Concerns about student performance are due in part to global competition and in part to the dissemination of a more comprehensive assessment of our educational system. Based on a national survey of Chapter 1 district-level coordinators in 1990, a major evaluation study found that federal requirements on funding compliance—supplementing, not supplanting, maintaining efforts, and adhering to comparability provisions—are all ranked as far less burdensome than procedures that affect instructional practices. Indeed, evaluation procedures, needs assessment, and student selection are viewed as the three most burdensome federal regulations that govern Chapter 1.[36] For example, very few districts develop reliable procedures for assessing the educational needs of students who remain in compensatory education for more than two years.[37]

In light of these concerns about classroom practices, the federal government and local school professionals began to look for ways to improve program effectiveness. Recent federal and local reform efforts are directed at issues that would forge a better linkage between community settings and instructional strategies in compensatory education.

Addressing "Concentration Effects"

The first reform is related to the "concentration effects" of disadvantaged pupils in poor neighborhoods.[38] According to a national assessment of Chapter 1, educational performance is just as adversely affected by living in a low-income neighborhood as by coming from a poor family. As the report pointed out, "[S]tudents were increasingly likely to fall behind grade levels as their families experienced longer spells of poverty, and . . . achievement scores of all students—not just poor students—declined as the proportion of poor students in a school increase[d]."[39] In other words, if both factors are present—a child comes from a poor family and lives in an impoverished neighborhood—the incidence of educational disadvantage is approximately twice as high as when neither factor is present. Similarly, a 1992 GAO report found that schools with a high concentration of poor children "have disproportionately more low achievers than schools with fewer children in poverty."[40]

Clearly, compensatory education is especially needed in neighborhoods where the incidence of poverty is very high. However, resources intended for needy students become diffused in a multilayered school policy system. Schools in which over 25 percent of students are from low-income families are eligible for Chapter 1 aid. Consequently, federal Chapter 1 funds are distributed to 64 percent of the nation's public schools instead of concentrating on the schools with the highest proportion of disadvantaged pupils. At the school level, the principal and teachers enjoy discretion in student selection. Although most of the students receiving Chapter 1 reading services are either low income or low achievers, a number of them do not fall in the disadvantaged categories. Indeed, according to the national assessment report, almost 10 percent of program participants are nonpoor students who achieved above-average performance.[41] Because of the diffused resource allocation pattern, the national assessment estimated that up to 60 percent of eligible students remained unserved in poor communities.

Although Congress has become increasingly aware of the concentration effects of poverty, it remains visibly resistant to any efforts that would reallocate Chapter 1 funds from more affluent to high-poverty districts. During the 1994 legislative session, the Clinton administration proposed altering the Chapter 1 formula and re-allocating about 8 percent of total program funds from low-poverty districts to high-poverty districts. This amounted to $500 million of a total $6.3 billion in fiscal year 1994. Not surprisingly, all members of the House Education and Labor Committee, except for two freshman Democratic congressmen from Texas, voiced their opposition to the proposed reallocation.[42] As one of the two supporters of the Clinton bill put it, "I'm not naive about politics, but I would hope we would put aside a selfish district interest to do what we're supposed to do for the whole United States. This is not a contract to build a lab somewhere, this is kids."[43] Instead, strong bipartisan support was behind a bill that would preserve the status quo with only minor reallocation of "additional" funds in future years.

Reducing Classroom Fragmentation

The second issue taken up by federal policymakers relates to curricular and instructional coordination within the classroom, thereby facilitating better learning opportunities for participants in the Chapter 1 program. Fragmentation is nothing new, and it was found to be counterproductive in meeting the educational needs of disadvantaged pupils. Schools that receive Chapter 1 funding often "pull out" program participants for special instructional purposes as a way to meet accounting requirements. A 1983 survey of district-level program coordinators found that 73 percent of the respondents used pullouts mainly to comply with auditing regulations. More often than not, pullout sessions offer inferior instruction, and students are held to low standards. "Only 18 percent of district administrators who used a pullout design indicated they believed it was educationally superior to any other mode of delivery."[44]

In the context of increasing public concern about competitiveness and reform, policymakers and local school professionals are beginning to shift their focus from administrative compliance to program effectiveness. As Kirst observed, federal publication of *A Nation at Risk* renewed concerns about blending Chapter 1 with a core academic curriculum.[45] Indeed, the Commission on Chapter 1 strongly urged that the federal program be redesigned at the school level in ways that would strengthen schools' overall organizational capacity in developing more comprehensive (instead of fragmentary) strategies for the disadvantaged.[46] To paraphrase the commission's central argument, federal policy should promote "good schools" and not merely provide good programs.

As we come to know more about learning patterns among disadvantaged students in Chapter 1 programs, there is heightened concern for better coordination at the classroom level. Evaluation studies showed that Chapter 1 participants made greater progress in math than in reading. Participants in the upper grades generally made slower progress than their peers in the lower grades.[47] To enhance program quality, Congress in 1988 adopted the Hawkins-Stafford amendments. The new legislation requires coordination of Chapter 1 with the regular instructional program, encourages parental involvement, allows schoolwide projects in schools with a high concentration of children in poverty (without asking for local matching funds), and directs the district to take steps to address ineffective programs. To promote these reforms, each state was given a modest grant of $90,000, which, in effect, amounted to a grant of only $2,000 per district. Although the effects of these federal initiatives remain uncertain,[48] some schools have already shown positive results.[49]

Several national trends in classroom organization have emerged following implementation of the Hawkins-Stafford amendments. First, an increasing number of Chapter 1 schools are beginning to combine pullout programs with in-class strategies, although the former remains by far the most popular instructional arrangement. Between 1985 and 1990, one study found that "there has been almost a 50 percent increase in the number of districts offering in-class instruction."[50] Another study reported that several districts have adopted computer-assisted instruction.[51]

Second, the Hawkins-Stafford amendments allowed for schoolwide projects in schools in which at least 75 percent of the student enrollment falls below the poverty level. This new flexibility has encouraged schoolwide programs, which increased from 621 schools in 1989 to 1,362 in 1990.[52] High-poverty schools are permitted to use federal funds to reduce class size, develop staff training, support parental involvement, and recruit new professional support personnel. Equally important is that schoolwide programs have, in some cases, contributed to instructional innovation. For example, in a 1990 survey of district coordinators, over 50 percent of the respondents reported that schoolwide projects had strengthened parent education programs, helped improve student placement in reading and math classes, and produced more heterogeneous student groups. The schoolwide reform has also facilitated district activities to promote parental involvement. Between 1987 and 1990, more districts reported "disseminating home-based education activities to reinforce classroom instruction" and using liaison staff to coordinate parent activities.[53] In light of these positive impacts, the Clinton administration urged an expansion of schoolwide projects by lowering the eligibility threshold from 75 percent to 50 percent low-income students in a school. The schoolwide project is creating an opportunity for high-poverty schools to allocate federal resources with few restrictions.[54] By 1995–96, over 8,000 schoolwide programs were in operation.

Although schoolwide reforms have become popular in high-poverty schools, coordination between Title I and the regular curriculum remains a challenge in most Title I schools. Coordination generally relies almost entirely on informal meetings, and staff planning sessions rarely occur. Further, local districts remain largely uncertain about student needs assessment and program evaluation, areas in which federal and state agencies can provide crucial technical assistance.

The somewhat mixed picture of the effectiveness of schoolwide programs illustrates the complexity of improving teaching and learning in the inner-city setting. A study of schoolwide programs in Minneapolis reflects the challenge.[55] That study made comparisons between schools with Title I schoolwide programs and the district as a whole to show how Title I students were distributed and what resources were available to them. In analyzing the data collected from the district office and the schoolwide programs in Minneapolis during 1993–94, three emerging trends were seen: school and classroom practices were, to some extent, shaped by recently adopted policies at the districtwide level; variation in instructional practices existed among the schoolwide programs; and these variations in practices may explain some of the differences in student outcomes.

Let us consider a few illustrations from Minneapolis. First, several recent districtwide policies have reinforced the intent of the schoolwide program, granting greater flexibility and programmatic autonomy in high-poverty schools. These include efforts toward site-based management that, among other things, enable schools to select their own textbooks; an increase in local tax revenues to reduce class size; and a push for a collaborative services model that encourages coordination of services between regular program staff and special-needs program staff. District policies thus support schoolwide programs in Minneapolis.

At the school-site level, instructional practices varied between schoolwide programs. In School 1, instruction was 100 percent pullout for Title I students in 1986. Beginning in 1989, the school began to experiment with collaborative services and team teaching, with the Chapter 1 teacher working in the classroom. Over the past two and a half years, the staff creatively used the computer lab to promote individualized instruction, accommodate students' different ability levels, identify each student's strengths and weaknesses, and place a focused emphasis on academic skill building. These instructional efforts produced reasonably good outcomes. Analysis of School 1 showed that student performance in vocabulary and reading was generally positive, with incremental gains over the years. Although "poor" students were performing at a lower level than "nonpoor" students, the former group made measurable progress over a four-year period. There was no significant difference in achievement scores between black and white students in School 1. Overall, this schoolwide program had an "equalizing" effect on the impact of race and poverty.

In contrast, School 2 did not undergo substantial restructuring. Practices and organization implemented during the 1980s were left largely intact—staffing assignments, team teaching, and ability grouping within the classroom. Teachers had not given much attention to curricular changes, student assessment, or instructional practices that integrate the at-risk student populations. The only major change that came with the schoolwide project was the flexibility for teachers to work with any student in the building. This change, however, was not enough to affect student performance. Indeed, students' gain scores in reading remained stable over time, and significant losses in math occurred. It should be noted that the lack of progress may also be related to the school size (with 1,000 students, it is the largest of the four schoolwide projects in the district) and its physical organization (it has no walls and uses white dividers to designate classrooms).

To sum up, new knowledge will accumulate as more systematic evaluations of schoolwide programs are disseminated in the policy community.[56] Given the climate of programmatic reform, local professionals are directing greater attention to instructional issues, such as whether pullout practices are educationally sound.[57] Overall, the federal categorical role has moved from excessive regulatory oversight in the 1970s to facilitating instructional effectiveness in the late 1980s and early 1990s.

MAKING BETTER USE OF FEDERAL RESOURCES

The federal government has relied primarily on categorical programs to address educational inequities. Given our multilayered policymaking system in education, I have identified three phases in the allocation of federal redistributive funding. This differentiated understanding offers a useful way to analyze resource allocation, as each phase involves different actors, issues, and politics. Legislative politics is clearly embedded in the partisan and institutional interplay between Congress and the president. Policy implementation is substantially shaped by professionalism, fiscal capacity, and other institutional factors at the state and district levels. At the school and classroom levels, federal resources are likely to affect teachers' work in terms of curricular organization and instructional strategies. Over the years, our understanding of the federal categorical role has been broadened to include policy issues at both the macro and the micro levels.

As we prepare to enter the twenty-first century, the federal government remains committed to social targeting in its educational policy. Categorical programs are likely to be used as major policy tools. If and when budgetary constraints loosen, we may see a significant increase in federal funding for Head Start, Title I, bilingual education, programs for the handicapped, and other socially redistributive services in education. As the federal focus on social targeting continues, a review of the federal experience over the last thirty years suggests that political conflict will occur periodically, and layering of rules will preserve previous allocative decisions.

A major challenge for the federal policymakers is to decide where to allocate resources that would bring about better life chances for all students, including the most disadvantaged. To reduce the mismatch between allocative practices and educational needs, I suggest two areas for greater federal attention. First, major federal support is needed to deal with the concentration effects in inner-city schools. Clearly, the ecological context of urban schools has changed significantly since the enactment of the original compensatory education legislation (ESEA Title I) in 1965. At that time, the nation had extensive rural poverty, its central cities were economically stable, and suburbs were emerging as viable communities. By the 1990s, we see a widening educational gap between the central city and its surrounding suburbs. This is especially evident in major metropolitan areas, where schools in outlying suburban communities are predominantly white and those in central cities serve primarily minority, low-income pupils. In 1990, minority groups made up over 60 percent of the central-city school enrollment, and whites accounted for almost 80 percent of the suburban school population in major metropolitan areas. In a typical public school in the metropolitan Chicago area, 73 percent of students are classified as low income, compared with only 12 percent in suburban schools.[58] As a 1985 report on metropolitan Milwaukee concluded, "[Our] study revealed two very different worlds of educational achievement; worlds separated by but a few miles, yet by much greater distances in terms of acquired skills, institutional success, and future prospects."[59] Similarly, Orfield and Reardon observed that metropolitan areas resemble "a structure of educational opportunity that is highly stratified at every level by both race and class" and by residential choices. They found that students in central-city districts "have a narrower range of course offerings and fewer opportunities for advanced and college-preparatory coursework than their suburban counterparts."[60]

Given the pervasiveness of metropolitan inequality, federal programs are particularly needed to narrow the educational gap between the haves and the have-nots. Clearly, to combat concentration effects in the classroom, schools in major urban centers need additional resources (federal and otherwise) to create incentives to attract highly qualified teachers, fill chronic staffing shortages in science and math, and strengthen professional development. Further, inner-city schools need more comprehensive support services. In an eight-district study on Chapter 1 resource allocation, large urban districts spent fewer dollars on the classroom because their students needed noninstructional support services. For example, Dade County and Detroit spent 14 and 22 percent of program funds, respectively, for parental involvement, in-house training, educational specialists, and supplies and equipment. In contrast, smaller districts allocated between 1 and 6 percent of Chapter 1 money for support services.[61]

The second area in which a federal role can make a difference is helping needy schools build their organizational capacity. A major first step is to reassess, and possibly reverse, the thirty-year trend of federal rule layering. Federal policy can be less regulatory but more supportive in technical areas. In this regard, federal programs should focus less on auditing compliance and more on within-school coordination. The current effort to have all Title I schools meet national standards in subject areas is one example. In high-poverty schools, the federal initiative to promote schoolwide programs is another good example. To that end, disadvantaged children would be better served if they were taught the core academic curriculum in regular classrooms, placed in heterogeneous groups, and asked to live up to higher academic expectations.[62] In sum, federal policy can be redesigned to move away from the "compliance mentality" and become a supportive partner in making a difference in classroom learning.

3
Mapping Interstate Variation in State Aid to Schools

Public education has always been a primary function of state and local governments. Over 90 percent of the funding for public schools comes from state and local taxes. Federal dollars account for only a small fraction of total school costs and, as chapter 2 shows, are targeted mostly for the disadvantaged. In 1990, public education ranked far above any other service in state and local appropriations—it accounted for almost one-quarter of the total state and local revenues.[1] Significantly, the relative contribution of state and local governments has changed over time. A reversal of responsibility between state and local governments occurred during the late 1970s and early 1980s. Due to local retrenchment, responsibility for funding education shifted from local to state sources. Since the mid-1980s, the state share of total school revenues has either exceeded or stayed close to the 50 percent level. When one considers the fifty state educational systems in 1995–96, the average state share comes to 49.9 percent of total school revenue. Back in 1958–59, the state share was only 38.3 percent. Clearly, efforts to shift greater fiscal responsibility to the state constitute a major allocative rule in public education.

The importance of state aid to local schools merits a more systematic examination of the development of the states' fiscal role. Such an understanding would be useful for rethinking the state role in equal educational opportunity, interdistrict disparity of fiscal capacity, and educational accountability. The state as a policymaker has taken on new prominence as districts across the nation have experienced financial and management crises in recent years. Districts have experienced teachers' strikes, adopted retrenchment practices, faced deteriorating physical stocks, and encountered political opposition to raising additional revenues. As more districts lack new avenues to fund their services, policymakers and the public look for solutions at the state capital. At issue is whether the state will assume primary responsibility for public education. A greater state role may signal a reallocation of fiscal responsibility among the levels of government in our federal structure.

Through a synthesis of two competing perspectives and the literature on state politics and education finance reform, I propose a more systematic way to understand the state role. Using a database on school financing from 1959 to 1996, this chapter pursues several questions on state–local relations in funding education:

1. How important is state aid to public education nationwide? Has the state share increased over time?
2. Are there significant interstate variations from the aggregate trends? How are urban schools affected by the variant patterns of state aid?
3. Can we identify political and institutional forces that have shaped interstate differences in state aid? To what extent is the state aid system tied to the decline in the political influence of cities? Above all, can we map the politics of state aid in education?

To examine these questions, I discuss the two competing perspectives on state aid, labeled the "progressive state" and the "reluctant state"; present a classification scheme that takes into account interstate variation; and relate state fiscal role to politics at the state level.

As the state emerges as an important funder, analysts are divided between two competing perspectives on state aid to public schools. The "progressive state" perspective endorses the notion of state activism, which can be defined in terms of the level of state fiscal support for public schools. According to this perspective, state governments at the aggregate level have shifted from a "parity" status (providing less than 50 percent) to a "dominating" role (providing over 50 percent of total school funds) in school financing.[2] With the emergence of the greater state role, some analysts argue that states are capable of taking over many of the federal educational functions, including services for the disadvantaged.[3] Consistent with this perspective, national policymakers during the Reagan years moved to consolidate federal categorical programs, trim federal regulations in social policy, and devolve decision making primarily to the states. Consequently, federal grants-in-aid in the late 1980s returned to the level of the early 1960s as measured in terms of the percentage of GNP.

In contrast, a second perspective greets the parity-to-dominance trend with caution. Analysts who adopt the "reluctant state" perspective are skeptical of the state's commitment to urban schools and their disadvantaged pupils. These concerns are grounded in the widening gap between needs in the big-city schools and resource allocation in the suburban-controlled state capitals. As state legislatures become increasingly dominated by suburban communities following the decennial reapportionment, major urban districts maintain a high concentration of children who come from low-income and minority backgrounds.

Instead of seeing state responsiveness to urban schools, numerous studies find that federal aid remains critical for disadvantaged pupils in urban areas. Even with federal direction, states and localities divert federal funds to noneligible purposes.[4] Consequently, many believe that federal leadership (and its alliance with cities) is necessary to make sure that the state supplements its own resources for urban educational services.[5] Indeed, federal programs for the handicapped, funding for pupils with limited English proficiency, and compensatory education have continued to direct state and local attention to national equity objectives.

This chapter argues that neither the progressive state nor the reluctant state offers an accurate picture of the state–local relationship in financing public education. Whereas the progressive state view is based largely on aggregate trends in the state role, the reluctant state perspective tends to exaggerate the pervasiveness of the structural constraints states encounter in making policy decisions. This chapter argues that a synthesis of the two perspectives offers a more accurate understanding of the changing state role. Although aggregate trends suggest increasing state support, they may conceal significant interstate variation, with many states providing only limited school funding.

This chapter draws on a fifty-state database compiled on state, local, and federal funding to public schools from 1959 to 1996. The database enables an examination of changes in state share of educational costs over a thirty-eight-year period: from the pre–Great Society liberal reforms of the 1960s, through the professionalization of state governments in the 1970s and the era of the Reagan-Bush retrenchment, and into the first term of the more activist Clinton-Gore administration. Instead of finding states converging toward activism, the state-by-state analysis shows significant diversity in the state fiscal role. Although the "parity to dominance" shift is clearly supported at the aggregate level, few states actually followed this pattern between 1959 and 1996. More important, each of the fifty states can be systematically classified into one of several distinct patterns based on the state's fiscal support status (parity or dominance) initially (1959) and whether state support has increased, remained stable, or decreased. Taken together, these distinct patterns of state fiscal support for education offer a more useful and comprehensive assessment than either the progressive state or the reluctant state perspective.

A key question is to what extent are changes in state aid for education shaped by political forces. Through a synthesis of the literature on state legislative politics, school finance reform, political culture, and interest groups, this chapter relates the state role to sources of constraints and facilitating factors. In the section on the progressive state, it examines state and local political factors that contribute to a greater state role in education financing. In the section on the reluctant state, it examines the ways in which political constraints account for persistent interstate variation. Among the constraints examined are the political culture of local autonomy, the decline of city influence in the state legislature, and the absence of a constitutional challenge to the school finance system. Finally, this chapter maps five major political patterns that shape state aid in education.

THE PROGRESSIVE STATE

The progressive state perspective offers the most persuasive characterization of aggregate changes in school support among the three levels of U.S. government over time. Since the 1980s, state governments have assumed a primary fiscal responsibility for public education. Equally significant is the fact that local governments have substantially reduced their contributions to public schools, while the federal role remains limited.

The trend toward state activism is clearly supported by the aggregate pattern of the states' share of school costs from the late 1950s to the mid-1990s. Because the main objective is to examine state responsibility relative to federal and local contributions, the key dependent variable is the state share as a percentage of total school revenues. Per pupil spending, a commonly used indicator in the study of school finance, is not used here because it does not measure the changing state role in the context of federalism.

As Table 3.1 shows, the state share of total school revenues increased from 38.3 percent in 1959 to 44.8 percent in 1975. Since 1982, state aid has stayed close to the 50 percent level. Although the recessions in early 1980s and early 1990s had a generally adverse effect on government finance, states maintained their dominance in school funding. Some analysts may object that this focus on the state share of school dollars underestimates total state support because of the provision of relief subsidies to property taxpayers in Michigan, Minnesota, Wisconsin, Oregon, and several other states.[6] However, these tax relief funds did not fundamentally shift the longer-term trend in the state fiscal role over the thirty-eight-year period. Further, owing to a lack of systematic documentation, the extent to which these relief funds actually went to schools, as opposed to other local services, remains unclear.

The increasing state support can be explained by the decline in both federal and local sources. As Table 3.1 indicates, local contributions to school expenses gradually fell from 56.6 percent in 1959 to 49.6 percent in 1968. This general decline continued until 1983, when local revenues accounted for only 41.5 percent of total school expenditures. Between 1984 and 1996, local support remained fairly stable at around 43 to 44 percent. Federal support rarely went beyond 10 percent of total school spending over the thirty-eight-year period. Interestingly, federal transfers jumped rapidly from 5 to almost 10 percent between 1965 and 1966, a year that marked the beginning of the Great Society reform with the pas-

Table 3.1. Percent Distribution of School Revenue among
the Three Levels of Government, 1959–1996

	State	Local	Federal
1959	38.3	56.6	5.0
1960	40.1	54.6	5.2
1961	40.7	53.9	5.4
1962	40.6	54.1	5.2
1963	40.4	54.5	5.0
1964	41.1	53.4	5.5
1965	40.7	54.0	5.4
1966	39.6	50.9	9.6
1967	39.6	50.5	10.0
1968	40.8	49.6	9.6
1969	41.3	49.5	9.2
1970	41.6	48.3	10.1
1971	41.7	49.7	8.7
1972	41.5	49.5	9.0
1973	42.0	48.6	9.5
1974	42.7	46.9	10.4
1975	44.8	46.0	9.2
1976	45.7	43.7	10.6
1977	44.8	44.0	9.1
1978	45.9	44.4	9.7
1979	46.5	43.5	10.0
1980	48.3	41.7	9.9
1981	48.6	42.0	9.4
1982	49.8	41.8	8.4
1983	50.3	41.5	8.2
1984	49.3	43.5	7.1
1985	50.0	42.8	7.1
1986	50.4	42.6	7.0
1987	49.9	43.3	6.9
1988	50.4	42.7	6.9
1989	50.0	43.1	7.0
1990	49.4	43.7	6.9
1991	49.5	43.7	6.8
1992	49.0	44.1	6.9
1993	48.6	43.9	7.5
1994	48.4	44.1	7.6
1995	49.4	43.3	7.3
1996	49.9	42.9	7.2

Source: National Education Association, *Estimates of School Statistics*
(Washington, D.C.: NEA, 1958–59 through 1995–96).
Note: Washington, D.C., is not included in the analysis. The total may
not equal 100 percent due to rounding.

sage of numerous antipoverty bills. Federal support remained stable at around the 10 percent level for over ten years. However, since the early 1980s, the federal role has steadily declined. By 1991, federal dollars accounted for less than 7 percent of school expenditures. In short, by the mid-1980s, states became the primary funder of public education.

Facilitative Factors in State Activism

The view that the state role has shifted from parity to dominance finds support from diverse sources, including writings on fiscal federalism, school finance reform, and interest-group dynamics.

Broader Fiscal Capacity

According to the literature on fiscal federalism, states have increased school support much faster than have localities because they enjoy a much broader revenue base. This broader fiscal capacity allows state governments to address interdistrict disparities in taxing and spending. An increasing number of states also provide targeted funds for the special-needs population.

When compared with local governments, states enjoy a broader revenue base.[7] Unlike localities, states do not rely on land value as a major source of taxation. Property tax amounted to only 1 percent of state revenue, whereas general sales tax provided one-third of total state revenue. One out of every five state dollars comes from a selective sales tax on such items as tobacco products and alcoholic beverages. Additional revenues are raised from lotteries.

Equally important, state governments have increasingly relied on both individual and corporate income taxes, both of which are based on the ability-to-pay principle.[8] For example, between 1962 and 1983, contributions to state revenues from these two sources increased from 13 to 22 percent. In a sharp departure from local taxing practice, where corporate tax is virtually absent, states have developed an elaborate system of taxation based on corporate earnings. Each of the forty-five states that levy taxes on corporate earnings has come up with its own rates and operating procedures, as if interstate competition were not a worry. In 1984, even among the twenty-nine states that had flat rates, these varied greatly, from 5 to 12 percent. This range of rates is not likely to be found in local property taxes in major metropolitan areas, where business and home owner migration is a real possibility.[9]

States also raise revenue through user charges (such as highway tolls), which are based on the "benefits-received" principle. But unlike personal income and corporate taxes, this revenue source has remained fairly stable. Its contribution to the state's revenue base increased from 13 to 16 percent between 1962 and 1983. This modest rise clearly contrasts with local trends. According to one account, local user charges amounted to 64 percent of all local tax revenues in 1983.[10]

These shifts toward a greater reliance on the ability-to-pay principle has several advantages. In times of economic prosperity, such as the 1960s and early 1970s, state treasuries would be able to bring in more tax revenue through their more elastic taxing mechanisms.[11] In California, Washington, and other states, fiscal surpluses became available for educational reform during the 1970s. State governments were able to continue to allocate additional funds even when local property tax revenue was stagnant, for example, in the aftermath of the local taxpayer revolt of the late 1970s and early 1980s. With a broader revenue base, state policymakers also enjoy greater allocative discretion. Thus, when pressure for property tax relief (such as California's Proposition 13) and demands for finance reform became imminent, state legislatures could use general revenues to address the inequity issues. Indeed, fiscal surpluses became facilitative factors in eighteen of the twenty-eight states that restructured their school finance systems between 1971 and 1981.[12] In Maine and Florida, state surpluses were used to increase subsidies to high-need districts without jeopardizing aid for the more affluent districts, the so-called leveling-up strategy.[13]

Judicial Actions

According to the literature on school finance reform, the increase in state fiscal support for public education has been driven by litigation and judicial actions. Since the 1970s, state courts have put pressure on legislatures to bring about a more equitable school finance system, virtually requiring an expanded state role.

As of 1998, state education finance systems had been overturned by the courts in eighteen states and upheld in another eighteen. Judicial involvement in reforming the statewide school finance system started in 1967 in California, when John Serrano and other parents, concerned about poor school services in the Los Angeles area, brought a class action suit against the state of California.[14] In the landmark ruling *Serrano v. Priest*,[15] often referred to as *Serrano I*, the California Supreme Court handed down a six-to-one decision in favor of the parents. According to this ruling, significant interdistrict disparities in school spending due to uneven distribution of taxable wealth violated the equal protection provisions of the state constitution. In this case, sharp disparity in school spending existed between the wealthy Beverly Hills district and the nearby Baldwin Park district. While the former had a tax rate that was less than half that of the latter, it spent twice as many school dollars per student during 1968–69. As the court opinion stated, "affluent districts can have their cake and eat it too; they can provide a high quality education for their children while paying lower taxes. Poor districts, by contrast, have no cake at all."[16] Shortly after the court decision, the California legislature adopted what became the first of several school finance reform plans during the 1970s.[17] Similar charges were filed by parent plaintiffs in several other states.

However, within two years, *Serrano I* was brought into question by a U.S. Supreme Court ruling in a Texas case. In *San Antonio v. Rodriguez*,[18] a five-to-four decision reversed a federal district court ruling. It concluded that since education does not constitute a fundamental interest under the U.S. Constitution, the state can choose to preserve local control by not interfering in interdistrict fiscal inequities. In line with *San Antonio*, the supreme courts of Arizona (1973), Washington (1974), Oregon (1976), Colorado (1976), Idaho (1975), and several other states ruled that the statewide system did not violate the state constitution despite interdistrict funding inequity.

Despite *San Antonio,* the pressure for a more equitable allocation of state funds continued. Among the most significant rulings that rejected the local control notion in *San Antonio* was *Serrano II* (1976) in California. In the post–*Serrano II* period, the state supreme courts in Washington, Wyoming, and several other states also ruled the state school financing systems unconstitutional. Costly services for special-needs students were brought to the states' attention by big-city districts in several lawsuits, including *Seattle v. Washington.* Further, the courts overturned the school funding systems in Texas (1989), Kentucky (1989), New Jersey (1990), Vermont (1997), Ohio (1997), and New Hampshire (1997). The New Jersey ruling (discussed further in chapter 4), in contrast to rulings in most other states, paid particular attention to the concentration of social needs in inner-city schools. The court in that case recognized the additional costs of addressing the needs of disadvantaged pupils in urban areas, estimating that programs to reverse the educational disadvantage such children started out with would cost about $440 million for the first year. Immediately following the court decision, the Democratic governor proposed $2.8 billion in new and increased taxes to fund new services for the poorest schools. However, the reform and tax-increase plan was substantially compromised following key Republican wins in the November election.

In many states, judicial pressure and, in some cases, perceived judicial challenges have brought about reform in state aid allocation. Utah, Washington, and California have "foundation programs" establishing a baseline revenue for students in poor districts. Districts are required to levy local property taxes up to a state-designated maximum. State dollars are channeled to make up the difference between local tax revenue and the minimum level of school spending. To supplement the foundation programs, many states have adopted complicated multitiered schemes. Under "power equalizers," state aid guarantees an equal amount of local tax returns at different levels of tax levy. Eight states use "resource equalizers" that either specify the state share of local spending (known as percentage equalizers) or equalize the return of taxes in districts to finance schools (known as district power equalizing). Unlike foundation programs, equalizing systems do not place a fixed dollar limit on state support.

Perhaps the more immediate outcome of litigation and reform is a greater state role. In comparing state support between the pre-reform year and the immediate post-reform year in the eighteen states that adopted reform measures during 1971 and 1975, Callahan and Wilken found that the eighteen-state average share of combined state and local spending rapidly increased from 39 to 51 percent.[19] Among the most dramatic increases were Kansas (from 30 to 48 percent), Minnesota (51 to 61 percent), North Dakota (32 to 46 percent), California (37 to 45 percent), and Arizona (42 to 55 percent). Except for Kansas, all these states followed the parity-to-dominance pattern. Further, the greater the interdistrict disparity in wealth and spending, the more extensive was the anticipated state role. This was the case in California, Texas, Michigan, New York, and Colorado. Limited additional aid was needed in states such as Florida and Utah, where interdistrict disparity was not as extensive.[20]

Besides fiscal concerns, some have argued that an increase in state aid is substantially shaped by political bargaining. In order to gain a legislative coalition for a reform package, policymakers often adopt the "leveling-up" strategy, whereby no districts suffer reductions in their state support. Taxpayer dollars may be more widely distributed in two-party competitive states where political elites want their constituencies to benefit from state allocation. In other words, an increase in state transfers to poor districts was not achieved at the expense of more affluent communities. These electoral concerns substantially shaped the final legislative outcome in Kansas, California, New Jersey, New York, and Washington.[21]

State Response to Federal Programs for the Disadvantaged

The prominent state role in school spending has been further encouraged by the adoption of legislation that promotes equal educational opportunity. In this regard, federal school policy during the Great Society era of the mid-1960s and 1970s played a crucial role. Although federal funds contribute less than 10 percent of all school revenues (see Table 3.1), federal programmatic guidance has clearly stimulated state activity in addressing special needs. Currently, all states are providing their own funds for special education. According to a 1990 survey, forty states spent $8.5 billion of state money on special education services.[22] Twenty-eight states funded compensatory education, and twenty-one states supported bilingual services.

During the 1980s, however, an increasing number of states shifted from the federal categorical model to an allocative system that weights special-needs students more heavily than others in the general aid formula. This alternative arrangement was used by only five states during the mid-1970s.[23] The shift from categorical to pupil weightings occurred at a time when states assumed greater autonomy in the climate of Reagan's New Federalism. By the 1980s, it had become a popular method of distributing funds for the handicapped. Currently, of the states that provide compensatory programs, thirteen adhere to pupil weighting, and fifteen retain categorical models. In bilingual education, six use pupil weighting, and fifteen allot funds through categorical grants.

Property Taxpayer Revolts

According to studies on constituent politics, the pressure to shift the state role from parity to dominance has been enhanced by citizen-based campaigns against local increases in the property tax levy. Within five years of California's Proposition 13, well over half of all states had enacted some form of legislation curbing governmental spending and restricting property tax increases. Between 1976 and 1990, thirty-six states experienced property tax revolts.[24]

Indeed, signs of taxpayer opposition to school levies had begun to emerge before the passage of Proposition 13 in 1978. As early as 1970, a majority of school bond requests failed to be approved by the voters nationwide.[25] In California, for example, local taxpayers were so dissatisfied with the sharp increase in local school contributions during Reagan's governorship that, between 1966 and 1971, they rejected 50 percent of all local tax increases for school operation and 60 percent of the school bond levies for capital improvements.[26] Discontent among property taxpayers became more widespread during the much-publicized campaign for Proposition 13. According to a national Gallup poll at the time, when respondents were asked to identify their dissatisfaction with various taxing sources for public schools, 52 percent mentioned property tax, compared with only 20 percent citing state sources.[27] In 1978 alone, voters in California, Colorado, Idaho, Montana, Nevada, Oregon, Utah, and several other states pushed for limitations on property tax increases. Consequently, major property tax limitation measures were adopted in California, Idaho, and Massachusetts.

Where the local taxpayer movement is well organized, there is evidence that the state begins to assume greater financial responsibility for local school costs.[28] After the passage of Proposition 13, California's share of nonfederal school revenues jumped from less than 50 percent to more than 70 percent. The state share also went up in Massachusetts and Idaho to make up for lost local revenues after the adoption of tax-limiting measures. The role of the state becomes more complicated where spending limits on both state and local sources are adopted, such as in Colorado, New Jersey, and Tennessee. In these states, it is more likely that both state and local spending on education will exhibit a slow growth pattern. However, a faster rate of decline at the local level may result in an increase in the state share.

In sum, the steady shift in the state role from parity to dominance in education financing can be explained by a combination of economic and political factors. This parity-to-dominance perspective is clearly useful in interpreting the aggregate trends, as suggested in Table 3.1. But how useful is this view in understanding the fiscal role of individual states? Are states converging toward dominance over time? Or are they diverging from the overall parity-to-dominance tendency? If so, what are the constraining factors?

THE RELUCTANT STATE

Despite the persistent increase in school aid share at the aggregate level, when one approaches the fiscal trends from the reluctant state perspective, interstate differences in school support become readily evident. In this regard, a useful summary statistic that estimates the extent to which states differ from the overall mean is the standard deviation. If states are converging toward the aggregate trend, the standard deviation will become smaller over time. If interstate differences increase, the standard deviation will rise accordingly. As Table 3.2 shows, the standard deviation has been remarkably stable over time, fluctuating within only a small

Table 3.2. Overall Mean and Standard Deviation in the State
Share of Total School Funds, 1959–1996

	Mean (%)	Standard Deviation (%)	Mean + 1 SD (%)	Mean – 1 SD (%)
1959	38.3	19.9	58.3	18.4
1960	40.1	18.8	59.0	21.3
1961	40.7	19.2	59.9	21.5
1962	40.6	19.0	59.7	21.6
1963	40.4	18.7	59.1	21.7
1964	41.1	19.0	60.1	22.1
1965	40.7	18.4	59.0	22.3
1966	39.6	16.1	55.7	23.5
1967	39.6	16.8	56.3	22.8
1968	40.8	16.4	57.2	24.4
1969	41.3	16.3	57.6	25.0
1970	41.6	15.1	56.8	26.5
1971	41.7	16.5	58.2	25.2
1972	41.5	16.3	57.8	25.3
1973	42.0	15.9	57.9	26.1
1974	42.7	14.2	56.9	28.5
1975	44.8	15.1	59.9	29.7
1976	45.7	14.1	59.8	31.7
1977	44.8	16.3	61.1	28.5
1978	45.9	14.3	60.2	31.5
1979	46.5	14.4	60.9	32.1
1980	48.3	14.9	63.3	33.4
1981	48.6	15.2	63.9	33.4
1982	49.8	15.6	65.3	34.2
1983	50.3	15.9	66.2	34.5
1984	49.3	15.5	64.9	33.8
1985	50.0	15.6	65.7	34.4
1986	50.4	15.8	66.2	34.6
1987	49.9	15.0	64.8	34.9
1988	50.4	14.8	65.3	35.6
1989	50.0	14.6	64.6	35.3
1990	49.4	14.9	64.2	34.5
1991	49.5	15.0	64.5	34.5
1992	49.0	15.3	64.4	33.7
1993	48.6	14.5	63.1	34.2
1994	48.4	13.7	62.1	34.6
1995	49.4	14.0	63.4	35.4
1996	49.9	14.4	64.3	35.5

Source: National Education Association, *Estimates of School Statistics*
(Washington, D.C.: NEA, 1958–59 through 1995–96).
Note: Washington, D.C., is not included in the analysis. The total may not
equal 100 percent due to rounding.

magnitude. Although the standard deviation was about 19 percent from the mean
from 1959 to 1965, it generally stayed at the 14 to 16 percent level. This finding
suggests neither a widening nor a converging tendency. In other words, interstate
differences that existed in the mid-1960s persisted through the mid-1990s. Despite school finance reform in the 1970s and late 1980s, the extent to which states
deviated from the overall mean remained stable. In 1966, for example, 67 percent

of all states were grouped between the 24 and 56 percent level of support (a 32 percentage point range). In 1996, the range shifted upward, but the difference between the upper and lower levels remained largely the same (a 29 percentage point range between 35.5 and 64.3 percent).

The relatively stable standard deviation at the aggregate level suggests that significant interstate variation in school support has persisted over the years. A more systematic examination of the state role in school financing merits a state-by-state analysis. Using data gathered between 1959 and 1996, I adopted a longi-tudinal approach. Instances of significant policy change often lead policy analysts to focus on the immediate pre- and post-reform years. Although the more focused research strategy helps magnify the politics in a critical period of policy change, it lacks a long-term perspective on policy development. A longitudinal analysis, in contrast, allows an examination of the extent to which state activism is sus-tained beyond the immediate reform period. Further, I propose a classification scheme that depicts distinct patterns of state support that can be defined in terms of a state's fiscal support status (parity or dominance) initially (the late 1950s) and whether state support has increased, remained stable, or decreased.

In light of the tremendous number of fluctuations in percentages of state aid for each state over the thirty-eight-year period, a linear regression was run on the thirty-eight data points for each state to help make interstate comparisons. The intercept of the regression line was then used as the state's fiscal support status at the beginning of the period, that is, 1959. The magnitude of the increase or de-crease in state aid for each year was provided by the slope of the regression line. The end value of the regression line was then calculated by multiplying the slope by thirty-seven, the number of interval years.

The parity-dominance status at both the beginning and the end of the thirty-eight-year period was determined in the following manner. If the intercept for a particular state fell below the 50 percent level, that state was considered to have held a parity status initially.[29] Likewise, states with an intercept that exceeded the 50 percent level were characterized as holding a dominance role at the beginning of the period. The same set of criteria applied to the end values of the regression line. Whether a state achieved parity or dominance status at the end of the period depended on whether the end value (for 1996) was above or below the 50 percent level.

Further, over the thirty-eight-year period, states were considered to have sig-nificant shifts in their fiscal support if they experienced at least a 10 percent change between the initial and the end points on the regression line. In other words, these states either increased or decreased their share of school costs by an annual incre-ment of at least 0.27 percent on average. States with less than a 10 percent change in their aid share over the years maintained a stable role.

Using these methods, each state was classified into a pattern of fiscal sup-port. As Tables 3.3 and 3.4 summarize, the six patterns are parity to dominance, parity strengthened, dominance strengthened, stable parity, stable dominance, and

Table 3.3. Classification of States' Fiscal Roles in Education in 1959 and 1996

	1996	
1959	Parity	Dominance
Parity		14
Strengthened	14	
Stabilized	8	
Subtotal	22	14
Dominance	4	
Strengthened		3
Stabilized		5
Weakened		2
Subtotal	4	10

dominance to parity. It should be noted that three of the patterns are not antici-pated by either the progressive state or the reluctant state perspective. Table 3.4 looks at these fiscal trends on a state-by-state basis.

The most pronounced state activism can be found in the fourteen states that shifted from parity to dominance status. These states were Iowa, Oklahoma, Idaho, California, Kansas, Indiana, North Dakota, Utah, Montana, Maine, Kentucky, Arkansas, Minnesota, and West Virginia. They increased their share by at least 16 percent in the thirty-eight-year period. Nine of these states experienced at least a 30 percent increase in their share of school funds over the years. The most re-markable example is Iowa, where the state share jumped from about 11 percent to over 57 percent of the total school cost. Oklahoma, Idaho, and California also stand out. The state share in California increased from about 32 percent to 71 percent during the same period. Clearly, Iowa led the rest of the nation in terms of the average yearly increase—at least 1.2 percentage points, as expressed by the slope in the regression line.

As Table 3.4 shows, several states in the parity-to-dominance pattern showed a more modest increase in state share. Minnesota and West Virginia, for example, experienced a smaller annual increase—less than half a percentage point, as ex-pressed by the slope in the regression line. Further, the linear regression analysis may underestimate the magnitude of annual fluctuations that states actually ex-perienced in reaching dominance status. Kansas, for example, maintained a stable state role until the early 1970s. Between 1972 and 1977, however, Kansas's state contribution increased from 27 to 45 percent. It was not until the early 1990s that Kansas actually moved from parity to dominance in state support. Arkansas and Oklahoma increased their support in a fairly steady manner, whereas most other states showed several significant shifts during the thirty-eight-year period. Equally important, as Table 3.3 shows, the parity-to-dominance pattern accounted for only fourteen states—the kind of evidence that the progressive state perspective is largely dependent on. However, most of the states that increased their fiscal sup-

Table 3.4. States Classified by Fiscal Pattern and Ranked by Annual Rate of Increase, 1959–1996

	Intercept (%)	Slope (%)	End Value (%)
All 50 states	38.25	0.36	51.75
Parity to dominance			
Iowa	10.64	1.21	56.69
Oklahoma	28.68	1.07	69.29
Idaho	28.30	1.06	68.73
California	32.07	1.02	70.71
Kansas	20.49	0.87	53.68
Indiana	28.97	0.86	61.67
North Dakota	22.73	0.84	54.73
Utah	28.10	0.84	59.93
Montana	22.59	0.84	54.36
Maine	26.59	0.77	55.98
Kentucky	48.78	0.64	73.08
Arkansas	41.08	0.59	63.61
Minnesota	40.89	0.46	58.30
West Virginia	49.46	0.44	66.19
Parity strengthened			
Nebraska	2.22	0.90	36.49
Ohio	21.92	0.71	48.93
Colorado	20.01	0.69	46.29
New Jersey	20.66	0.66	45.59
South Dakota	7.13	0.61	30.25
Massachusetts	19.90	0.58	42.09
Illinois	24.90	0.43	41.33
Rhode Island	27.90	0.42	43.98
Arizona	38.06	0.27	48.21
Oregon	23.16	0.32	35.44
Wyoming	33.21	0.31	44.98
Connecticut	28.57	0.32	40.58
Vermont	24.78	0.30	36.03
Wisconsin	29.14	0.29	40.13
Dominance strengthened			
Hawaii	70.69	0.66	95.67
Washington	54.37	0.54	74.71
Alaska	52.74	0.50	71.86
Stable parity			
Missouri	31.59	0.21	39.74
Maryland	35.40	0.12	40.04
Tennessee	47.84	0.03	48.88
New Hampshire	8.02	-0.01	7.49
Pennsylvania	46.16	-0.04	44.60
Virginia	38.57	-0.07	35.86
New York	43.60	-0.08	40.53
Michigan	44.71	-0.15	39.02
Stable dominance			
New Mexico	65.49	0.19	72.61
Alabama	62.63	0.14	68.06
Mississippi	54.48	-0.01	54.08
Florida	53.97	-0.04	52.29
North Carolina	67.95	-0.12	63.26
Georgia	63.99	-0.36	50.42
Delaware	78.93	-0.42	63.12
Dominance to parity			
Texas	51.67	-0.20	44.01
Nevada	52.21	-0.43	35.75
Louisiana	67.75	-0.47	49.61
South Carolina	69.01	-0.55	48.06

Source: National Education Association, *Estimates of School Statistics* (Washington, D.C.: NEA, 1958–59 through 1995–96).
Note: Strictly speaking, Georgia, Delaware, Nevada, Louisiana, and South Carolina experienced significant declines (over 10 percent) in state share and can be said to have followed a stable pattern.

port for public schools did not follow the parity-to-dominance pattern. Rather, other patterns emerged.

The reluctant state perspective is supported by the parity-to-parity fiscal trends in twenty-two states. These states can be further divided into two groups. Although they experienced a significant increase in school aid, fourteen states retained parity status over time (that is, parity was strengthened). All these states increased their share of total school costs by 10 percentage points over the years. Nebraska, in particular, showed significant gains in state support, increasing from a mere 2 percent at the intercept to 36.5 percent at the end point. Two states, Ohio and Arizona, were slightly short of attaining dominance status in 1996, as suggested by the regression analysis.

Eight other states showed a stable fiscal role within the realm of parity (that is, stable or declining parity). None of these states increased its share by over 8 percentage points in the entire period, and five states—New Hampshire, Pennsylvania, Virginia, New York, and Michigan—actually provided a lower level of support in 1996 than in 1959. Whereas Tennessee fell slightly short of assuming a dominant role, New Hampshire maintained its status as providing the lowest level of state aid among all fifty states during the thirty-eight-year period. With the exception of 1965, 1966, and 1970, the state portion of school revenues in New Hampshire never exceeded 10 percent. Of the states in the stable parity group, Michigan showed the greatest drop, a decline of almost 6 percentage points, as indicated by the regression analysis (see Table 3.4). Indeed, plagued by a declining economy based on the auto industry, Michigan showed a persistent decline in state school support since the mid-1970s. Consequently, localities assumed a greater fiscal burden until 1994, when the state adopted major restructuring of the school finance system.

Three patterns are not readily anticipated from the two perspectives. Four states—Texas, Nevada, Louisiana, and South Carolina—moved from dominance to parity status between 1959 and 1996. This suggests a nonlinear fiscal pattern— one that could not have been detected had the study focused on a shorter period. South Carolina, for example, had a 21 percentage point decline in state aid support over the years. Louisiana and Nevada reduced their state shares by 17 and 16 percentage points, respectively. Texas decreased its state share by over 7 percentage points.

Three states (Hawaii, Washington, and Alaska) held a dominance status as early as the late 1950s, and they increased their support levels even further over the years. All three states were above the national mean at all times. The state share in Washington and Alaska jumped by 20 and 19 percentage points, respectively, over the thirty-eight-year period. Consistent with the state's centralized system, schools in Hawaii received 96 percent of their revenues from the state in 1996.

Finally, seven other states, though maintaining their dominance status, provided either stable or declining support for public schools over the years. Georgia and Delaware experienced significant declines in state support, with Georgia experiencing a 13 percentage point decline, and Delaware showing a 16 percentage point drop in state share.

Effects of State Role on Urban School Finance

An important policy question is whether the six fiscal patterns influence the way public schools are financed in urban districts. Do urban districts in activist states receive greater state support? Do their schools rely less on property taxes? To examine the fiscal effects on urban districts, this study drew on another database of financial information for 422 school districts with an enrollment of at least 15,000 students in 1995. Districts were then classified in terms of the fiscal patterns, and the financial characteristics of urban districts across the categories were compared.

Urban districts varied in their financial characteristics, depending on the specific fiscal role of the state. As Table 3.5 shows, states that maintained a dominance status paid a greater share of the total expenses in urban schools. On average, the states with stable dominance or parity-to-dominance patterns supported urban schools at above the 50 percent level. In contrast, the parity states in 1995 provided less than 50 percent of educational costs. On average, states in the parity-strengthened and dominance-to-parity groups provided 43 percent of school costs.

Further, variation in state share was correlated with the dominance versus parity patterns. The higher the level of state aid (that is, dominance status), the smaller the interdistrict variation in the level of state support, as suggested by the coefficient of variation in each category in Table 3.5. Finally, districts in the more activist states were generally less dependent on property taxes as a revenue source. Indeed, urban schools in states with either dominance-stabilized or parity-to-dominance patterns were less dependent on property tax revenues. Interdistrict variation in

Table 3.5. Financial Characteristics of Urban Districts as Differentiated by State Fiscal Pattern, 1995

State Fiscal Pattern	Number	State Aid as Percent of Total Cost	Coefficient of Variation	Property Tax as Percent of Total Cost	Coefficient of Variation
Parity to dominance	127	54.4	0.205	30.4	0.353
Parity strengthened	59	42.5	0.331	43.3	0.355
Dominance stabilized	81	52.3	0.220	28.1	0.541
Dominance to parity	57	42.8	0.385	41.7	0.446

Sources: Based on school funding data as reported in the U.S. Bureau of Census, *Public Education Finances 1995* (Washington, D.C.: U.S. Government Printing Office, 1995).
Note: Urban districts are defined as having an enrollment of at least 15,000 pupils. States for which data were unavailable have been excluded. The dominance-strengthened and stable-parity patterns had too few districts for this analysis.

local revenues, however, did not neatly fit the dominance-parity categories. For example, districts in dominance-stabilized and dominance-to-parity groups showed a greater variation in reliance on property taxes.

Although the fiscal role of the states has an impact on urban districts overall, it remains unclear whether similar effects can be found in the largest central-city districts. Special attention is given to these districts because they share a disproportionate amount of educational problems due to concentrated poverty, a high percentage of minorities and new immigrants, and aging facilities. As Table 3.6 suggests, nineteen of the twenty central-city systems had a higher percentage of students in poverty than the statewide average. For example, whereas 75 percent of students in Boston were eligible for free and reduced-price lunch programs, only 13 percent of students in Massachusetts fell in the poverty category. Similarly, Chicago exceeded the statewide student poverty average by 55 percentage points. In addition, Milwaukee, Baltimore, Atlanta, and San Antonio exceeded their statewide poverty averages by over 50 percentage points.

Because of their greater needs, central-city districts would be expected to receive more state aid. To examine whether state allocation of funding was proportional to city systems' poverty characteristics, I developed a state support index that takes into account the interplay between concentrated poverty and the state share of total educational spending. The index was derived by considering the city versus statewide differences in both state aid and the proportion of students in poverty (column B minus column A in Table 3.6). A negative index suggests that the state fiscal contribution to the urban system fell short of the district's share of students in the poverty category. Using this index, I examined whether the twenty districts received a fair share of state aid. Contrary to the expectation that more state aid would go to the larger urban districts, Table 3.6 shows that eighteen of the twenty districts did not have a favorable state support index in 1994. In other words, only two districts received state aid at a level that was proportional to their student poverty share. When the concentration of students in poverty was controlled for, urban districts by and large did not receive a fair level of support from their states, regardless of whether the states belonged to parity or dominance groups. For example, all three large districts in California (a parity-to-dominance state) had unfavorable state support indexes when poverty was controlled for. Likewise, in the parity-strengthened group, five of the six districts had unfavorable state support indexes. Further, only seven of the twenty central-city districts received over 50 percent of their revenues from state sources. But of these seven districts, six had such high concentrations of children in poverty that their state support indexes remained unfavorable. In short, the parity and dominance differentiation at the state level has a limited effect on state funding support for big-city schools.

In sum, the fifty states do not follow a single fiscal pattern when it comes to supporting public education. Fourteen states provided over 50 percent of school expenditures in 1959, long before the public paid attention to state activism. Clearly,

Table 3.6. Poverty and the State Role in Twenty Large-City Districts, 1994

State Fiscal Pattern	District	Percent of Pupils in Poverty	Statewide Percent of Pupils in Poverty	Difference (A)	State Aid as Percent of Total Cost	Statewide Average on State Aid (%)	Difference (B)	State Support Index (B – A)
Parity to dominance	Los Angeles, CA	73.2	23.5	49.7	59.7	54.5	5.2	-44.5
	San Diego, CA	64.2	23.5	40.7	41.7	54.5	-12.8	-53.5
	San Francisco, CA	64.6	23.5	41.1	30.3	54.5	-24.2	-65.3
Parity strengthened	Tucson, AZ	30.4*	29.6	0.8	46.7	42.2	4.5	3.7
	Chicago, IL	71.2*	16.5	54.7	35.8	32.2	3.6	-51.1
	Boston, MA	75.0*	13.1	61.9	27.7	37.0	-9.3	-71.2
	Milwaukee, WI	65.9	10.4	55.5	56.6	41.1	15.5	-40.0
	Columbus, OH	49.0*	24.2	24.8	34.4	42.0	-7.6	-32.4
	Denver, CO	50.6	11.2	39.4	28.0	44.6	-16.6	-56.0
Dominance strengthened	Not applicable							
Stable parity	Baltimore, MD	65.2	14.9	50.3	57.8	39.0	18.8	-31.5
	New York, NY	64.7*	25.0	39.7	40.8	39.1	1.7	-38.0
	Philadelphia, PA	40.1*	15.8	24.3	50.6	42.3	8.3	-16.0
	Detroit, MI	63.4	15.7	47.7	79.1	68.5	10.6	-37.1
Stable dominance	Atlanta, GA	74.0	19.6	54.4	26.2	51.5	-25.3	-79.7
	Albuquerque, NM	28.7*	32.2	-3.5	77.2	66.1	11.1	14.6
Dominance to parity	Houston, TX	60.4	22.5	37.9	26.2	43.4	-17.2	-55.1
	Dallas, TX	64.9	22.5	42.4	22.9	43.4	-20.5	-62.9
	Fort Worth, TX	53.3	22.5	30.8	43.3	43.4	-0.1	-30.9
	San Antonio, TX	79.8	22.5	57.3	58.7	43.4	15.3	-42.0
	Memphis, TN	52.1*	20.6	31.5	41.8	49.9	-8.1	-39.6

Sources: Poverty data are measured in terms of students who are eligible for free and reduced-price lunch programs and were compiled from *The Condition of Education in the Great City Schools* (Washington, D.C.: Council of Great City Schools, 1990) and National Center for Education Statistics, *Characteristics of the 100 Largest Public Elementary and Secondary School Districts in the United States: 1995–96* (Washington, D.C.: Office of Education Research and Improvement, U.S. Department of Education, 1998), pp. 98–214. State poverty data were compiled from National Center for Education Statistics, *Digest of Education Statistics* (Washington, D.C.: U.S. Government Printing Office, 1997), Table 20: Household Income and Poverty Rates by State, 1996. State aid and data were compiled from National Center for Education Statistics, *Digest of Education Statistics* (Washington, D.C.: U.S. Government Printing Office, 1997).
* Poverty data are for 1990.

the longitudinal database offers a more balanced assessment of the changing state role in financing education. Further, an exclusive focus on the aggregate trend is likely to overlook significant interstate differences in school financing. Whereas changes in the overall mean over time may suggest a convergence toward state activism, the state-by-state analysis shows that significant variation has persisted. I have shown how these different state roles can be systematically classified into six distinct patterns and how they affect urban district finances. Equally important is to find explanations for the patterns of stable and declining state support. What, then, are the constraints on a greater state role?

Sources of Constraints on State Activism

Given the pervasiveness of parity states and the dominance-to-parity pattern, it is useful to look for explanations. The more restricted state role over time can be related to political culture, state legislative politics, structural economic constraints, and the legal context.

Localism

State variation in school support is often said to be rooted in each state's distinct political culture and history. In his examination of thirty-six school policy areas in the early 1970s, Wirt proposed the concept of a centralization score for assessing the state government's role in public education.[30] The lowest level of centralization (or highest local autonomy) scores zero (0.0), and the highest level of state policy control scores six (6.0). The average score for all fifty states was 3.56, which suggests that state governments generally exercise a fair amount of control over local districts. This pattern comes as no surprise. From a constitutional perspective, local districts are seen as agencies of the state educational system. The states enjoy substantial control over compulsory attendance, accreditation, curriculum, graduation standards, and such housekeeping matters as calendar, records, and accounting procedures. Localities generally maintain more discretion over district organization, guidance and counseling, pupil-teacher ratios, staff recruitment, and extracurricular activities.

Interstate variation in centralization scores is closely related to differences in cultural disposition.[31] According to Wirt, twelve "traditionalistic" southern states had contributed much to support local schools. Fourteen of the "moralistic" states in New England and the northern plains had a more limited fiscal role, thereby preserving a great deal of local autonomy. Case studies on individual states provide further empirical support for this cultural explanation.[32]

Although the degree of centralization seems to be useful in understanding the traditional state role (at least up to the early 1970s, when Wirt collected the data), it remains unclear how this factor interacts with other crucial variables in the changing political context since the 1970s. Perhaps the tradition of localism was substantially undermined by judicial and federal pressure for financial equity and by the taxpayer movement. Even in the early 1970s, Wirt found that practices in sixteen states were not consistent with the cultural explanation.[33] Nine of these states, for example, enjoyed extensive authority over school issues but had a limited fiscal role. Another seven had limited programmatic control but allocated a higher level of financial resources. In other words, political tradition should be considered one of several crucial sources of constraints on increases in state aid to local schools. These limitations notwithstanding, political culture can be relevant. States with a strong tradition of local autonomy are likely to exhibit a more restricted role over time. Even in the face of judicial pressure, these states are reluctant to increase their share of school costs.

Fragmented Power in the Legislative Process

A limited state fiscal role can be related to difficulties in gaining political support for a reform package in the legislature. Because they are related to revenue and spending issues, school finance reform bills are often parts of larger revenue packages. Given the fact that over 80 percent of state money is distributed through formulas written by lawmakers, the legislative process can be highly competitive.

Difficulties in forming the needed political coalition are likely to be magnified under two circumstances in the legislative process. The first occurs when the legislative authority structure in education is fragmented. In their comparative state study, Rosenthal and Fuhrman found interstate variation in legislative priorities in education.[34] Often, education committee chairs do not overlap with the membership on the ways and means and the appropriations committees. In each budgetary cycle, education has to compete with other major domains such as welfare assistance, transportation, and higher education. Given this fragmentation, newly adopted education programs may not be fully implemented due to insufficient funding. Likewise, partisan splits between the legislature and the governor's office, as well as between the two houses of the legislature, are likely to present political obstacles to enacting spending and taxing bills.

Moreover, legislative division can be aggravated by the big city–suburban split within the legislature. An example is Illinois, where the legislative feud between Chicago and the rest of the state has been a crucial factor in explaining state revenue and spending policies. Suburban and rural legislators rarely voted for tax increases to provide additional aid to the fiscally stressed Chicago schools. It is likely that the limited state role is illuminated by urban-suburban-rural contentions. Racial factors may further contribute to these cleavages. In other words, in states with major cities (such as Chicago in Illinois), state aid allocation can be substantially determined by complex political alignments.

Fiscal Constraint

Even when challenged by court decisions, the state policy response may be tempered by a restricted taxing structure, lack of surplus for dealing with extraordinary circumstances, and economic recession. States are subject to two sources of taxing and spending limitations. The first limitation is the extent to which a state relies on a limited set of revenue-raising mechanisms. In 1988, there were four states that did not have a general sales tax and one that did not rely on selective sales tax. More important, personal income tax was absent in six states, and corporate tax was not used by four states. For example, without a state income tax and with no revenue surplus, Connecticut adopted a reform package that was not backed by an increase in the state share of school costs.[35] Second, some states are subject to formal limits on revenues and spending. As of 1990, ten states operated under a set of constitutional limits on state finance, and another ten states had statutory limits.[36] In other words, when these formal fiscal constraints are present, states are less likely to play a greater role in school financing.

Constitutionality

When judicial pressure for finance restructuring is absent, the state share remains more stable over time. Between the late 1960s and the early 1980s, twenty-six states had no lawsuits pending against the school funding system.[37] Of the twenty-four states that were challenged, only five states were found to have violated their own constitutions by the states' highest courts as of 1981. Although the courts had overturned eighteen state funding systems by 1998, the courts upheld the legality of the financing systems in eighteen other states, including Arizona, Colorado, Georgia, Idaho, Maryland, Michigan, New York, Ohio, Oklahoma, Oregon, Pennsylvania, Rhode Island, and Virginia. Further, when courts find that reform has substantially addressed funding inequity, the state share becomes increasingly stable. This is true even for states that have gone from parity to dominance. An example is California. In April 1983, the high court in California ruled that the state system was in compliance with the judicial decree.[38] This decision, coupled with the recession, contributed to a 19 percent decline in the state share between 1982–83 and 1983–84.

MAPPING THE POLITICS OF STATE AID

Having identified various facilitating factors and constraints, I now attempt to correlate various political variables with each of the fiscal patterns. Table 3.7 presents a summary of this analysis. These findings are not meant to establish a statistically significant relationship but rather to specify the circumstances under which a particular state support pattern is most likely to emerge. Given the small number of states in each category, I caution against overgeneralization of the findings. Further, not all the variables are useful in understanding each pattern. Although similar factors exist across patterns, they may have different meanings when placed in the proper political context. To make sure that no group contained too few cases, the six fiscal patterns were consolidated into five groups of states, and each is associated with a distinct kind of politics. In other words, interstate variation in state funding can be explained by different types of politics. Generally speaking, and fairly consistent with the expectation, facilitating factors are found in states that have experienced a significant increase in funding share. States that have not experienced a significant increase in funding share are more likely to have constraining factors present.

Reallocative Politics

States that follow the parity-to-dominance pattern tend to associate with the politics of reallocation, where responsibility for funding schools is gradually shifted from the local to the state level. The process of reallocation has been driven by several factors, as suggested in Table 3.7. Seventy-one percent of these states experienced local taxpayer revolts. The public's discontent with the property tax burden gained further support as the high courts in 36 percent of the states in this group ruled against the constitutionality of the school funding system. Whereas two-party competition in the legislature in 43 percent of the states may facilitate higher state expenditures in education, organized interests (as indicated by union membership) tend to promote an activist state role. Consequently, half of the parity-to-dominance states were able to overcome the fragmentation of local governments and move toward school finance reform.

California offers a good example of reallocative politics. The combined effect of the *Serrano* decision (which overturned the funding system) and the passage of Proposition 13 (the property tax limitation referendum) has been a steady expansion of the state role in educational funding. Further, Proposition 98 stipulates that 41 percent of the state's general revenues go to public schools and community colleges. Naturally, teachers unions, urban districts, suburban communities, and other interest groups target their lobbying activities at the state capital. Unlike in many states, politics in California is substantially shaped by urban interests. Urban lawmakers dominate influential legislative offices and committee chairs—the speaker of the house, the president pro tempore of the senate, the chair of the assembly's ways and means committee, the chair of the senate appropriations committee, and the chairs of the education committees in the two houses.[39] To respond to their urban constituencies, the legislative leaders have funded a wide range of categorical programs. Indeed, on average, 26 percent of the urban districts' total school funding is from state categorical sources, compared with only 13 percent in the suburban districts.[40] For example, whereas Los Angeles receives 31 percent of its school revenues from state categoricals, Palos Verdes obtains only 8 percent of its funds from categorical programs. In the case of California, the parity-to-dominance trend has been beneficial to urban districts.

Table 3.7. Relation between Key Explanatory Variables and State Fiscal Patterns of Support

	PARITY TO DOMINANCE (N = 14)		DOMINANCE STRENGTHENED/ STABLE (N = 10)		DOMINANCE WEAKENED/ TO PARITY (N = 4)		PARITY STRENGTHENED (N = 14)		PARITY STABLE/ WEAKENED (N = 8)		TOTAL (N = 50)	
	N	%	N	%	N	%	N	%	N	%	N	%
Facilitating Factors												
1. System overturned	5	36	2	20	1	25	7	50	3	38	18	36
2. Local tax revolt	10	71	6	60	4	100	10	71	6	75	36	72
3. Black elected officials:												
Over 10	9	64	7	70	4	100	10	71	7	88	37	74
Over 100	3	21	5	50	3	75	3	21	7	88	21	42
4. Hispanic officials	9	64	6	60	3	75	12	86	5	63	35	70
5. Finance reform	7	50	1	10	1	25	3	21	3	38	15	30
6. Union membership:												
1983	5	36	4	40	0	0	5	36	4	50	18	36
1996	5	36	4	40	1	25	5	36	5	63	20	40
7. Two-party competition:												
In legislature	6	43	6	60	3	75	8	57	4	50	27	54
In governorship	5	36	2	20	2	50	3	21	4	50	16	32
8. Democratic win in governorship	3	21	6	60	1	25	3	21	2	25	15	30
9. Democratic win in houses	4	29	5	50	1	25	2	14	3	38	15	30
Constraints												
10. System upheld	4	29	3	30	0	0	6	43	5	63	18	36
11. Limits on state taxing/spending	6	43	3	30	4	100	5	36	3	38	21	42
12. More than 10% enrollment:												
Black	3	21	6	60	3	75	4	29	7	88	23	46
Black plus Hispanic	6	43	8	80	4	100	10	71	7	88	35	70
13. Middle-class income	5	36	7	70	2	50	11	79	7	88	32	64
14. Fragmentation of local units	11	79	4	40	1	25	8	57	4	50	28	56

Table 3.7 footnotes

1. As of 1988, courts in eighteen states had overturned the school finance system. See Education Commission of the States, "Litigation in Progress and Unsettled Lawsuits," www.ecs.org, November 1998.

2. Between 1976 and 1990, thirty-six states experienced property tax revolts. See Daniel Mullins and Phillip Joyce, *Tax and Expenditure Limitations and State and Local Fiscal Structure* (Bloomington: Center for Urban Policy and Environment, School of Public and Environmental Affairs, Indiana University, December 1995).

3. Total number of black elected officials in 1993 as reported in table 458, *Statistical Abstract of the United States*, Bureau of the Census, www.census.gov, November 1998.

4. Total number of Hispanic elected officials in 1994 as reported in table 459, *Statistical Abstract of the United States*, Bureau of the Census, www.census.gov, November 1998.

5. Fifteen states adopted major school finance reform legislation between 1991 and 1998. See Mary Fulton, "School Finance System Changes," Education Commission of the States, www.ecs.org, November 1998.

6. States whose union membership was above the national average of 17.2 percent of the total employed in manufacturing in 1996, as reported in table 690, *Statistical Abstract of the United States*, Bureau of the Census, www.census.gov, November 1998.

7. States where neither the Republican Party nor the Democratic Party controlled both houses in 1990, 1992, 1994, and 1996. States where neither the Republican Party nor the Democratic Party won all the gubernatorial elections in 1990, 1992, 1994, and 1996, as reported in tables 452 and 454, *Statistical Abstract of the United States*, Bureau of the Census, www.census.gov, November 1998.

8. States where the Democratic Party won the governor's races in 1990 and 1996. See note 7 above.

9. States where the Democratic Party controlled both houses in the state legislature in 1990 and 1996. See note 7 above.

10. As of 1998, courts in eighteen states had upheld the constitutionality of the school finance system. See Education Commission of the States, "Litigation in Progress and Unsettled Lawsuits," www.ecs.org, November 1998.

11. States in which state spending and tax limitations were adopted between 1977 and 1989. Stephen Gold, *The State Fiscal Agenda for the 1990s* (Denver: National Conference of State Legislatures, 1990), pp. 48–49.

12. Based on fall 1995 enrollment figure as reported in table 45 of the *Digest of Education Statistics*, National Center for Education Statistics, www.nces.ed.gov, November 1998.

13. States where per capita income exceeded 90 percent of the national average in 1997. See *Bureau of Economic Analysis*, www.bea.doc.gov, November 1998.

14. States where the number of local government units exceeded 1,000 in 1996, as reported in table 475, *Statistical Abstract of the United States*, Bureau of the Census, www.census.gov, November 1998.

Progressive Politics

States that belong to the dominance-strengthened and dominance-stable groups can be combined into a category broadly labeled as progressive. Over the years, state activism has been sustained by two political forces. First, some of the states enjoy a tradition of strong state government. For example, Hawaii has no local school districts, and all educational services are provided by the state. As suggested in Table 3.7, only 40 percent of the states in the progressive group have a relatively large number of local governmental units. This limited degree of local fragmentation is indicative of the traditionally strong state role in this fiscal group. The second facilitating force is the recent emergence of black political power, particularly in the southern states. Almost half of the dominance states have over 100 black elected officials. Sixty percent of the states have a public school enrollment that is over 10 percent black. Black representation may have contributed to Democratic control over both houses in 50 percent of the states and to Democratic victories in gubernatorial races in 60 percent of the states. Working within the Democratic Party caucus, blacks have gradually gained influence over educational policy.

An example of progressivism that blends with a traditionally strong state government is Mississippi. Among the poorest states in the nation, Mississippi has always ranked near the bottom in total educational spending on a per capita basis. Given the state's weak fiscal capacity, it is interesting to note that Mississippi ranks sixteenth in state funds for public education. In recent years, the state's active role in education and other social policy has been facilitated by biracial coalitions. During Governor Ray Mabus's administration in the 1980s, blacks were recruited to key leadership roles. As a result of redistricting, both houses saw significant gains in black representatives in the 1992 election. The newly empowered black caucus, with thirty-two representatives and ten senators, has taken a more aggressive stand on social programs by presenting its own budget. Black representatives call for higher state spending in historically black colleges and more funds to raise teachers' salaries in public schools.[41] Regardless of the impact of black leaders on the state budget, there is unlikely to be a reversal in the state's commitment to schools.

Sectoral Rivalry

Rivalry between two powerful sectoral interests is likely to exist in states that follow the patterns of dominance weakened and dominance to parity.[42] One faction calls for increasing state spending and consists of blacks and their representatives. Indeed, all states in this group have at least ten black elected officials. However, unions are not likely to be influential, as suggested by the low level of union membership. The other faction, which demands budgetary restraint, seems to be gaining influence. This opposing coalition is predominantly middle class and is able to impose limits on taxing and spending by the state government (as occurred in 100 percent of the states).

Texas offers a good example of the politics of sectoral rivalry. In 1989, the Texas educational finance system was ruled unconstitutional. In a nine-to-zero reversal of the appellate court's ruling, the state supreme court pointed out, "Districts must have substantially equal access to similar revenues per pupil at similar levels of tax effort. Children who live in poor districts and children who live in rich districts must be afforded a substantially equal opportunity to have access to educational funds."[43] The ruling set off fierce partisan conflict and interest-group contention that lasted three years. Having gone through various reform plans, the Republican governor and the Democratic-controlled legislature produced a compromise bill in 1990. The senate bill would have provided $500 million more to the state's 1,056 districts; in other words, no district would come out a loser. However, the seemingly modest increase in state support and the scattering of these funds prompted a district judge to reject the plan.[44] The prospect of school finance reform was substantially enhanced with the election of a Democratic governor, Ann Richards, whose campaign included state educational funding as a key issue. After numerous delays and last-minute give-and-take, the governor and the legislature produced yet another legislative proposal in June 1993. The proposed reform called for the state to reallocate "excess" local tax revenues from the richest 10 percent of the districts to support the statewide teacher retirement system, thereby freeing more state funds for the poorest districts. The plan would use property taxes collected from affluent communities to support schools in fiscally depressed communities. Although the plan was shaped by the Robin Hood principle, it did not commit additional state tax dollars. In other words, the state's political leaders remained constrained by middle-class concerns and made no serious attempt to call for an increase in state taxes to fund schools.

Fragmentary Politics

States that have increased their share of school costs within the parity realm (parity strengthened) are likely to be governed by fragmentary politics. Although policymakers and the public may prefer a greater state role, the process of building a reform coalition is far from complete. Indeed, efforts to shift greater responsibility to the state are likely to be tempered by contending racial, ethnic, and income groups, as suggested by a strong presence of Hispanics, blacks, and the middle class (see Table 3.7). Further, two-party competition in the legislature is found in 57 percent of these states. Finally, local governmental units are functionally specialized and territorially scattered to the extent that state aid is highly contested among suburban and city service providers.

Illinois is a good example of how school finance reform can be frustrated by fragmentary politics. In 1992, voters opposed a constitutional referendum that would have directed the state to be the primary funder in public education. The initiative was supported by 57 percent of the voters—3 percent short of what is needed to enact a constitutional referendum. As expected, support was the strongest from Chicago, and opposition came mainly from the surrounding middle-class suburbs. Indeed, the city–suburban rivalry was exacerbated by racial and income differences. Whereas whites constituted only 12 percent of the enrollment in the Chicago public schools, students in the suburban schools predominantly came from white middle-class families. With a fiscally conservative Republican governor and the senate under the leadership of a Republican from a middle-class suburb west of Chicago, it seemed unlikely that the state legislature would launch any major reform in school finance. Then politics took a dramatic turn in 1997 when the governor reversed his earlier position on school finance reform. When the legislature rejected his proposal to increase state income tax to lower the local tax burden in funding schools, the governor returned with a new reform package that would rely on user fees and sales taxes. The 1997 "compromise" reform legislation would guarantee a foundation level of $4,225 to every student in the state for three years, beginning in the fall of 1998. At least for a brief period, fragmentary politics gave way to coalitional politics in Illinois.

Politics of Non-Issue

States that assume a limited role in financing public education—the parity-weakened and parity-stable groups—are likely to be shaped by the politics of non-issue, where progressive reform is not placed on the legislative agenda. Seven of the eight states are dominated by middle-class interests, with a general reluctance to expand the state's fiscal role. Six of the eight states experienced local taxpayer revolts. The courts in 63 percent of these states upheld the legality of the school funding system, as Table 3.7 shows. Further, black representation is weak, and local governmental units are fairly scattered—the kinds of constraints that frustrate a statewide coalition for school finance reform.

Michigan, at least up to 1993, illustrates what happens when state aid to schools does not receive political support. In part due to the recession and the decline of the auto industry, Michigan experienced the steepest decline in state share in school costs among the parity-stable group. The state's limited role is seen in two different examples, one related to Detroit and the other to a small rural district. Detroit, the state's major city, is clearly isolated from the governing institutions at the state level. State–city relations have deteriorated during the long tenure of Mayor Coleman Young. In addition, the demographics have worked against the city. Whereas Detroit maintained 22 percent of the house seats in the 1960s, it controlled less than 14 percent of the seats in the 1980s. The suburban communities now hold 30 percent of the house seats. Just as Detroit's influence was declining, the state legislature became increasingly reluctant to provide additional aid to the city schools. In 1973, for example, the state legislature raised the minimum level of required local levy, which was substantially higher than Detroit's rate at the time.[45] To avoid risking a significant loss in state aid, Detroit had to impose a higher millage on its already shrinking property tax base. Although Detroit presently receives more than half its revenues from the state, there is limited political support for a more activist state in general. The latter point is illuminated by the failure of the state to intervene in the rural Kalkaska district in the northwestern lower peninsula area.[46] The district's levy proposal has been rejected three times by residents, who are mainly retirees with no school-age children. In response to the district's appeal for $1.5 million in state aid to keep the school open for ten more weeks, the state legislature cited the fact that the current state codes cannot force the district to stay open (unlike California laws). In the absence of a state subsidy, the district was forced to close the schools ten weeks early. In short, even in a fiscal crisis like the one in Kalkaska, the state has decided not to step in and assume greater responsibility in educational funding.

In late 1993, Michigan politics took a dramatic turn when the Republican governor and the legislature produced a compromise that would replace two-thirds of the local property tax revenues with state taxes. Among the facilitating factors for the bipartisan reform was the fact that Michigan's property tax burden was 30 percent higher than the national average.[47] Michigan voters subsequently approved a measure that raised the state sales tax from 4 to 6 percent, increased the tax on cigarettes threefold, and created other user fees.[48] The adopted measure also slightly reduced the state's personal income tax from 4.6 to 4.4 percent. Clearly, the plan reduced the property tax burden for home owners and, to a limited extent, business property owners as well. It remains to be seen whether the shift to a greater state role will actually reduce the disparity between the have-nots (such as Detroit and rural districts) and the haves (such as suburban communities outside of Detroit).

This chapter has identified several distinct patterns of state fiscal support in education between 1959 and 1996. Although the progressive state perspective finds support at the aggregate level, only fourteen states actually followed the parity-to-dominance path. States that have increased their share can be differentiated into two other patterns: dominance strengthened and parity strengthened. At the same time, the reluctant state perspective is useful for explaining the fiscal trends in the twenty-two states that have remained in the parity realm over the thirty-eight-year period. These fiscal patterns tend to be perpetuated by political and institutional factors. While the politics of reallocation has facilitated the parity-to-dominance trend, political fragmentation and the politics of non-issue have tended to perpetuate a reluctant state.

From a broader perspective, the presence of distinct state roles suggests a lack of policy convergence, despite the finance reform movement, the effects of the Great Society, and taxpayer pressure for a greater state assumption of public services. This state-by-state analysis has not found states converging toward activism, as many policy analysts have assumed in the context of federal and local retrenchment. Although the overall mean has persistently gone up, interstate divergence in the state support level has remained fairly stable during the thirty-eight-year period. Even in 1996, twenty-six states maintained a parity status, including four states that had shifted from dominance to parity. In other words, the "structure" of state aid to schools is neither "progressive" nor "reluctant," as the current literature suggests. Rather, state–local fiscal relations in the fifty-state systems consist of a set of fairly stable, yet distinct, fiscal patterns over time. An understanding of these variant fiscal patterns should lay the groundwork for efforts toward greater state support for urban schools. Having specified the development in the state role, in the next chapter I examine how state dollars are used to address equity issues.

4

Politics of Leveling Up Spending at the State Level

Efforts to create a more equitable distribution of school resources have gained ground in the states since the 1970s. In 1990, New Jersey's supreme court ended nine years of litigation by ruling that the state's educational finance system was unconstitutional. In Texas and Kentucky, lawmakers began to restructure their school funding systems after similar court decisions in 1989. In a 1989 decision in Montana, the court required equal access to "quality" instead of "basic" education. In 1997, the high courts in both Vermont and New Hampshire found the state funding systems unconstitutional. At least a dozen states have ongoing litigation over the constitutionality of the state finance system.

As of 1998, state education finance systems had been overturned by the high courts in eighteen states (involving twenty-one decisions) and upheld by the courts in another eighteen states (involving nineteen decisions). Reform in school finance, however, is not limited to the first group of states. This chapter examines the ways in which states have responded to the challenge of equity in school financing. Funding reforms are shaped by two concerns in public elementary and secondary education. First, state governments can address *interdistrict inequity* in spending caused by disparity in local taxable wealth. Second, state governments can act like the federal government and focus on *social inequity* caused by the presence of special-needs populations within a district. Although they often overlap, the two challenges and their associated policy strategies can be distinguished analytically.

The policy priority for the states is to address interdistrict disparity in spending. States, in general, are keen on allocating resources to level up spending in poor districts, thereby reducing the interdistrict gap in fiscal capacity. Social targeting, a dominant decision rule at the federal level, remains a secondary strategy at the state level. The state's two-tiered allocative strategies are shaped by various political and institutional factors. As I will argue, politics has a cumulative effect in sustaining two-tiered decision rules at the state level. In this chapter and the next, states' leveling-up and social strategies are systematically distinguished. They differ in terms of the financing mechanisms employed and the institutional and political factors that facilitate the state's role. The distinction between these two concepts offers a basis for a more differentiated understanding of the states' decision rules. These concepts are also useful in reviewing reform activities during the 1990s. This chapter looks at interdistrict equity, and the next discusses the emerging but limited state role in social targeting.

LEVELING UP AS A PRIMARY ALLOCATIVE STRATEGY

While the federal government pursues social redistribution, states have assumed the primary task of reducing interdistrict disparity in educational spending. It should be noted that there have been several failed attempts to increase the federal role in addressing the spending gap between wealthy and poor communities. The most publicized effort was a case in Texas that led to a 1973 landmark ruling by the U.S. Supreme Court. In *San Antonio v. Rodriguez,*[1] the U.S. Supreme Court in a five-to-four decision reversed a federal district court ruling. It concluded that since education does not constitute a fundamental interest under the U.S. Constitution, the state can choose to preserve local control by not interfering in interdistrict fiscal inequities. Despite *San Antonio,* the pressure for a more equitable allocation of state school funds has continued.

To be sure, the state handles a wide range of important educational policies—teacher certification, textbook policy, and graduation requirements, among others. By focusing on interdistrict equity issues, the state is distinguished from the other two levels of government in its allocative practices. Only the state devotes a significant amount of resources to address interdistrict inequity. This decision rule becomes even more significant in light of the increasing reliance on state sources of school funding in recent years. As discussed in chapter 3, state funding in public schools has become prominent in the context of federal and local governmental retrenchment. By the early 1980s, states became the primary funders of public education. To be sure, the shift toward a greater state role has been going on since World War I, when the state share was only 17 percent, as opposed to the 83 percent provided by local sources. But as Benson pointed out, only during the late 1970s and early 1980s did the "state government for the first time [become] the primary supplier of revenue" for public schools.[2]

The leveling-up strategy is designed to allocate state aid in ways that would favor localities with low property values and high tax burdens. The distribution of state dollars is formula based and is inversely correlated with the district's own taxing capacity, as commonly measured by the per student assessed valuation of taxable property. Although the poorer districts receive much greater amounts of state funds than their more affluent counterparts, the legislature enables as many districts as possible to be eligible. But before we discuss the politics, let us look at the trend in the states' allocative practices.

Trends in Two-Tiered Funding Strategy

On average, almost four out of every five dollars in the states' public education budgets went to address interdistrict inequities by the late 1980s and early 1990s. As Table 4.1 shows, less than 8 percent of the total school aid was specifically targeted for the socially disadvantaged. The remaining 14 percent was distributed according to the number of students in each district; in other words, these were flat grants that did not consider equity issues. Toward the end of the 1980s, the state role in equity issues gained prominence. As suggested in Table 4.1, in 1972, grants that lacked an equity focus accounted for almost 30 percent of the total state aid. These flat grants provided an equal amount of state dollars per pupil without regard to either the disparity in local wealth or the special needs of various student populations. By the late 1980s, however, funding for equity purposes represented 86 percent of the total state allocation. While aid to poor districts continued to rise from 68 to 78 percent of total state appropriations, socially targeted funding also increased from 2 to almost 8 percent. In short, state governments have adopted a two-tiered strategy in resource allocation.

These patterns are based on an analysis of finance data collected from eighteen state departments of education during early 1990. The sampled states vary

Table 4.1. Interdistrict Equity and Social Targeting as Percentage of Total State School Aid: Average for the Eighteen States

	Interdistrict Equity	Social Equity	Equity Total	Nonequity Total
1972	68.0	2.1	70.1	29.9
1988–1990	78.4	7.8	86.2	13.8
Percent difference	10.4	5.7	16.1	−16.1

Sources: Classification for 1988–1990 is based on an analysis of funding data supplied by state departments of education in Kentucky (1989–1990), Alaska (1987–1988), Minnesota (1987–1988), Utah (1987–1988), Delaware (1987–1988), Indiana (1986–1987), Idaho (1987–1988), Arkansas (1988–1989), Arizona (1987–1988), Ohio (1989–1990), Kansas (1987–1988), Colorado (1987–1988), Oregon (1986–1987), Wisconsin (1988–1989), Illinois (1986–1987), Texas (1989–1990), New York (1988–1989), and Michigan (1989–1990). Classification for 1972 is based on an analysis of funding data from U.S. Office of Education, *Public School Finance Programs: 1971–72* (Washington, D.C.: U.S. Office of Education, 1972). The Minnesota data were for 1972–73. The percentage calculations and categorization are my own.
Note: I had difficulty classifying territorial funds in five of the eighteen states. In Arizona, Indiana, and Delaware, the state's territorial-based allocation formula includes additional weighting for handicapped students. In Illinois and Minnesota, low-income pupils are assigned additional weights in the general formula. Disaggregated data in these five cases are not available. These methodological limitations, however, are not likely to have a significant effect on the spending trends.

by the level of state contribution, regional location, and population size. Phone interviews were conducted with key staff in charge of school finance in each sampled state. These interviews, lasting from twenty minutes to an hour, gave an overview of each state's approach to aiding public schools. Additional detailed information was received about the formulas for making appropriations. Using these documents and the information from the interviews, I delineated the key purposes of state subsidies to local schools. Allocation based on the assessed valuation of the districts is classified as territorial aid. Social equity funding includes programs for various disadvantaged groups, such as early childhood programs and exceptional education, bilingual, and compensatory services. Transportation and other items that count every student as equal in dollar terms are considered as distributive (or flat grant) funding.

To be sure, there are interstate variations. To some extent, the states' emphasis on equity can be related to their share of overall school expenditures. As I discussed in chapter 3, interstate divergence in state support level has remained fairly stable over the past four decades. Table 4.2 reports the changes in state aid for the sampled eighteen states in terms of the parity versus dominance framework developed in chapter 3. By the 1990s, nine states maintained a dominant fiscal role (the parity-to-dominance and dominance groups), and nine others remained in the parity realm. Clearly, the leveling-up strategy dominates the way state resources are used. Regardless of their dominance versus parity status, all but one state allocated between 55 and 98 percent of their school aid to address interdistrict fiscal inequity in the late 1980s and early 1990s. Two states, Delaware (a dominance state) and Arizona (a parity state), exhibited significant increases in aid to low-spending districts between 1972 and 1988–1990.

Although none of the sampled states reduced both leveling-up grants and social targeting during the study period, three states—Delaware, Alaska, and Wisconsin—increased both kinds of funding. All three states showed significant growth in their interdistrict equity allocation. Delaware, in particular, increased allocation to low-spending districts from less than 3 percent to almost 80 percent of the total state education budget.

Departing from the eighteen-state aggregate trend, most states tended to adjust their social equity spending upward by slightly reducing the portion for leveling-up purposes. Of the nine states in the parity group, five increased their social share while reducing their aid to low-spending districts in terms of the percentage of total school aid. Ohio increased social funding from 4 to 21 percent while reducing its leveling-up allocation from 82 to 63 percent. Similarly, of the seven states in the parity-to-dominance group, five saw growth in their social spending over time. For example, Utah cut its aid to low-spending districts from 82 to 55 percent while increasing its social spending from less than 2 to 12 percent of the total budget. In other words, social spending has received more attention over the last two decades in the state capital. Chapter 5 examines the state politics of social targeting in greater detail.

Table 4.2. Percent Change in State Aid to Schools for Interdistrict Equity and Social
Targeting, 1972 and 1988–1990

State Fiscal Role, 1959–1996	INTERDISTRICT EQUITY			SOCIAL EQUITY		
	1972	1988–1990	Percent Change	1972	1988–1990	Percent Change
18-state average	68.0	78.4	10.4	2.1	7.8	5.7
Dominance						
Alaska	59.6	82.4	22.8	0.0	13.9	13.9
Delaware	2.7	78.2	75.5	0.0	1.4	1.4
Parity to dominance						
Idaho	99.2	85.8	-13.4	0.0	7.8	7.8
Kansas	93.4	81.0	-12.4	3.0	12.1	9.1
Indiana	77.1	95.5	18.4	1.1	1.1	0.0
Utah	81.8	54.8	-27.0	1.6	11.8	10.2
Kentucky	98.8	75.2	-23.6	0.0	1.1	1.1
Arkansas	86.6	97.9	11.3	0.5	0.4	-0.1
Minnesota	82.2	70.0	-12.2	3.3	9.8	6.5
Parity						
Ohio	81.6	62.5	-19.1	4.3	21.3	17.0
Colorado	85.9	98.4	12.5	5.1	1.6	-3.5
Illinois	79.1	62.6	-16.5	7.7	13.1	5.4
Arizona	8.3	98.1	89.8	1.8	1.4	-0.4
Oregon	13.7	25.4	11.7	4.6	3.0	-1.6
Wisconsin	46.8	80.9	34.1	6.8	16.6	9.8
New York	92.6	70.0	-22.6	2.3	11.8	9.5
Michigan	82.2	79.3	-2.9	3.3	13.8	10.5
Texas*	65.6	59.7	-5.9	2.4	25.8	23.4

Sources: Classification for 1988–1990 is based on an analysis of funding data supplied by state departments of education in Kentucky (1989–1990), Alaska (1987–1988), Minnesota (1987–1988), Utah (1987–
1988), Delaware (1987–1988), Indiana (1986–1987), Idaho (1987–1988), Arkansas (1988–1989), Arizona
(1987–1988), Ohio (1989–1990), Kansas (1987–1988), Colorado (1987–1988), Oregon (1986–1987),
Wisconsin (1988–1989), Illinois (1986–1987), Texas (1989–1990), New York (1988–1989), and Michigan
(1989–1990). Classification for 1972 is based on an analysis of funding data from U.S. Office of Education,
Public School Finance Programs: 1971–72 (Washington, D.C.: U.S. Office of Education, 1972). The
Minnesota data were for 1972–73. The percentage calculations and categorization are my own.
Note: I had difficulty classifying territorial funds in five of the eighteen states. In Arizona, Indiana, and
Delaware, the state's territorial-based allocation formula includes additional weighting for handicapped
students. In Illinois and Minnesota, low-income pupils are assigned additional weights in the general
formula. Disaggregated data in these five cases are not available. These methodological limitations,
however, are not likely to have a significant effect on the spending trends.
*Texas followed the dominance-to-parity pattern.

Leveling-Up Funding Tools

The specific leveling-up mechanisms are complicated and vary from state to state.
The funding mechanisms can change from one legislative session to another.
Despite these shifts, I identified several grant types that states adopted to address
interdistrict spending disparity during the early 1990s. For analytical purposes, I
grouped the funding mechanisms as follows: foundation programs (thirty-three

states), resource equalizers (eight states), and a combination of the two (eight states). Only one state, Hawaii, assumes full funding and taxing responsibilities for local schools.[3] Over the years, regardless of partisan and political changes, the primary intent of these funding tools has remained largely intact.

Thirty-three states have foundation programs—nine use instructional units, and twenty-four use individual pupil counts as the basis for revenue distribution. These foundation programs can be traced back to the 1920s, when George Strayer and Robert Haig proposed such an allocation system for New York State.[4] As its label suggests, the foundation program establishes a baseline expenditure for each pupil or each instructional unit throughout the state. The state in effect guarantees a level of school support that poor districts could not otherwise afford. In most cases, districts are required to levy local property taxes up to a state-designated rate level, often referred to as the required local effort. State dollars are then channeled to make up the difference between local tax revenue and the preset minimum level of per pupil spending. In Iowa, for example, the state stipulated $2,250 as the per pupil foundation from state and local sources in 1988. In districts with a high tax burden or a low assessed land value, state aid makes up the difference between the foundation level and the revenues raised through the required local tax efforts.

Under the foundation arrangement, a state's responsibility is limited to providing the minimum level of school support. State aid does not go beyond the foundation level, although that can be adjusted annually. In many cases, however, the foundation level is far from sufficient to provide adequate school services. Instead of adhering to a restrictive fiscal role, an increasing number of states have developed funding mechanisms designed to allow for "equal access" to educational resources—namely, per pupil spending and taxing revenues. Local districts decide how many dollars are adequate for school services, and the state subsidizes either the local budget or the local tax yields. Eight states use primarily "resource equalizers" that either specify the state share of local spending (known as percentage equalizing) or equalize the tax returns of districts to finance schools (known as district power equalizing or guaranteed tax yield). Unlike foundation programs, equalizing systems do not place a fixed dollar limit on state support.

The concept of "percentage equalizers" was popularized by Charles Benson.[5] The state assumes a percentage of the district's total budget. The specific amount of state aid takes into account the difference between local and statewide averages in assessed property value on a per pupil basis. Some states use a "power equalizer," or guaranteed tax base (GTB).[6] Under this scheme, state aid helps to equalize the taxing capacities among districts. State aid, in effect, guarantees an equal amount of local tax returns at different levels of tax levy. For example, Wisconsin, one of the first states to adopt power equalizers, guaranteed a local tax base of $283,000 per student during 1988–89.

Another eight states have adopted a multitiered subsidy approach, supplementing the foundation with some kind of equalizers. This strategy is designed to address a major shortcoming in the foundation programs—a widening gap between the haves and the have-nots. Although the foundation level by itself is often inadequate to provide services in poor districts, rich districts use the required local tax effort to raise revenues well above the minimum level. These problems can be addressed by the multitiered subsidy strategy, which compensates poor districts above the foundation spending level. The Colorado legislature established an equalized tax yield at $66.33 per pupil per mill of local property tax in 1987. Districts with a lower yield per local tax mill received state subsidies up to the statewide average. At the same time, districts that were able to raise more than $66.33 per mill received a modest amount of state aid. Missouri supplements foundation allocation with a GTB. The foundation is 75 percent of the statewide average per pupil expenditure. The GTB was set at the ninetieth percentile of pupils, which was $66,682 for fiscal year 1987. The state subsidy is based on the difference between local tax yields and the expected yield from the state average GTB.

Use of district fiscal capacity as the primary basis for state funding allocation has been supplemented by the considerations of other jurisdictional differences, such as low or declining enrollment, transportation, and capital construction. Thirty-one states compensate districts with low population densities.[7] For example, Arizona provided additional funds to districts with fewer than 600 pupils, California allotted extra dollars to districts with fewer than 2,501 pupils, and Minnesota gave supplemental aid to high school districts with fewer than 500 students. Another twenty-four states take into consideration rapid enrollment loss. Vermont used the average enrollment over a two-year period as the basis for allotment. Declining districts in Ohio used the enrollment average over a three-year period to calculate state entitlements. In reimbursing local transportation expenses, all fifty states consider the number of pupils transported and the population density. For example, Wisconsin dispensed aid according to a sliding scale of mileage ($30 per pupil for a distance of two to five miles, and $85 for over eighteen miles). New York supported 90 percent of approved busing costs. Finally, Washington, Vermont, New York, and a few other states reimbursed capital construction costs on the basis of local wealth. Most other states considered only district size and enrollment for reimbursement of capital funds.

POLITICAL INSTITUTIONS AS A LAYERING PROCESS

Because states play such a prominent role in leveling-up strategies, much of the literature on the state politics of education can be said to describe the politics of reducing interdistrict disparity. This literature includes studies on the legislative process, constituency factors such as the taxpayer movement, and school finance reform in response to constitutional challenges. From these studies, the circumstances that facilitate states' pursuit of interdistrict equity can be specified.

A state's propensity toward interdistrict equity is affected by five institutional and political factors: constitutional challenges to the school finance system, local taxpayer protest movements of the late 1970s, state mandates on school improvement in the 1980s, political factionalism in the state legislature, and local control of schools. Taken together, political changes have resulted in the layering of state decision rules addressing interdistrict spending disparity.

Litigation

School finance litigation has directed the attention of the public and policymakers to interdistrict inequalities almost exclusively. Court rulings on school funding issues primarily address interdistrict funding gaps.[8] Clearly, evidence of interdistrict inequity can be cogently presented. The structure of the plaintiffs' argument is seemingly straightforward—disparity in local taxable wealth is closely linked to spending differences, which contribute to inequities in educational quality. In virtually all judicial challenges, taxpayers in districts with low property values were found to carry heavy tax burdens. Students in these high tax–low wealth districts do not seem to benefit from the fiscal well-being of the state as a whole. By the late 1980s, twenty-six states had faced legal challenges, and state courts found that twelve of them had violated state constitutional provisions of equitable education.

Using information reported by the Education Commission of the States (ECS), I analyzed the decisions made by state high courts as of 1998. As Figure 4.1 suggests, court rulings have shifted in favor of the plaintiffs in the last three decades. The number of decisions in favor of the defendant states declined from seven in the 1970s to six in both the 1980s and the 1990s. At the same time, the number of court rulings that declared state funding systems unconstitutional increased from five in both the 1970s and the 1980s to eleven in the 1990s. In 1997 alone, the courts found the funding systems in Ohio, Vermont, and New Hampshire unconstitutional. Consequently, the eighteen states that violated their constitutions had to restructure their funding systems to reduce interdistrict inequity.

Judicial impact has not been confined to the eighteen states where the state funding cases were successful. As Brown and Elmore pointed out, the pace of the diffusion of finance reform measures among states was surprisingly rapid.[9] In response to the *San Antonio* ruling, thirteen states adopted reforms in 1973 alone. By the early 1980s, a total of twenty-eight states had adopted reforms to address interdistrict inequities. During 1991 and 1998, fifteen states adopted major legislation to revamp their school funding systems.[10] The proliferation of reform measures resulted in part from legislators' concern over the perceived cost in the event of an unfavorable court ruling. Further, school finance reform was encouraged by a "national network" whose members included both education policy insiders

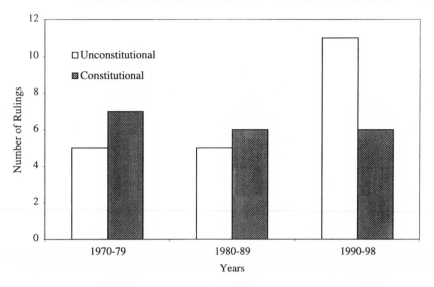

Figure 4.1. State high court rulings on school funding systems, 1970–1998. (Compiled from Mary Fulton, "School Finance System Changes," Education Commission of the States, www.ecs.org, November 1998)

and other advocates.[11] Communication among members of this network helped policymakers in several states learn from what had been tried elsewhere. Even in the absence of judicial pressure, legislatures adopted finance reform measures in Florida, Illinois, South Carolina, Wisconsin, and several other states.[12] In those states, finance experts associated with the network drafted the legislative proposals. According to one count, state officials in eleven of the twenty-eight reformed states and members of special task forces in all twenty-eight states were closely associated through this extensive national reform network.[13]

Taxpayer Protest

Leveling up as the primary mechanism for addressing school funding inequity is, in part, a response to the local taxpayer movements of the mid and late 1970s. Discontent with property taxes was evident. According to a 1978 Gallup poll, when asked to identify their dissatisfaction with various taxing sources for public schools, 52 percent of the respondents mentioned local property taxes, 21 percent cited federal taxes, and 20 percent named state taxes.[14] Consequently, between 1978 and 1983, of the sixty-seven tax or spending limitation measures on state ballots, thirty-nine were approved.[15] These taxpayer campaigns, in turn, put pressure on the state legislatures to distribute aid so as to ease the tax burdens of virtually all districts.[16] In allocating state dollars to the district, the legislature reinforces the jurisdictional authority of the district over its taxpayers.

Equally important, taxpayers' preferences for a lower tax burden, spending control, and better public-sector performance generated new pressure on state governments to reassess the magnitude of many of their social welfare programs. In a comprehensive assessment of tax revolts, Citrin concluded that "Proposition 13 has modified the culture of policy-making. Austerity and self-reliance have become new symbols of legitimacy. Politicians increasingly speak the language of trade-offs and constraint rather than progress and social reform."[17] A similar reversal of policy preference was found in a series of statewide surveys following the 1980 passage of Proposition 2½ in Massachusetts. Although its central goals were to obtain lower taxes (particularly property taxes) and more efficient government, the vote for Proposition 2½ seemed consistent with the nationwide trend of taxpayers' opposition to financing welfare and other public assistance programs.[18] For example, both pro- and anti–Proposition 2½ voters "thought that [the] greatest cuts could be made in the welfare and public assistance" programs among a list of fifteen major state and local services.[19] However, current service levels in various traditional municipal areas, such as education, were strongly supported.

This selective policy preference (anti-redistribution but pro-education) in Massachusetts, a state with a strong liberal tradition, was similar to that observed in studies of taxpayer movements in Michigan and California.[20] Consequently, five years after Proposition 13, California's expenditures on welfare and health programs dropped from 36 to 33 percent of the state's total budget.[21] Other studies found that AFDC recipients were among the major losers in the aftermath of a successful tax limitation initiative.[22] Because cities have a greater concentration of welfare recipients, they are expected to be adversely affected by these new budgetary realities.

In contrast, general funding for education did not suffer major cuts, because tax revolts do not necessarily mean that voters are critical of the local schools. According to an ECS survey in Idaho, for example, 75 percent of the voters did not want to see schools suffer as a result of the anti–property tax Proposition 1.[23] Moreover, voters in the states that rejected these antitax measures often enjoyed substantial state support in school finance. Without exception, teacher associations and other public employee groups formed the core of the coalition against the tax relief drive. According to an ECS study, the Colorado spending limitation referendum would have been rejected even if its proponents had had enough money to launch a statewide campaign. This is because a majority of Coloradans were more satisfied with both governmental and educational spending than were people elsewhere.[24] In 1978, Oregon's Measure 6 (similar to Proposition 13 in California) was rejected by a narrow margin of 52 to 48 percent, a sharp reversal of an earlier 66 to 22 percent support margin based on a preelection poll. This tax limitation drive was seriously contested by a broad-based coalition consisting of the governor, education interests, and other public employee groups, and there was widespread media opposition to Measure 6.[25] In 1992, Oregon voters finally supported Measure 5, a constitutional amendment to limit taxes that is likely to have long-term adverse impacts on both public schools and higher education institutions.

Given the message of anti-redistribution in many tax revolts, state legislatures are not likely to use state funds to promote major reallocation of educational resources. The taxpayers have sent the message that a continual increase in education funding is acceptable, as long as all the dollars are not channeled to the needy. By focusing on districts with high local tax burdens, state policymakers can distribute resources widely, protect services for their constituencies, and reduce political risk in the next election.

Mandates

Recent state efforts to achieve greater school accountability have also contributed to the decision rule that uses the district as the unit of state funding allocation. The late 1980s saw a series of lawsuits for greater interdistrict equity, including those in Alaska, Connecticut, Indiana, Oregon, North Dakota, Michigan, and Minnesota. The climate is different from that of the 1970s, however. Whereas reforms of the 1970s were motivated largely by concerns for equal access to education, the latest lawsuits represent local efforts to make the state government pay for new state mandates for school improvement.

Indeed, in response to public concerns about educational excellence, state legislatures have become actively involved in school reform. During the first wave of reform immediately following the 1983 publication of the federal report *A Nation at Risk,* states rapidly imposed higher standards on local districts. Virtually all states raised the graduation requirements for public school students. Two-thirds of the states instituted statewide pupil testing at certain grades. This phase of top-down reform gave way to the second wave of state legislation. Since the mid-1980s, an increasing number of states have paid attention to issues related to classroom instruction and curriculum. Many states now require additional instructional time in the classroom. Others have begun to provide assistance for prospective teachers. More recently, several states created curricular frameworks in various subject areas that guide teaching in the classroom. In light of public concerns about declining school performance, districts are required to report fairly detailed student performance outcomes, which are included in the annual state report card.

There is no question that the reform agenda is dominated by state legislatures and state school boards. Proposals that come from both the legislature and the state school board have the greatest chance of being adopted. According to an analysis of a 1985 survey, out of the 174 major reform proposals being considered in California and twelve other states, 53 (30.5 percent) were initiated in legislatures, and 63 (36.2 percent) came from state school boards.[26] Governors submitted 9 percent, various task forces and commissions were responsible for 13.8 percent, and state education agencies and chief school officers proposed 9.8 percent of all policy innovations. Of the 174 submitted proposals, only 89 were finally adopted. Of them,

83 (93.3 percent) were traced to either the legislature or the state school board. Policy initiations from other sources, including the governor, largely failed in the legitimization process. The prominence of state legislators in the current reform is largely consistent with the literature on education policymaking in the United States. According to a six-state study, state lawmakers who specialize in education are most capable of influencing their colleagues in voting on school matters. These influential legislators are appropriately labeled "the insiders."[27]

Altogether, these mandates have not only placed enormous demands on existing local resources but have also provided a legitimate basis for mobilizing broad support for additional state subsidies to all districts. In particular, state funds are needed for planning and evaluation, professional development, and curricular improvement.

Legislative Representation

State aid to districts is linked to the way power is distributed in the state legislature. State legislatures, the institutions with primary authority for writing allocation formulas, are structured by geographic representation. To attain the legislative coalition needed to pass a school finance package, lawmakers are likely to adopt territorial strategies in which no district suffers a reduction in state support. This leveling-up strategy is consistent with the electoral concerns of legislators. They are keenly aware of the territorial impacts of spending decisions. Legislators are community bound and have an obligation to secure program benefits for their own constituencies as defined by a set of geographic boundaries.[28] Their support for territorial policy is likely to yield both electoral gains for themselves and tangible benefits for their constituencies. In New York, for example, the senate, which traditionally plays a stronger role in education than the assembly, has successfully disbursed state aid to all but 9 of the state's 708 districts. As Berke, Goertz, and Coley observed in New York, "the legislative design for the distribution of state aid to education continues to mirror the distribution of power in the legislature rather than the educational needs of the state."[29]

Equally important, the district-by-district distribution of state funds creates incentives for lawmakers to overcome two structural barriers that often jeopardize major spending and taxing decisions in education. The first lies in the fragmented legislative authority structure on educational matters. Each lawmaker is assigned to membership on several standing committees, each of which can exercise enormous influence on the passage of appropriations bills. In a multistate study, Rosenthal and Fuhrman found significant interstate variation in educational concerns among the legislative leadership.[30] In many cases, education committee chairs are not members of the ways and means committee. In addition, partisan splits between the governor's office and the legislature or between the two houses are likely to make the adoption of spending and taxing bills difficult. Policy disagreements across legislative committees were found to be quite frequent in a study of over 400 bills handled by six legislative committees in the 1985 legislative session in Oregon.[31] Although 70 percent of the education bills were reported out of the education committees in both houses, 12 and 29 percent of the committee bills in the senate and house, respectively, were killed in other committees. The second barrier comes from regional splits. Acting to protect their benefits, suburban lawmakers often vote against state aid packages that primarily address the needs of the central-city schools. Having observed legislative politics in several states, Cronin concluded, "States stood by as city school boards wrestled with unions, neighborhood school champions, special interest groups, and others who opposed cutbacks in budgets or services as enrollments dropped and retrenchment became necessary."[32] Racial factors may further contribute to these regional cleavages.

When leveling-up grants are broadly distributed, lawmakers have incentives to build legislative coalitions that bypass structural and regional factionalism. One state where creative legislative compromise fostered the scattering of school funds is New York.[33] Low-tax-effort districts in upstate and rural areas are treated "as if" they fulfill the state-required minimal tax level. Affluent downstate districts are protected by save-harmless provisions so that they, too, receive state subsidies. At the same time, New York City is considered to be five separate boroughs and hence is entitled to a substantially higher level of state funding.

Local Control

Finally, legislatures tend to adopt interdistrict equity reform because they can address inequity without undermining local autonomy in instructional and curricular matters. District-based aid does not impose additional programmatic directions on local schools, does not tighten accountability procedures, and does not expand the state's regulatory presence in the classroom. Once the state aid goes to the district, the local staff can use the additional money for general purposes. In short, schools and their programs remain under local control.

WHEN POLITICS CONTRIBUTES TO LEVELING-UP STRATEGY

Given the facilitating factors, it is not surprising to find that the most popular kind of equity reform during the 1990s centered on reducing the interdistrict spending gap. Several examples can be cited. Nebraska's unicameral legislature overrode the governor's veto and adopted a reform package that would level up school spending in all districts. The new financing system was designed to favor districts with a weak tax base. At the same time, the plan did not restrict voter-approved increases in local spending in the more affluent districts. Voters endorsed this territorial approach to school finance in the next election by ousting the incumbent governor from office and rejecting two measures that would have halted the reform.[34] When fully implemented, the new funding arrangement will shift the burden of funding public education from the local property tax to state sales and income taxes. The state's share will increase from 23 to 45 percent of total school spending.

The leveling-up strategy also figures prominently in states where the highest courts have overturned the education finance systems. In June 1989, the Kentucky Supreme Court decided that "students in property poor districts receive inadequate and inferior educational opportunities as compared to those offered to those students in the more affluent districts. . . . Children in 80% of local school districts in this Commonwealth are not as well-educated as those in the other 20%."[35] The legislative response to the court ruling, known as the Support Education Excellence in Kentucky (SEEK) program, provided additional aid to all districts. The reform also allotted additional resources to districts with a concentration of low-income students. Under the original legislative proposal, the affluent districts would have been given fewer state dollars if they chose to exceed the state-designated base spending level by over 15 percent.[36] But under intense lobbying from those affluent districts, the legislature revised the package and allowed them to spend up to 30 percent more than the state-designated base without jeopardizing their state aid.[37] As a result of the leveling-up efforts by the state, interdistrict spending inequity decreased. According to one evaluation, the correlation between per pupil spending and the district's property wealth declined from 0.87 in pre-reform 1989–90 to 0.48 in post-reform 1992–93.[38]

Interdistrict inequity is also a major concern in Texas. Its education finance system was ruled unconstitutional by a unanimous court decision in 1989. In reversing the appellate court's ruling, the state supreme court pointed out, "Districts must have substantially equal access to similar revenues per pupil at similar levels of tax effort. Children who live in poor districts and children who live in rich districts must be afforded a substantially equal opportunity to have access to educational funds."[39] Having gone through various reform plans, the legislature and the governor finally resolved their many differences and agreed on Senate Bill 1, which would have provided $500 million more to the state's 1,056 districts. However, the seemingly modest increase in state support and the scattering of these funds prompted a judge to reject the plan.[40] As the opinion stated, under Senate Bill 1 "the rich can still raise revenue through local property taxes and the poor cannot. The poor will receive state funds to equalize the difference, but only up to a level of bureaucratically and legislatively determined 'adequate,' not to the level of the real difference in educational opportunity."[41] Following rounds of political negotiations, the Texas legislature adopted a reform bill in 1993 that provided several options for resource-rich districts to share part of their revenues with resource-poor neighboring districts.

In February 1997, the high court in Vermont declared the state's funding system unconstitutional. The ruling was based on extensive evidence that showed funding disparity between affluent districts near the state's ski and recreational resorts and poor rural districts. For example, Peru was able to tax handsomely on its $2.2 million per student valuation and spent $6,476 on each student. In contrast, Richford was able to spend only $3,734 because of its more restricted tax base of $140,000 per student. In a prompt response to the court ruling, the legislature and the governor adopted a seemingly sweeping reform that established a $5,000 block grant for each pupil and basically replaced the district-based property tax with a statewide property tax. Act 60, as the reform bill was labeled, also provided property tax relief to property owners who earned less than $75,000 per year. However, owners of second homes, which are disproportionately located in resort towns, and small businesses were not given tax relief. Consequently, the 40 resort towns are likely to bear a higher tax burden than the remaining 220 towns.[42]

In short, reform efforts during the 1990s were largely consistent with a leveling-up strategy. A "reformed" state aid system compensates for inequalities in the tax base among jurisdictions. Taxpayer equity continues to dominate the policy debate. Often, the state legislature distributes new tax dollars to property-poor districts without reducing its existing support for affluent districts. To a large extent, only limited attention has been paid to meeting the educational needs of special-needs pupils, an issue that chapter 5 addresses.

LIMITS OF THE LEVELING-UP STRATEGY

Size of the Spending Gap

A key policy question is whether the state's leveling-up strategy has the effect of narrowing the gap in fiscal capacity among districts. To be sure, there are variations from state to state. If one considers the nationwide picture, the intended policy effects seem to be largely mixed. According to a 1990 survey conducted by the Congressional Research Service, the highest-expenditure districts spent almost three times as much per student as the lowest-expenditure districts in many states.[43] In New York, the gap was 2.6 to 1; in Ohio, it was 2.8 to 1. In Illinois, the ten richest elementary districts spent an average of $6,300 per pupil, compared with $2,000 in the ten poorest districts in 1987. Similar patterns of interdistrict disparity were documented in a report prepared for the House Committee on Education and Labor.[44] The report showed that Montgomery County in Maryland outspent the city of Baltimore by over 50 percent on a per student basis, even though the latter received substantial federal and state aid. Clearly, Maryland's school aid policy did not significantly narrow the gap between the more affluent districts (for example, the wealthiest 10 percent) and the rest of the state.

Using the latest available state-by-state information (1994), I analyzed the extent to which disparity persisted between the fifth and ninety-fifth percentiles of the districts in each state. To standardize the measure of interdistrict inequity,

I developed the spending gap index, derived by dividing the excess per pupil spending in the wealthier districts by the statewide per pupil spending. As Table 4.3 shows, the spending gap index for all fifty states in 1994 averaged 0.544 (or 54.4 percent of the statewide per pupil spending), which was slightly higher than the 1991–92 gap of 24 percent that the GAO reported.[45] My analysis showed that nine states had a modest disparity gap of less than 25 percent between the haves and the have-nots. In seven of these nine states, the state fiscal role assumed a dominance status (see chapter 3). These seven states were Hawaii (with a state centralized funding system), two parity-to-dominance states (California and West Virginia), and four stable-dominance states (Delaware, Florida, Mississippi, and North Carolina). In contrast, seven states maintained a substantial level of interdistrict inequity in which the wealthiest districts outspent the poorest by over 100 percent. Four of the seven were states that maintained a parity fiscal role, namely, Nevada, Nebraska, Oregon, and Arizona. The other three states were all in the dominance group by 1996, including Montana, which shifted from parity to dominance but had the largest spending gap index (2.09) among all fifty states. Most of the states, however, fell in the moderate range of interdistrict spending gap. As Table 4.3 shows, twenty states had a spending gap index between 0.26 and 0.50, and another fourteen states had wealthy districts outspending their poorer counterparts by about 50 to 100 percent of the average statewide per pupil spending.

The persistence of this spending gap is due in part to the widening disparity in local taxable wealth. Urban districts with a declining economic base and a high concentration of children in poverty are unable to raise more local tax dollars for education.[46] At the same time, affluent districts, with a healthy tax base, are able to spend more on their schools regardless of how the state allocates its aid. Indeed, state aid does not seem to have much effect on spending and taxing practices in wealthy districts. These districts have continued to spend a lot more at a faster rate than the rest of the state. According to one analysis, educational spending is highly correlated with the district's wealth in thirty-seven states.[47] In other words, a state's decision rules seem to run into structural limitations—the state's effort in leveling up the lower-spending districts is far from effective in narrowing the gap between wealthy and poor districts.[48]

Adequacy in Schooling Opportunities

Disparity in interdistrict spending has contributed to unequal access to key services for disadvantaged children. Some analysts argue that inadequate support for student learning may provide a sound justification for court intervention.[49] The notion of adequacy is complementary to efforts to promote interdistrict equity, in that a certain level of resources must be available to poor districts to create the instructional conditions to meet state- or districtwide educational standards. In an extensive study of New Jersey, a congressional investigation found that wealthier districts are able "to offer from their own resources a greater range of programs

Table 4.3. Classification of States by Spending Gap Index between 5th and 95th Percentiles of Districts in per Pupil Spending, 1994

	Spending per Pupil, 1996 (A)	Disparity between 5th and 95th Percentiles, 1994 (B)	Spending Gap Index* (B/A)
U.S. average	$5,660	$3,044	0.54
2.01 or greater			
Montana	$5,202	$10,858	2.09
1.01–1.25			
Nevada	$4,855	$6,072	1.25
Nebraska	$5,725	$6,526	1.14
North Dakota	$4,717	$5,144	1.09
Oregon	$5,736	$6,155	1.07
Arizona	$4,481	$4,771	1.06
Washington	$5,868	$6,018	1.03
0.76–1.00			
Wyoming	$5,808	$5,681	0.98
Kansas	$5,384	$4,548	0.84
Alaska	$8,238	$6,701	0.81
Texas	$5,245	$4,197	0.80
0.51–0.75			
Idaho	$4,287	$3,190	0.74
Utah	$3,645	$2,707	0.74
Vermont	$6,690	$4,045	0.60
Illinois	$6,267	$3,766	0.60
South Dakota	$4,315	$2,580	0.60
Minnesota	$5,816	$3,446	0.59
New Hampshire	$6,098	$3,495	0.57
Maine	$5,955	$3,371	0.57
Oklahoma	$4,788	$2,683	0.56
Missouri	$4,689	$2,502	0.53
0.26–0.50			
New York	$8,442	$4,247	0.50
Colorado	$5,051	$2,398	0.47
Ohio	$5,663	$2,516	0.44
New Jersey	$9,644	$4,171	0.43
Massachusetts	$7,128	$3,047	0.43
Michigan	$6,540	$2,758	0.42
Wisconsin	$6,247	$2,546	0.41
New Mexico	$5,533	$2,073	0.37
Louisiana	$4,342	$1,568	0.36
Arkansas	$3,303	$1,185	0.36
Pennsylvania	$6,881	$2,330	0.34
Connecticut	$8,343	$2,762	0.33
Virginia	$5,614	$1,819	0.32
Iowa	$5,461	$1,747	0.32
Tennessee	$4,832	$1,466	0.30
Rhode Island	$7,151	$2,139	0.30
Alabama	$4,302	$1,235	0.29
Georgia	$5,935	$1,677	0.28
Kentucky	$5,245	$1,451	0.28
Indiana	$5,866	$1,552	0.26
0.00–0.24			
South Carolina	$4,581	$1,150	0.25
North Carolina	$4,941	$1,195	0.24
Florida	$5,270	$1,210	0.23
Mississippi	$3,948	$896	0.23
California	$5,034	$1,102	0.22
Maryland	$6,115	$1,320	0.22
Delaware	$6,903	$1,312	0.19
West Virginia	$5,742	$861	0.15
Hawaii	$5,131	$0	0.00

Source: Based on data reported in Education Week 17 no. 17, Jan. 8, 1998, pp. 86–87.
*The spending gap index is derived by dividing the disparity figure by per pupil spending.

and to serve a higher percentage of eligible pupils than poor districts."[50] For example, although Englewood has a high concentration of poor children, the property-rich district funds many programs for the disadvantaged, including all-day kindergarten, an after-school program, a social worker, elementary counselors, and high school programs in dropout prevention and substance abuse. In contrast, property-poor districts are unable to fund programs for their disadvantaged pupils. East Orange and Camden cannot afford an all-day kindergarten. In Trenton, there are not enough resources (local or state) to support social workers, counselors, or prekindergarten programs.

There is mounting evidence that spending variations among districts have contributed to disparity in the learning and instructional setting. Consider the supply of experienced teachers. In Pennsylvania, where property value strongly correlates with district spending, Hartman found that teachers in wealthier districts have three years more experience than those in the lower-spending districts.[51] Similarly in New Jersey, teachers in districts with a lower socioeconomic status (SES) have an average of twelve years'experience, compared with fifteen years for those who stay in high-SES districts.[52] Further, the quality of curriculum is vastly different. In a 1990 ruling, New Jersey's high court pointed out that the Princeton district provides one computer for every eight children, whereas the resource-poor Camden schools have one computer for every fifty-eight children.[53] Resource-rich districts are also able to offer art and music programs in preschool. Poorer districts, according to the New Jersey ruling, can rarely afford art programs. In Montana, science classes in poor districts are filled with outdated equipment and inferior facilities.[54] In Kentucky, poor districts lag far behind in mathematics, science, foreign languages, music, art, and specialty programs.[55]

POLITICAL RESISTANCE AGAINST CLOSING THE GAPS

Leveling-up allocation is likely to continue as long as the current institutional practices remain intact. Clearly, to close the gap between rich and poor districts, the state would have to adopt systematic reform that goes beyond the leveling-up strategy. It would require a major redistribution of resources from affluent to poor districts. Naturally, attempts at any kind of Robin Hood redistribution have met with staunch political opposition from the haves.

A good example of political resistance against redistribution is New Jersey. In *Abbott v. Burke* (1990), the New Jersey Supreme Court unanimously ruled that the state's school finance system was "unconstitutional as applied to poorer urban school districts." The court directed the legislature to address the special education needs of the poorer urban districts so that their funding would become "substantially equivalent to the average of that of property-rich suburban districts." The court paid particular attention to the concentration of social needs in inner-city schools in the state's twenty-eight poorest urban districts. Redistribution of resources was clearly at the center of the remedy pushed by Governor James Florio immediately following the court's ruling. The governor's plan, which was known as the Quality Education Act and was signed into law on July 3, 1990, proposed using all additional state aid for property-poor districts with concentrated poverty. The school reform plan would be financed by $2.8 billion in new and increased taxes. It would reduce state aid to over 200 wealthier districts by phasing out subsidies for personnel pensions, a move that drew opposition from the teachers union and the School Boards Association.[56] A major portion of the new state funds would be distributed to thirty "special-needs" urban districts. Administrators in Newark, for example, planned to use their $54 million in extra state aid on "high-impact" intervention programs, including dropout prevention.

Optimism for the reform was substantially dampened after the November 1990 election, when U.S. Senator Bill Bradley, a close ally of Governor Florio, narrowly survived a Republican challenge. This came at a time when the governor's own popularity had declined substantially. Taking seriously this measure of voter dissatisfaction with his reform and tax-increase plan, Florio indicated his willingness to reconsider the package.[57] A compromise that included a much lower level of resource redistribution was adopted by the state legislature. At the end of his first term, Florio was defeated by Republican Christine Todd Whitman, who promised to reduce the state income tax by 30 percent in three years.

The New Jersey story took another dramatic turn on July 12, 1994, when the state supreme court ruled for the third time in two decades that the state's school finance system was unconstitutional.[58] This latest decision required the state to develop a funding plan to address the disparity between poor and wealthy school districts by September 1996. By the fall of 1997, the governor and the lawmakers adopted a reform plan that would allocate an additional $140 million in state aid to the twenty-eight poorest districts. These new dollars, which were substantially less than what the lower court had called for in an earlier ruling, would be targeted for whole-school reform and other curricular strategies that were designed to improve student performance. This latest legislation was indicative of the state's efforts to broaden the definition of *remedy* from an exclusive focus on equalizing the spending gap to the notion that the state is responsible for providing "substantially equivalent" funding for the poorest and the most affluent districts.[59] The latter suggests that as long as the state provides an "adequate" level of support toward meeting educational goals, the plaintiffs' complaints will be considered addressed by the state. Given this latest round of negotiations between the judiciary and the state, one would not expect to see institutional politics cease to shape the state's decision rules in school funding.

The decades-long litigation in the New Jersey case suggests the difficulty of finding a policy solution when governance is highly fragmented. Spending inequity among districts, according to the Congressional Research Service, is most severe in industrialized states with a sizable minority population.[60] New York, with 28 percent minorities, has a spending disparity ratio of 2.6 to 1 between rich and poor districts. In Illinois, where minority children make up 26 percent of the enrollment, the gap is 3.1 to 1 in elementary schools. In Texas, with 36 percent minorities, the spending disparity is 2.8 to 1 among unified districts.

The relationship between the minority population and the spending gap suggests the conjoint influence of race and income on schooling opportunities—the concentration of minority populations in resource-poor communities in metropolitan areas. In the 1990s, six out of ten students in central-city districts came from minority groups, and eight out of ten suburban students were white. Given the pervasiveness of metropolitan inequality, policy analysts argue for a major restructuring of local school finance by moving toward a metropolitan- or statewide funding system.[61] At issue is whether a new kind of constructive politics can be created so that fragmentation (be it racial or regional in nature) can be replaced by a broad-based coalition for greater redistribution of resources to address the rich-poor gap. The first key step is for governors to be willing to take risks in promoting a collective vision for the next generation, despite resistance from taxpayers. In the unlikely event that a state is willing to pay greater attention to narrowing the gap between the haves and the have-nots, policymakers can take a lesson from the ways resources are currently used to address social inequity.

5
The Emerging State Role in Social Targeting

Decision rules designed to improve social equality are no longer the exclusive domain of the federal government. Although the federal government has been most active in social targeting (as chapter 2 argues), states have increasingly allocated their own funding to implement programs to meet the educational needs of the disadvantaged. Over time, state guidelines on social targeting constitute another layer of decision rules, operating in ways that tend to be fairly independent from federal direction. How does this distinct role of the states come about? And how are the states' policies shaped by state politics? These questions are examined in this chapter.

Since the 1960s, states have broadened their involvement in social equity issues. Although less prominent than their leveling-up strategies, targeted services for disadvantaged students have received an increasing amount of state resources (as suggested in chapter 4). In distinguishing social targeting and interdistrict fiscal capacity as two separate policy matters, I argue not only that disadvantaged pupils concentrate in less affluent districts (as expected in most cases) but also that their needs place additional service demands on the district (both wealthy and poor). Subsequently, state resources are used in supplemental services for various groups of educationally disadvantaged children across the state.

Spending priorities for social targeting vary from state to state, and they differ in terms of the concentration of particular needs. Overall, by the early 1990s, state provisions for special education were extensive. In some states, state-funded programs in exceptional education predated the 1975 passage of the Education for All Handicapped Children Act (P.L. 94-142).[1] Yet states seemed less active in programs for students with limited English proficiency, for low achievers from low-income families, and for other categories of disadvantaged children. In this chapter, I first highlight the development in state social strategies. Then I examine the politics of social targeting. Finally, I connect state resources to instructional activities at the classroom level. Using data collected from schools with high concentrations of disadvantaged students in four states, I map the macro-micro linkages in state-funded programs for special-needs students.

GROWING DISTINCTIVENESS FROM FEDERAL POLICY

The distribution of state resources addressing social inequalities has changed in recent years. During the 1960s and 1970s, state fiscal policies for compensating social inequity tended to imitate the federal categorical arrangement. In fact, categorical aid became the prevalent way of providing state-funded services to special-needs populations. Resource targeting and "pullout" classes were common practices at the school and classroom levels.

During the 1980s, however, an increasing number of states diverged from the federal categorical model. Currently, state social equity policy is distinct from federal social policy in three ways. First, states have shifted from the federal categorical model to an allocative system that weights special-needs students more heavily than others in general state aid formulas. The shift from categorical to pupil weightings occurred when states assumed greater autonomy over policy decisions in the climate of Reagan's New Federalism. Whereas this alternative arrangement was used by only five states in the mid-1970s,[2] in the 1990s, a majority of the states use pupil weighting in the general formulas for special-education students. Several states use reimbursement methods, subsidizing local districts for the approved excess cost of the special services. States that provide bilingual and compensatory services are fairly evenly divided between those using pupil weighting and those using categorical grants. Of the states that provide compensatory programs, thirteen adhere to pupil weighting[3] and fifteen retain categoricals.[4] In bilingual education, six use pupil weights,[5] and fifteen allot funds through categorical grants.[6]

Using additional weights as allocative criteria does not necessarily govern the specific use of state dollars at the district and school levels. Indeed, policymakers can choose various targeting options for the local use of supplemental state funds.[7] At one extreme, the state can make no targeting provisions at all, allowing districts or schools to decide on specific allocations. This option reflects the strong public support for local control in education. At the other extreme, the state formula can stipulate that districts target the supplemental aid to serve only a particular category of students. To make sure that districts and schools comply with state guidelines, states are expected to develop and implement an elaborate accountability framework. As will be discussed later, states vary in their choice of targeting provisions in promoting social equity.

The second distinction is that state-funded programs have become more independent of federally funded programs. Even in the early 1980s, at the beginning of Reagan's New Federalism, Moore, Goertz, and Hartle found that for compensatory education, none of the five sampled states blended state appropriations with federal funds.[8] Instead, three states operated programs that were administratively and substantively distinct from federally funded compensatory education. The remaining two states had procedures that allowed for programmatic coordination, but resource allocation and priority setting remained separate from the federal program. These observations led the authors to conclude that state agencies respond not just to federal policy signals but also to state political values. To maintain their identity in social policy, states have developed their own accounting procedures, hired their own staff, and implemented their own reporting requirements.

Third, consistent with a climate of state assertiveness, more states are defining participant selection mechanisms for their special-needs programs. Among state-funded compensatory education programs, for example, an increasing number of states have moved away from the federal model of funding for the economically disadvantaged. Instead, many states now use performance-based criteria in allocating funds for special-needs students.[9] These state practices are likely to become even more popular as the concept of accountability in the public sector becomes increasingly defined in terms of outcome-based performance.[10]

POLITICS AND STATE SOCIAL EQUITY

Facilitating Factors

The overall increase in social support from 2 percent to almost 8 percent of total state aid in the eighteen-state sample between 1972 and 1988–1990 (see Table 4.1) suggests that social equity has received more attention from policymakers in recent years. Several factors have fostered a greater focus on social equity in state finances. Taken as a whole, these institutional and political changes have the cumulative effect of sustaining the state decision rule in social targeting.

Federal Rule Layering

Federal social equity policy has stimulated state funding increases in programs for special-need populations. The prominent state role in school spending has been encouraged by the adoption of legislation that promotes equal educational opportunity. In this regard, federal school policy during the Great Society era of the mid-1960s and 1970s played a crucial role.[11] Although federal funds have contributed to less than 10 percent of all school revenues (as discussed in chapter 2), federal programmatic guidance has clearly stimulated state activity in addressing special needs. In no area in school policy is the exercise of federal judicial and enforcement power more important than in the racial desegregation of school districts. Most visibly in the Deep South, state compliance with federal judicial guidelines significantly reduced racial segregation in the region's public schools by the late 1970s.[12] Outside of the South, to comply with federal standards, state funding increased for programs in transportation, staff training, and special school projects that facilitated desegregation in Detroit, Milwaukee, Cincinnati, Boston, and St. Louis.[13]

Further, in compensatory instruction, Native American programs, and bilingual education, state legislation is modeled after federal policy. By the early 1980s, twenty-four states were allocating their own state revenues for compensatory education, supplementing federally funded projects in the poorest neighborhood schools.

State programs for students with limited English proficiency were encouraged by the 1970 Department of Health, Education, and Welfare guidelines against native-origin discrimination, ESEA Title VII assistance to language minorities, and the 1974 U.S. Supreme Court decision in *Lau v. Nichols*. In *Lau,* the Court ruled that school districts are responsible for providing instructional programs to students with minimal English proficiency. Thirty states either mandated or permitted bilingual programs, although only twenty-one states provided funds for bilingual projects. In addition, California, Montana, Alaska, and Washington adopted statutes in the area of Native American education.

Finally, unlike bilingual and compensatory education, instructional programs for the handicapped between the ages of five and seventeen are now mandated by all fifty states. Often, state provision of special programs is promoted by well-organized interest groups in the state capital, as this chapter discusses later. All states provide funds for these services above and beyond the federal funding through the Education for All Handicapped Children Act and its subsequent legislation, although their allocation mechanisms differ.[14] Sixty percent of the states allocate state aid on the basis of the size of the classroom or personnel unit. Eight states assign additional weights to the handicapped, and eleven states provide for the excess cost of the special services.

As the federal government shifted toward devolution of program responsibility during the Reagan years, most states maintained the allocative practices they had established years before. Many states, for example, continued to fund major categorical programs. Numerous states provided additional funding for curricular reform and teacher training in response to public concern about declining performance following the publication of *A Nation at Risk*.[15] A few states took the opportunity during the Reagan era to eliminate politically unpopular programs such as school desegregation. Others streamlined the administrative process. For example, the legislatures in Utah, Washington, and Arizona consolidated major single-purpose programs into more broadly defined block grants, thereby allowing greater local discretion in setting priorities for special-needs programs.[16] Despite these changes, the state's social equity role has remained basically intact.

Advocacy Groups

In the past three decades, advocacy groups for the handicapped, migrant children, and minorities focused on bringing about reform through new legislation or court action. As Murphy described these lobbying activities, "they have helped to raise the consciousness of various groups about their needs; they have helped to change common perceptions about the scope of governmental responsibility for solving problems; they have helped to spur the growth of special interest groups in the states."[17] Interest groups range from intergovernmental lobbying groups, such as the Council of Great City Schools, to highly specialized interests, such as The Association for the Severely Handicapped (TASH). As Reynolds observed, "TASH has been most effective in producing a full array of trainers, researchers, and policy advocates from within its own ranks. They conduct research, develop policies, and advocate very aggressively for their policies."[18] Advocacy groups for urban clientele are likely to be extensive. For example, according to a survey on educational advocacy organizations governed by minority-dominated boards, there are two that represent the interests of American Indians, three for Asians, eight for blacks, and fifteen for Latinos in the Chicago area alone.[19] To be sure, legislative successes have been uneven. Many state-funded services for the handicapped preceded P.L. 94-142. In bilingual and compensatory education programs, however, state programs followed federal initiatives.

Minority Representation

An increase in minority political representation has facilitated state social spending in education. The civil rights movement of the 1960s gave rise to a new class of black officials, who tend to share a strong commitment to social redistribution. Because blacks make up a disproportionate share of the poverty population, black officials are advocates of public programs to alleviate the economic deprivation of their constituencies.[20] In education, for example, black school board members are instrumental in reducing "second-generation discrimination" for black students.[21] Of the thirteen states in the eighteen-state sample that increased social spending between 1972 and 1988–1990, 54 percent had a greater level of black representation (with at least ten black elected officials) in the education policy arena in the late 1980s. Only one of the five states that reduced social grants had greater black representation.

Constraining Factors

Although politics has facilitated social targeting in some states, there are institutional and political constraints on the state role to promote social equity.

Dependence on Federal Funding

States have traditionally relied on federal funding to address social targeting. Federal educational support for the disadvantaged has been fairly stable, in large part as a result of a strong "benefits coalition," whose key players include intergovernmental actors, lobbyists who represent the interests of various disadvantaged groups, and veterans of Congress in the area of education policy.[22]

Concerns about Adequacy

There is controversy as to how much additional state aid is "adequate" for the various types of special-needs students. This was a key contention in several court cases that focused on cost differentials between "regular" and special-needs students. One example is the debate over the concept of "municipal overburden."[23] In 1974, four of the largest cities in New York (New York, Buffalo, Rochester, and Syracuse) joined the lawsuit as plaintiffs-intervenors in *Levittown v. Nyquist*. The four cities argued that the state aid formula had overstated their taxable wealth but understated their educational burden. Four types of overburdening were cited: municipal service costs due to higher needs of city populations for police, fire, welfare, and other services; higher operating costs in urban schools; higher absenteeism costs, thus reducing state aid based on attendance instead of on enrollment; and higher concentration of the disadvantaged in city schools.[24] In 1982, the Court of Appeals of New York overturned the lower court decisions and ruled that those funding inequities did not violate either the federal or the state constitution. Funding reform, the court ruled, remained the responsibility of the state legislature. In addition, policy analysts remain skeptical of the overburden concept. For example, a three-state study provided evidence that cities have access to a broad revenue base and that a portion of a city's tax burden can be exported to noncity residents.[25]

The notion of "adequacy" in social responsibility has gone beyond the debates among the legal and educational professions. As the taxpaying voters grow increasingly skeptical of the benefits they receive from governmental programs, they become more vocal in supporting service retrenchment for the disadvantaged. Through a series of statewide referenda beginning in the mid-1990s, voters sent strong signals to the state leadership that they prefer educational policy to be both fiscally and socially conservative. In this regard, Californians led the nation by passing statewide referenda that terminate affirmative action in college admissions, end educational services for children of undocumented migrants, and place a one-year limit on bilingual education programs for children with limited English proficiency. Voters in several states, including Washington, are likely to adopt similar measures. As their taxpaying constituencies reassess the scope of the government's social responsibility, politicians are likely to take a fiscally cautious approach to social equity.

Legislative Process

Coalition building for targeted social funding can be difficult when the state legislative process strongly favors using the district as a whole in allocative decisions. During the fiscally stressed 1980s, special-needs interest groups were less influential than taxpayers who wanted to reduce their tax burden. Instead, broad-based coalitions in support of "omnibus" legislative packages seemed crucial to school spending decisions.[26] Under enormous public pressure to lower taxes, the

Arizona legislature adopted a comprehensive school reform package in a 1980 special session. This legislation was approved after extensive bargaining among over 100 interest groups from the taxing community, the professional sector, and municipalities.[27] In other words, single-issue interest groups find it difficult to operate effectively in a retrenchment climate. Moreover, there is city–suburban contention over aid to the disadvantaged. In Illinois, for example, the 1978 legislature reduced the weights assigned to poor students, which decreased state aid to inner-city schools. Of the eighty-six lawmakers who voted for the bill, eighty-five represented districts outside of the city of Chicago. In contrast, forty-seven of the sixty-five legislators from both major parties who voted against the measure came from Chicago. In short, regional cleavages tend to undermine coalition building for social redistribution.

Partisan Politics

The allocation of state resources for socially disadvantaged students can be blocked by partisan politics. The most prominent example is New Jersey, where Democratic governor James Florio was voted out of office in part because he wanted to increase state taxes to improve educational quality in the state's poorest districts. As discussed in chapter 4, in *Abbott v. Burke,* the New Jersey Supreme Court unanimously ruled that the state's school finance system was "unconstitutional as applied to poorer urban school districts."[28] The New Jersey ruling is significant because it paid particular attention to the concentration of socioeconomic needs in inner-city schools. Additional costs to address the needs of disadvantaged pupils were recognized. The court estimated that programs to "reverse the educational disadvantage the children start out with" in urban districts would cost about $440 million for the first year. Some examples of intervention programs included better libraries, additional guidance programs, alternative education programs for potential dropouts, and intensive preschool programs.

Social equity was clearly at the center of the remedy plan pushed by Governor Florio immediately following the court's ruling. The governor proposed a "Robin Hood" plan, under which more than 200 affluent districts would lose state aid and the poorest thirty districts would receive most of the revenues from the $2.8 billion in new and increased taxes. One-quarter of the state's public school pupils reside in the thirty special-needs districts. As Commissioner of Education John Ellis put it, "This is the most exciting effort to improve urban education that the nation has ever seen."[29] Additional resources also drew new state regulations. As Florio pointed out in the signing ceremony, "Without the right tools, the right safeguards, indeed the right attitudes, additional money alone may not improve our schools."[30] To make sure that the money went to improve education, the state established a monitoring system with internal and external review teams, a new inspector general on education spending, and an urban advisory group to oversee implementation of the reform.[31] Under public pressure to improve school performance, districts looked for effective ways to channel resources for educational improvement. For example, administrators in Newark planned to use their $54 million in extra state aid on "high-impact" intervention programs, including dropout prevention. Other special-needs districts were likely to spend the new resources on reducing class size, preschool programs, and parental involvement programs.[32]

However, the 1993 election of Governor Christine Todd Whitman, a fiscally conservative Republican, virtually halted the redistributive efforts of the previous three years. After several years of negotiations and legal actions, Governor Whitman and the legislature proposed a reform package in 1997. The plan was finally approved by the high court and would provide an additional $140 million to support whole-school reform in the twenty-eight poorest urban districts. The level of additional state funding for social targeting, however, was less than half that called for by a lower court. The compromise also enabled the state to set its own pace in moving toward the goal of equalizing spending between rich and poor districts. In short, the history of New Jersey reform illustrates the complicated tasks state political leaders have to confront to meet courts' equity standards within budgetary constraints.

MAPPING THE CLASSROOM EFFECTS OF STATE SOCIAL TARGETING

As an increasing number of states address social equity policy, the effects of supplemental dollars on promoting learning opportunities for the disadvantaged at the school and classroom levels become a key policy concern. What is the relationship between decisions on appropriations made in the state capital and instructional organization in the classroom, including the use of ability grouping and curricular coordination between the targeted services and the mainstream setting? To what extent do state funding strategies impede instructional services for the disadvantaged? What kinds of funding strategies facilitate a more effective instructional environment? To better understand these macro-micro linkages in the process of producing learners, I examined the implementation of state-funded programs for the disadvantaged in a sample of inner-city schools in four states. In this section, I trace the different kinds of funding strategies from the state, through the urban district, and into the school and classroom, where students are placed in bilingual and compensatory education programs.

Divergence from the federal model has encouraged greater variety in state programs for the disadvantaged. This diversity provides an opportunity for more systematic inquiry into the relationship between state socially oriented strategies and classroom practices. However, the classroom effects of the different state strategies have not received much attention from researchers and public policy analysts. There are at least three reasons for this absence of systematic research. First, researchers who are interested in redistributive issues have focused almost exclusively on federally funded programs.[33] Even though state funding for these purposes has become important in recent years, its level continues to lag behind federal support. For example, the 1987 national assessment of Chapter 1 reported that only about 10 percent of the poorest schools were heavily dependent on state-funded compensatory programs. In the late 1980s, state aid in compensatory education amounted to less than 30 percent of the combined federal and state funding for this purpose. In bilingual education, state funding constituted less than 50 percent of total program funds.[34] Consequently, research questions on the state role are often overshadowed by concerns about federal policy. Research that does look at state provisions tends to focus on how state and federal programs can be coordinated to achieve federal goals rather than disaggregating the distinctive impact of state programs.[35]

Second, even in the literature on state finance, most studies focus on the impact of wealth disparity among school districts, or on territorial inequities (see chapter 4). Since *Serrano* in the late 1960s, the school finance litigation has directed the attention of policymakers and the public almost exclusively to territorial inequalities. State courts use a territorially defined standard of equality and a uniform set of measures to assess the interdistrict equity of state aid.[36] Remedies are designed to reduce the gap in property tax yields between affluent and poor districts. No single standard or set of commonly accepted measures exists, however, for evaluating state spending for social equity.[37] With the notable exception of the *Abbott v. Burke* decisions (1990 and 1994) in New Jersey, court rulings on school funding issues seldom pay primary attention to social inequities.

Third, the few studies that do focus on state-funded special-needs programs largely ignore the classroom as a unit in the multilevel policy organization. Indeed, there are few systematic studies about how state aid to special-needs programs affects the school and the classroom.[38] In evaluations of state compensatory programs in Connecticut,[39] Georgia,[40] Louisiana,[41] and South Carolina,[42] distribution of services and student achievement were the major concerns. Three of these studies described instructional arrangement options and class size, but none provided further classroom information. School district evaluations in Austin, Texas,[43] Dade County, Florida,[44] New York City,[45] Portland, Oregon,[46] and Saginaw, Michigan[47] also minimized the discussion of classroom variables. In other words, instructional practices fall outside the boundaries of most of the current work on state-funded programs. The linkages between state policy and the classroom remain largely unexamined.

Understanding Macro–Micro Linkages

In light of the limitations of the current literature, the remainder of this chapter seeks to fill both a conceptual and an empirical gap. I hope to generate discussion about the importance of state-funded programs (as distinguished from their federal counterparts) for special-needs populations and examine the evidence for macro-micro (from state policy to classroom) linkages. Accordingly, this study examines the impact of state-funded programs on the education of two groups of students: pupils meeting state-specified criteria of economic or academic disadvantage, and pupils identified as having limited English proficiency (LEP). State compensatory and bilingual programs are fiscally and administratively distinct at the state level. In school districts and in schools themselves, these programs are sometimes amalgamated with their federal and local counterparts to produce one set of services. The task is to identify and document those services that state funds have purchased for the disadvantaged at selected program sites. In this study, a preliminary attempt is made to link state policy to instructional arrangements. By comparing aspects of the funding of state programs, hypotheses are generated about the organization of instruction in schools.

In constructing an analytical framework, two policy strategies are used to characterize state programs. The first is program targeting. In order to dichotomize the spectrum of targeted programs, I use a narrow definition of the term: a targeted program is one in which specific resources are distributed for the benefit of identified and eligible students only. All other programs are nontargeted. This definition is consistent with the literature. Funkhouser and Moore rely on the same criterion to distinguish their set of state compensatory education programs from others that weight students in general aid formulas without "attaching strings to the use of the funds generated by the additional weight."[48] This distinction is also drawn by McDonnell and McLaughlin[49] and by Fuhrman.[50]

The second policy strategy I consider is the level of state funding in social programs. States appropriate different amounts for their special-needs programs. Many states do not fund such programs at all. The School Finance Collaborative reported that twenty-eight states have state compensatory education, and twenty-one states support bilingual education (including both states that support the teaching of English as a second language [ESL] only and those that also encourage native-language instruction).[51] Among those states that do supply compensatory or bilingual programs, student need influences spending levels.[52]

The two policy strategies—targeting and funding—can be linked to the organization of instruction for compensatory and bilingual students. First, through targeting provisions, the state establishes accountability mechanisms that govern the use of program resources. The tighter the targeting provision, the greater the likelihood that eligible students will be identified and grouped so that they alone receive program resources in the classroom. The presence of targeting provisions is likely to produce an identifiable structure, and their absence a nonidentifiable structure, for special-needs students. Specific needs at individual schools are less likely to shape resource allocation in targeted programs.

Second, in both identifiable and nonidentifiable structures, the amount of state aid determines the amount and kinds of instructional services provided to pupils. In appropriating supplemental funding, the state program absorbs the costs (such as salaries) of providing additional educational services for needy students. Compensatory services, for example, are estimated to cost 1.6 to 2.4 times more than regular classroom instruction.[53] Given these cost differentials, one would expect to find that disadvantaged pupils receive additional instructional attention as state programs receive higher levels of funding.

This framework, as depicted in Table 5.1, connects two aspects of state policy—targeting and funding level—to instructional arrangements for special-needs students. These arrangements differ in the degree of organizational discreteness of the service structure. Four types of instructional arrangements are recognized: distinct (self-contained classrooms), intermittent (pullout classes), enhanced (smaller class size), and diffuse (in-class assistance). The variation in classroom organization occurs in response to conditions that are made possible by the state policy.

Table 5.1 presents the four patterns of instructional organization. I hypothesize that targeted programs produce identifiable program structures in schools. These instructional structures are maintained in accordance with state regulations. State programs enjoying a high level of targeted funding (cell A, Table 5.1) are likely to evolve into stable, distinct structures that parallel mainstream organization. For instance, self-contained instructional programs, sometimes referred to as "replacement" programs, have their own chain of command, with project managers at the district level, resource specialists at district offices and in schools, and teachers and aides in classrooms. For compensatory programs, a high level of targeted state funds may result in self-contained classrooms with augmented staffing. For bilingual programs, these policy strategies are likely to provide a "maintenance" curriculum that develops both the students' native language and English language skills. A language maintenance program may consist of a separate track of classrooms for LEP students only.

In states where modest amounts of targeted revenues (cell B, Table 5.1) characterize special-needs policies, instructional services are likely provided through structures that are identifiable only periodically. The most commonly used intermittent structure is the pullout class; others include after-school programs, summer school, and district instructional centers. In pullouts, resource teachers take small groups of students out of their regular classrooms for a period and give them specialized instruction. Compensatory students are usually pulled out for extra reading or math instruction.[54] LEP students often have pullout classes in ESL.[55] A different form of intermittent structure is the instructional service center, where

Table 5.1. Expected Patterns of Instructional Arrangements for Special-Needs Programs under Varying State Social Targeting Strategies

	STATE FUNDING MECHANISMS	
Level of State Funding	Targeted Programs	Untargeted Programs
High	(a) Structurally distinct	(c) Schoolwide enhancement
Low	(b) Intermittent arrangements	(d) Structurally diffuse

special instruction is provided to disadvantaged pupils from different schools during part of the day. Service centers are an economical way to instruct special-needs pupils scattered throughout the district.

Diffuse instructional forms are common in states without targeting provisions for funding. Again, two kinds of organizational arrangements are differentiated, depending on the level of state aid. Schools that receive a high level of untargeted state funding (cell C, Table 5.1) are likely to have a great deal of flexibility in determining the use of program resources. Instead of focusing on a particular instructional unit, the school may choose to enhance the overall conditions that affect the education of the disadvantaged. State funds may be used to reduce class size by hiring an additional teacher. Lab equipment may be upgraded, and more students may have access to computers. The supplemental state funds can also be used to hire additional staff in the area of greatest need, for example, a resource teacher in the science area. Consequently, state funds are distributed to improve the school's overall quality, and no distinct program structure can be identified. In these circumstances, local priorities figure prominently in allocating state funds.

Another form of diffuse structure can be found when the state distributes limited resources for special-needs students without targeting the funding (cell D, Table 5.1). Schools receiving this sort of aid may provide students with special assistance within the mainstream setting. For example, an instructional aide may be assigned to tutor a small group of low-achieving, low-income students. Similarly, schools can hire bilingual staff members (teachers and aides) for the mainstream program to help LEP students in their classes informally (not in organizationally distinct ways). For LEP and low-achieving students in mainstream classrooms, teachers' decisions about ability grouping and the use of differential curricula according to group may either restrict or advance their learning.[56]

In short, I argue that state decisions about targeting and funding special-needs programs are likely to influence the organization of instruction in schools, even when these decisions result in diffuse organizational structures. The objective of this study, then, is to evaluate this set of policy-based hypotheses about program instruction through case studies of urban elementary schools in four states: Illinois, Michigan, New Mexico, and Oklahoma.

Data Collection: States, Districts, and Program Sites

The investigation began by identifying state special-needs programs with the four combinations of funding levels and funding mechanisms specified in Table 5.1: highly funded and targeted programs, poorly funded and targeted programs, highly funded and untargeted programs, and poorly funded and untargeted programs. *School Finance at a Glance* provided clues about the targeting issue.[57] Data from the Education Commission of the States on 1987–88 appropriations for state bilingual and compensatory programs and on the number of students receiving either bilingual or compensatory instruction in the state revealed a preliminary per pupil funding ratio. To adjust for variations in state educational support and service costs, the per pupil figure for the program was divided by the 1987–88 average per pupil expenditure of the state. These procedures resulted in a set of candidate programs for the study.

Next, state administrators of the candidate programs were interviewed to verify that the identified targeting provisions and funding levels were accurate. The major difficulty at this stage was assigning degrees of "targeting" according to the narrow definition specified earlier. After refining the list in this way, a final selection was made (see Table 5.2): Illinois bilingual education is targeted and has high funding, Michigan bilingual and compensatory education are targeted but have limited funding, Illinois compensatory education is nontargeted and has high funding, and New Mexico and Oklahoma bilingual education are nontargeted at lower support levels. Table 5.3 summarizes the funding characteristics of these programs.

In order to study one or both special-needs programs in a state, an urban district was selected where the programs in operation could be examined. In general, this study was carried out in the state's largest city. Where that was not possible, other urban districts were used. District administrators were then consulted about school selection. Because of the nature of social equity policies, schools offering one or both of these state programs often have a higher concentration of minority and poor students than the district as a whole (see Table 5.3).

For each state program, data collection proceeded in three steps. First, through brief interviews with state program and finance officers, requests for materials, and follow-up questions, the state special-needs programs were categorized according to current levels of support and degrees of targeting. The mechanisms for funding the state program and the legislative mandates governing the use of program funds were also identified.

Second, district administrators were interviewed and materials collected about programmatic and budgetary aspects of the state programs in their schools. On the programmatic side, the following district information was sought: program goals and history, implementation guidelines, program organization and descrip-

Table 5.2. State Special-Needs Programs and Program Sites Included in the Study

| Level of State Funding | STATE FUNDING MECHANISMS | |
	Targeted Programs	Untargeted Programs
High	Illinois bilingual (Chicago School 1) (Chicago School 2)	Illinois compensatory (Chicago School 1) (Chicago School 2)
Low	Michigan bilingual (Lansing School 1) (Lansing School 2) Michigan compensatory (Lansing School 3)	Oklahoma bilingual (Oklahoma City School 1) (Oklahoma City School 2) New Mexico bilingual (Albuquerque School 1)

Table 5.3. Characteristics of Selected State Programs, 1990–91

	STATEWIDE			SELECTED DISTRICTS		
	Funding*	Students Served†	Per Pupil Funding	Funding*	Students Served†	Per Pupil Funding
High funding, targeted						
Illinois bilingual program	$50.8	63,568	$798.71	$28.0	41,751	$670.64
High funding, untargeted						
Illinois compensatory program	$445.2	343,871	$1,294.84	$264.0	282,269	$935.23
Low funding, targeted						
Michigan bilingual program	$4.2	18,369	$229.30	$0.1	569	$229.30
Michigan compensatory program	$23.5	74,783	$314.51	$0.4	1,032	$349.96
Low funding, untargeted						
Oklahoma bilingual program	$3.6	7,546	$477.07	$0.6	1,735	$345.82
New Mexico bilingual program	$17.9	71,302	$250.80	$6.9	23,623	$290.52

*In millions of dollars; figures are rounded.
†Due to differences in accounting, the number of students served is not necessarily comparable from state to state.

tions, monitoring procedures, and evaluation reports. Program officers often advised about school selection as well. On the budgetary side, sources and amounts of program revenues were identified, as were the numbers of students served by the state program, the numbers of students served by the total district program, the distribution of program revenues to schools, and district summaries of student, teacher, and school characteristics.

Third, at the selected schools or program sites, the principals, program coordinators, teachers, and instructional aides were interviewed. Classroom observations were conducted in both regular and other instructional settings. Principals were asked about general school characteristics, the use of program resources, program participants and personnel, and measures of achievement for the program's students and for the school as a whole. Program coordinators were asked about the details of program organization and operation and about the program's history in the school. Other program personnel were asked less formally about their roles in the school and about points of interest arising from the interviews or from classroom observations. When questions remained after the main research effort (usually a one-week visit to a district between December 1990 and May 1991), answers and clarification were sought through district contacts.

VARIATIONS IN STATE SOCIAL TARGETING STRATEGIES

To better understand the variation in state funding mechanisms, I chose to focus on two socially redistributive programs that have received state support: the compensatory education program and bilingual instructional services. Interstate variation in funding strategies can be illuminated with examples from Illinois, Michigan, New Mexico, and Oklahoma. Social equity programs in these states were selected to show the kinds of funding decisions made at the state level. Specifically, there are four types of funding strategies, based on state funding levels and the degree of targeting to a well-defined group of eligible students (see Table 5.1). In the following sections, I describe how each of these fiscal strategies may affect educational opportunities for the disadvantaged, and then I map their effects on instructional activities at the school and classroom levels in the sampled states.

Targeted and Highly Funded

Illinois' bilingual program is funded at a high level and targets eligible LEP students. After being identified as a child whose English proficiency is below average for age or grade level, a bilingual student must be enrolled in one of two programs: a transitional bilingual education (TBE) program using both the native language and English, in attendance centers with twenty or more bilingual students of one native language; or a transitional program of instruction (TPI) in English, in attendance centers with fewer than twenty bilingual students of one native language. When a district has fewer than twenty LEP children, it may establish either a TBE or TPI for them; students must not, however, go unserved. Student proficiency in speaking, comprehension, reading, and writing skills is tested annually. The expected length of program participation is three years. Those students whose skills are still not approaching grade-level fluency after three years may continue in the program for up to six years, subject to district discretion and parental approval. Program regulations are rigid, and targeting provisions are very clear; programs are monitored frequently by both state and district administrators in the sample district, Chicago.

Due to an increase in state income taxes, the level of state reimbursement for bilingual programs in Illinois grew from 30 percent of excess costs in fiscal year 1989 to almost 90 percent in fiscal year 1990. As Table 5.3 shows, state funding amounted to $670 for each eligible student in Chicago, and about $800 per pupil statewide.

Targeted with Low Funding

Bilingual education in Michigan is targeted but with low funding levels. Identified LEP students who are receiving bilingual instruction commensurate with their English skills and grade level qualify for the state program, and they can be funded for up to three years. Districts with fewer than twenty LEP students are not required to have a program. Districts receiving state bilingual funds must provide native-language assistance, especially when the child cannot understand content-area instruction in English. The extent of native-language and English programming is not specified by state legislation, however. Program monitoring is light; the report for the 1987–88 school year, citing the many responsibilities of the Office of Bilingual Education, stated that staff members made only thirty school visits that year. The per pupil funding for Michigan's bilingual education during 1990–91 was about $230.

Like the bilingual program, state compensatory education in Michigan is targeted and funded at relatively low levels. It is designed to work in conjunction with the federal Chapter 1 program to supplement the instruction of low-achieving students. The state guidelines specify that student eligibility depends solely on performance measures, rather than on indices of poverty. The Michigan program is funded for districts in which at least 12 percent of the kindergarten through tenth-grade enrollment demonstrates a need for substantial improvement in basic cognitive skills. Students in those grades who show extraordinary need for special assistance, usually through low performance on statewide assessment batteries or other standardized tests, are eligible to participate. Since the Michigan program complements federal Chapter 1, the two compensatory programs are often administered together in larger districts. District monitoring is ongoing, and schools are expected to be monitored once every three years.

In the early 1990s, the Michigan legislature capped appropriations for the compensatory education program at $300 per eligible student. Because of this low ceiling, a district may choose to concentrate its services by selecting a subset of participants from among the eligible students. Consequently, the actual per pupil expenditure for Michigan's compensatory education program for the 1990–91 school year was about $315.

Untargeted and Highly Funded

Compensatory education in Illinois is an example of nontargeted aid provided at a high funding level. Although part of the compensatory funding is distributed to schools in accordance with the federal free and reduced-price lunch counts, none of it is identified with the needs of particular students or designated exclusively for their instruction. Often, all the students in a school are beneficiaries of the compensatory funds. Districts are required to submit an annual plan for the proposed use of the funds. There is a great deal of latitude with respect to acceptable program expenditures, and program monitoring in the schools is infrequent (about once every seven years in Chicago). Using federal Chapter 1 eligibles as the count of students served, Illinois state compensatory funding stood at almost $1,300 per pupil ($935 in Chicago) during 1990–91—a very high level of untargeted assistance.

Untargeted with Low Funding

New Mexico's bilingual education has been expanded from kindergarten through sixth grade to kindergarten through twelfth since 1987. In part because of the larger eligible population, the program provided a limited level of state funding for each bilingual student statewide ($251 during 1990–91). In Albuquerque, the state aid was $291 per bilingual pupil. The state aid formula assigns an additional 0.35 weight to each bilingual student, who is defined as "culturally and linguistically different" (that is, his or her home language is not English). This definition has also enlarged the eligible population, since all students with a home language other than English are included, regardless of need. The state program, which began in the aftermath of *Lau v. Nichols* in 1977, has three broadly defined instructional components that are designed to address the multicultural needs of schools with linguistically diverse student bodies. The home-language component enables a school with predominantly native Spanish speakers to use Spanish in content-area instruction. The ESL component provides assistance to LEP students in achieving English proficiency. The state also supports multicultural activities that promote understanding and acceptance of cultural differences among students. Teachers in the bilingual program are required by the state to receive bilingual endorsement, which includes twenty-four hours of bilingual education course work and a passing grade on a Spanish proficiency test. Within these state guidelines, districts are given a lot of discretion in program design and operation. To be eligible for funds, each school must prepare a bilingual program proposal that complies with state guidelines. The proposal is approved by the district before going to the state for approval. In Albuquerque, between 70 and 90 percent of the bilingual funds go directly to the schools. Evaluation is not extensive, and the state visits Albuquerque schools about once every three years. Especially in Albuquerque, where school-based management has been in place since 1986, schools exercise substantial autonomy over the use of state bilingual resources.

Similarly, Oklahoma's bilingual program does not specify targeted services and is funded at a low level. In 1990–91, the state allotted $477 per bilingual student; the districts received that money, without any targeting strings, as part of their general aid. State administrators admit that state bilingual funds may subsidize other school programs, because there are no regulations specifying that all the state funds generated from counts of bilingual students must be spent on bilingual services. A State Board of Education policy (approved July 24, 1986) gives each district the authority to establish its own bilingual program under the broad guidelines listed in a three-page document. The instructional arrangements of bilingual programs are not specified. Oklahoma City has in-class programs and language centers. Smaller districts, such as Tulsa and suburban Putnam City, use language centers and pullout classes. The nontargeted regulations of Oklahoma's bilingual program give districts a great deal of freedom in providing bilingual instruction.

LINKING SCHOOLING OPPORTUNITES TO STATE TARGETING AND FUNDING STRATEGIES

These case studies have generated two major findings that provide fairly strong support for the proposed framework. First, the targeting requirement produces identifiable structures for the education of the disadvantaged. When state aid is untargeted, regardless of the level of state funding, diffuse forms of instructional organization can be found. Second, in both the identifiable and the diffuse structures, the level of state support further differentiates the scope of supplementary services for the intended population groups. In this section, the evidence linking state funding strategies to classroom practices is examined.

Discrete Organization in Targeted, High-Level Funding

This framework holds that a targeted approach, together with high levels of state funding, produces discrete instructional arrangements such as self-contained classes. To substantiate this claim, findings are presented on the implementation of state bilingual education in two elementary schools in Chicago.

The Chicago public schools received $670 per bilingual student from the state program during 1990–91. The state bilingual funding significantly increased as a result of the passage of a temporary income tax surtax in 1989. These funds, which constitute the primary support of bilingual education in Chicago, are used to provide either TBE programs or TPI in over 300 schools. Since 1975, TBE programs have been offered in schools where there are twenty or more LEP students of the same language background. Ninety percent of the district's LEP students are served through TBE. Beginning in 1986, TPI has been offered in schools where there are nineteen or fewer LEP students of the same or different language backgrounds.

The state strategy has produced a regulatory framework that governs district administration. In response to the state targeting requirement, the district operates a technical unit to provide assistance to schools that have been unable to comply. A 120-page implementation handbook is distributed to school staff. The district's Office of Internal Audit also regularly reviews school information about the number of students served, the number of state-funded instructional positions, and staff qualifications. District–state relations can become acrimonious over the interpretation of program guidelines. During the early 1990s, for example, the state found numerous implementation problems and demanded a refund of $350,000 for noncompliance with staff qualification, student assessment and placement, and programmatic regulations.

A "School within a School"

To examine bilingual services, I conducted case studies of two Chicago elementary schools (grades kindergarten through eight). School 1 has approximately 450 students, all of whom are low income (that is, they qualify for free or reduced-price lunches). About 65 percent of the students are black, and the majority of the rest are Asian. With few exceptions, the LEP students at this school speak one language. At the end of the field study (February 1, 1991), eighty students were full-time participants in the bilingual program (grades one through eight), and thirty-two more were part-time program students. Their numbers grew almost daily during the fieldwork period (late December 1990 through February 1, 1991) because many new immigrant families took up residence in the neighborhood of School 1.

The Illinois bilingual program funds several staff members at School 1 and is the major source of regulations about the curriculum, testing, and so forth. The state program cannot be distinguished from the school's overall bilingual program. Rather, it works in conjunction with federal and other sources of support to forge a discrete instructional setting for School 1's bilingual students.

The bilingual classes are organized into a "walking bilingual program" in which five teachers and three assistants teach all subjects from first through eighth grade. Bilingual students change classes, moving to and from the classrooms of the five teachers. For most subjects, students of all ages are grouped into classes of basically one ability level. A third grader, for instance, may attend the first-grade English class, the fourth-grade native language arts class, and the third-grade science class. Consequently, each bilingual student has an individualized schedule, and even students who have officially exited from the program can take advantage of one or two bilingual classes while spending most of the day in their mainstream classrooms.

The bilingual program is clearly a discrete part of the school's organization. Although bilingual classrooms are not self-contained, they do form a parallel track, separate from mainstream classrooms. In fact, the bilingual program operates like a "school within a school." There are numerous differences between the bilingual and the mainstream programs. Bilingual class size is smaller than mainstream classes. Although the school as a whole has a heterogeneous grouping philosophy, the bilingual teachers group almost all their classes homogeneously. Aides in both mainstream and bilingual classrooms facilitate instruction, but bilingual aides also teach lessons (not just reviewing or providing individualized attention) to small groups. The bilingual students change classes every period, whereas mainstream students rarely leave their homerooms. Primary students in the mainstream program attend a computer "writing to read" lab, and those in the middle and upper grades have departmentalized science instruction. Bilingual students do not benefit from either of these programs. In sum, bilingual classrooms differ from nonprogram classrooms on the following points: faculty, students, class size, grouping practices, roles of paraprofessional staff, scheduling of the school day, and student access to specialized faculty and facilities.

A Mix of Classroom Arrangements

School 2 also has a discrete bilingual program, but with different instructional arrangements. This school is smaller than the first. It has about 280 students, 90 percent of whom qualify for free or reduced-price lunches. Between 80 and 85 percent of the children are Hispanic, and almost all the rest are black. The school's bilingual program serves seventy-eight Spanish-speaking students, including bilingual kindergartners.

The organization of the school's bilingual program is conditioned by both the low bilingual enrollment at each grade level and the belief of several key staff members that ESL meets their students' needs better than native-language instruction. The afternoon kindergarten is a bilingual class, and there is another self-contained bilingual class with twelve first graders, four second graders, and seven third graders. The rest of the bilingual program in this school consists of intermittent structures. Primary students who are approaching grade-level English proficiency are pulled out of their mainstream classrooms for small-group instruction in ESL. Similarly, all bilingual students in the middle and upper grades are pulled out for ESL, and a few also have grade-level pullout classes in Spanish language arts and content areas taught in Spanish (often reviewing or coordinated with what is being taught in their mainstream classes).

The self-contained kindergarten and primary classes in School 2 fit my proposition based on Illinois' bilingual funding, but the numerous pullouts do not. The state bilingual program funds only one teacher; her duties include providing ESL and native-language instruction to the middle and upper grades, as well as coordinating the school's bilingual program. This school also relies on informally extended bilingual services with Spanish-speaking teachers and aides working in mainstream classes. Because of the small bilingual enrollment and the preference of some staff members for an all-English program, only students in grades kindergarten through three attend self-contained bilingual classes in this school.

The two case studies in Chicago generally support the hypothesis that discrete instructional arrangements would result from high levels of targeted funding for special-needs programs. This is definitely the case at School 1, where the bilingual program functions much like a school within a school. School 2 also shows this pattern for the primary grades. Bilingual instruction for the middle and upper grades, however, is intermittent (pullout classes) at School 2. School size— or at least the size of the school's target population—and educator attitudes about bilingual instruction at School 2 work to counter the funding and targeting attributes that encourage discrete service provision. These two cases, then, show that a targeted special-needs program funded at a high level produces distinct, identifiable instructional structures, even though they also show that other factors can influence the program's organization.

Intermittent Arrangements in Targeted, Low-Level Funding

My framework suggests that targeted programs funded at low levels foster intermittent structures, such as pullout classes. This proposition is supported by the findings from three schools in Michigan.

Bilingual Education in Lansing

In Lansing, the state bilingual allotment has not changed since the program began in the mid-1970s. With its growing refugee and immigrant populations and its fixed state bilingual aid, the district supplies the bulk of the revenues for bilingual education. State bilingual funds account for 13 percent of the district's program costs, and an additional 18 percent is supported by the state's migrant funding. State funding thus totals about 31 percent of the bilingual budget in Lansing. Most of the state bilingual money is used to pay the salaries of program administrators and teachers assigned to district instructional centers.

The district has centralized English services for LEP children at six bilingual instructional centers. Three are located in the high schools and serve high school students, two are in middle schools and serve middle-school students on the northern side of the city, and the sixth center serves elementary students (grades kindergarten through five) and middle-school students from the southern half of the city.

One administrator handles the coordination, promotion, and budgeting for all the bilingual centers and effectively serves as principal for the elementary center. In addition to the teachers at the bilingual instructional centers, four teachers and one aide work with bilingual children in mainstream programs.

School 1 is a Lansing elementary school with 369 students. It has a poverty rate considerably above the district average, and the principal cites the rise in student mobility as one of the school's major challenges. The student body is diverse; about 19 percent of the students are bilingual, and of these, 10 percent are classified as LEP and receive ESL services. Many of the school's bilingual students are Hispanic, and about 11 percent are Asians who speak Hmong, Lao, or Vietnamese.

Bilingual children attending School 1 benefit from one of two state-funded instructional programs, both intermittent structures. Those School 1 students who know virtually no English, usually kindergartners and first graders, attend the elementary bilingual center (School 2) for half the school day. Also, a state-funded bilingual teacher spends two days a week at School 1. She is the only bilingual staff member at School 1 and teaches a total of thirty-five bilingual students, most of whom scored below the fortieth percentile on the reading section of the Stanford Achievement Test. All her classes are small, half-hour pullouts, during which she gives grade-level instruction in English. She usually focuses on writing, but she also presents certain lessons in math or other content areas when teachers discuss them with her. In addition to teaching, she assists with the identification and placement of LEP students, coordinates bilingual and multicultural activities at the school, and serves as a liaison between students' homes and the school.

School 2 is Lansing's elementary bilingual instructional center, which is also an example of an intermittent arrangement. The center enrolls about 190 students, all of whom are categorized as LEP by (1) the use of another language at home, especially for students in kindergarten through grade two who have not taken the Stanford Achievement Test; (2) a score at or below the nineteenth percentile on the Stanford reading scale; or (3) a score at or below the tenth percentile on the Language Assessment Battery. School 2's students come from twenty-six different home schools. They spend half the school day at School 2 and the other half at their home schools. Buses transport the students to and from their homes, their home schools, and School 2.

School 2 has a bilingual curriculum specialist, five classroom teachers with bilingual endorsements in Spanish and English, and five bilingual or trilingual paraprofessionals: a Spanish speaker, an Arabic speaker, a Vietnamese speaker, a speaker of Hmong and Lao, and a speaker of Lao and Vietnamese. The paraprofessionals take on different classroom roles to fulfill the teacher's needs and requests, including the instruction of individuals or small groups. They change classrooms according to a daily schedule, but they are also on call during and after school for translation. One paraprofessional said that she speaks English regularly to all the children and tries to facilitate their using it with one another. All lessons are presented in English at School 2. In general, a child's native language is used only to clarify concepts that are problematic for the student in English. For example, the home-school teacher may ask School 2 personnel to reteach a difficult mathematical concept in the student's native language.

Students are placed in classes by grade and English proficiency. In an effort to minimize some of the problems inherent in the pullout instructional arrangement, School 2's administrator has decided that students should remain in one class with one teacher during their half day at School 2. Moreover, she asks School 2 teachers to use the same basal curriculum as the home-school teachers in order to improve the articulation of instruction between schools. School 2 teachers integrate both ESL and whole-language reading techniques into their classes. In the middle grades (three through five), they also teach a content area—science, math, or social studies. Although there is often an overcrowding problem at the beginning of the school year, the average class size usually drops to around twenty students. During the morning session, School 2 offers a kindergarten class; two beginning English classes—one for first and second graders, and the other for third through fifth graders (with a few middle-school students as well); an intermediate class of first and second graders; and an advanced first- and second-grade class. For the new shift of students after lunch, School 2 offers an intermediate class and an advanced class for third, fourth, and fifth graders, as well as three kindergarten classes. On average, students attend School 2 for two to three years before being completely mainstreamed at their home schools.

In Lansing, the pullout classes at School 1 and the bilingual instructional centers, such as School 2, fit the hypothesis about the organization of instruction for targeted state programs with low funding.

Compensatory Education in Lansing

Michigan's compensatory program provides a third example of a low-funded state program that is targeted. District allocations are based on student performance on a statewide assessment battery, and in Lansing, students' scores have been rising. Consequently, in each of the last two school years, the district has taken a 20 percent cut in its state compensatory allocation. During 1990–91, 1,032 Lansing students were eligible for the Michigan compensatory funding, and the district received about $361,000 in revenues from the state program. In contrast, Lansing's federal Chapter 1 aid, based on the district's AFDC count, totaled almost $3 million. Hence the state compensatory program provided only about 11 percent of the district's compensatory funds.

About half of the 1990–91 state compensatory funding was applied to central costs, including program administration, program monitoring and evaluation, one centrally funded media teacher, and a contribution to the maintenance of a districtwide teaching resource room with educational materials for the use of parents and teachers of low-income children. In addition, approximately $10,000 was reserved for ninth and tenth graders identified as at risk of dropping out. Supplemented by a $35,000 carryover from the 1989–90 program budget, the remaining funds were distributed to schools for the instruction of eligible low achievers. A few years earlier, Lansing program administrators had decided to dichotomize their compensatory funding by distributing federal Chapter 1 funds only to schools with a greater proportion of low-income students than the district average and Michigan compensatory funds only to schools below the district average on that indicator. Accordingly, in 1990–91, program participants at twelve elementary schools, two middle schools, and all three high schools had a claim on state compensatory money.

Given the untargeted nature of state compensatory funds, schools used the resources differently. A few schools chose to fund part-time positions for resource teachers or to buy computer hardware or software, but most hired instructional assistants to work in classrooms or to teach remedial pullout classes. School 3 elected to spend its state compensatory funds for 1990–91 to hire a paraprofessional to give pullout math classes—an example of intermittent organization. School 3 has the lowest AFDC rate of any Lansing elementary school—just 2 percent—so it receives state-funded compensatory services, not federal Chapter 1. The neighborhood is middle class, but the principal reports that a housing project near the school accounts for 15 to 17 percent of School 3's 394 students. About half the students are black, about one-third are white, and the rest include Hispanics, Asians, and a few American Indians.

In 1989–90, the state compensatory program served forty-three children at School 3 through additional classes in reading and math. In 1990–91, because of cuts resulting from Lansing students' higher achievement, only twenty-nine targeted students received program-funded benefits. Since so few children could participate, teachers at School 3 decided to give priority to serving poor achievers in the lower grades.

One instructional assistant, teaching at School 3 only in the mornings, uses calculators, innovative manipulatives, and games to work on math concepts. She elicits student participation in creating their own math games and problems, and she says that they enjoy this approach. On average, she meets with four students at a time for twenty to twenty-five minutes. Her students come only from kindergarten through grade-four classrooms. She pulls out most of her students on a daily basis, but the third- and fourth-grade group meets every other day.

As hypothesized, the targeted, modestly funded Michigan compensatory program fosters intermittent instructional arrangements in Lansing schools. Often, instructional assistants are trained to provide remedial pullout classes in math and reading. The district's policy of dichotomizing compensatory monies according to schools' rates of low-income students, plus its success at improving student achievement so that it receives less state program funding, intensifies the tendency for state resources to be spent in small, supplemental ways in Lansing schools.

Schoolwide Enhancement in Nontargeted, High-Level Funding

When the state distributes a high level of nontargeted funding, school administrators are likely to use the additional resources in accordance with their own programmatic priorities. Often, state funds are channeled to enhance the overall quality of the school or to reduce class size and upgrade equipment. The propositions outlined earlier seem to be supported by the use of nontargeted compensatory revenues in two Chicago schools.

Compensatory Education in Chicago

Special-needs programs that receive substantial state support without targeting constraints allow for either district or school discretion over the use of resources. Illinois has this type of compensatory funding, and in Chicago, spending decisions about the state program rest largely with the school. During 1990–91, Chicago received $935 per eligible pupil from the state program. About 60 percent of these funds were distributed to schools based on poverty count, and the remaining 40 percent on school membership. Schools can use the state funds in a number of broad educational areas, including early childhood programs, reduction of class size, enrichment programs, attendance improvement, remedial assistance, and other supplemental instructional activities.

Because of the untargeted nature of the state program, the district is not required to closely monitor program implementation. Indeed, as a result of the Chicago school decentralization legislation enacted in 1988, locally elected school councils enjoy substantial discretion over the use of these funds. Neither the district's central office nor the state vigorously monitors program implementation. The central office has only four staff members to monitor the program in over 500 schools. In essence, the schools run their own programs and conduct their own evaluations.

The two Chicago schools discussed earlier in reference to their bilingual programs also benefit from state compensatory money. The state uses the free and reduced-price lunch counts as a poverty measure (although some of the funds are currently distributed without reference to poverty). Accordingly, the levels of poverty at the two schools—100 percent at School 1 and 92 percent at School 2—ensure that they are recipients of Illinois compensatory funds. In both cases, the state funds are used to meet a variety of needs.

At School 1, the state compensatory program provides the following: an assistant principal freed from her half-time instructional responsibilities, a science teacher for the upper grades, three aides at the primary level, and some extra supplies for the science lab and for other classrooms. The school uses the funds to strengthen both its early childhood program and its science curriculum in the upper grades. Interestingly, these state funds complement the Illinois bilingual funds. The state bilingual program serves only LEP students, and the state compensatory funds supplement programs available to the remaining 70 percent of the school population. This division of resources reinforces the conceptualization of School 1 as two structurally distinct units under one administration.

At School 2, the Illinois compensatory program supports two Spanish-speaking aides—one for the primary grades and one for the upper grades—and it also provides half-time positions for the following full-time staff: the assistant principal, the gym teacher, the ESL and fine arts teacher, and the bilingually certified librarian. Unlike the division of state resources characterizing School 1, compensatory funding at School 2 helps augment its bilingual program by supporting four Spanish-speaking staff members. In short, the state compensatory funds provide supplementary services to bilingual students, the area of greatest need at School 2.

In these two schools, the state compensatory money neither provides for nor is used to expand traditional "compensatory" classrooms. Consistent with my expectation, this program pays for no identifiable compensatory structures. Instead, the schools have elected to expand programs of their choice to meet students' needs. The virtual absence of student targeting restrictions at the state level turns the Illinois compensatory program into general aid for supplementary purposes at the school level. Use of state dollars is determined by varying needs in individual schools. These examples of schoolwide enhancement support the hypothesis about well-funded, untargeted state programs.

In-Class Strategy in Nontargeted, Low-Level Funding

A more localized (or classroom-specific) form of diffuse organization can be found in programs that receive low levels of nontargeted funding. As the case studies in New Mexico and Oklahoma suggest, paraprofessionals are assigned to work with students with special needs in the regular classroom setting.

Bilingual Education in Albuquerque

Albuquerque's bilingual program is supported by a moderately low level of state funding. The state allocation to the district—$291 per bilingual student—is based on both the student count and the amount of language instruction given to each LEP student. For example, a one-and-a-half-hour program generates $192 for each student; thus, each student in a three-hour language program received $384 in 1990–91. Not all of the state allocation goes to the classroom. Using a needs-based formula for schools with students identified as "culturally and linguistically different," the district channels somewhere between 70 and 90 percent of the state aid to the schools. The rest covers expenses at the district level. The district serves 24,000 LEP students, 90 percent of whom speak Spanish.

The untargeted character of the state program allows the district to exercise control over program operation. In Albuquerque, budget allocations for bilingual programs are school based. In 1990–91, the district used state aid to hire 133 teachers, ninety-eight assistants, and twenty-five part-time tutors in the forty-eight schools that operate bilingual and multicultural programs. One teacher is assigned to every forty-five identified LEP students. Schools with twenty bilingual students share one teacher, and schools with fewer needy pupils receive tutoring services. According to district administrators, the school principal plays the key role in deciding who participates in decision making, program planning, and budgeting. At some schools, the bilingual program is highly participatory, with teachers and principal working together. At others, it is dominated by the principal.

The school that was visited has a total of 562 students in grades kindergarten through five. Over 90 percent of the students are classified as "culturally and linguistically different." The instruction of bilingual students involves both pullout and in-class strategies, thus providing partial support for the hypothesis. ESL pullout classes serve about one-third of the LEP students, who receive single or mixed grade-level English instruction for forty-five minutes to one and a half hours each day. An ESL class averages twelve students, and the students are not grouped according to language ability. The ESL teacher plans classroom activities on an individual level. Pullout classes are also provided to teach Spanish language arts to fifteen students with no or limited English proficiency. Spanish is usually team taught in the classroom with the bilingual resource teacher. Each classroom teacher is responsible for the cultural component of the program.

Two-thirds of the LEP students receive instruction in the regular classroom setting. The bilingual instruction is done in the mainstream class because many teachers are proficient in Spanish. In a second-grade classroom, the regular teacher, who is bilingual, teaches content areas in both English and Spanish without using a bilingual aide. Sometimes, she separates the twenty-four students into groups based on language ability—three students are monolingual English speakers, seven are English dominant with limited Spanish proficiency, nine are fully bilingual, and five are monolingual Spanish speakers. To help the monolingual Spanish pupils learn, the teacher uses lots of manipulatives. In this classroom, English-proficient students also learn Spanish through formal Spanish instruction, by speaking to and assisting one another in Spanish, and by listening as the teacher uses both languages throughout the day. In another classroom, most of the students are bilingual and handle both languages fairly well. Spanish is team taught, using the in-class strategy with ability grouping. By and large, the case study in Albuquerque supports the proposition that low state funding facilitates a more diffuse organizational structure.

Bilingual Education in Oklahoma City

Oklahoma City also receives limited state funding ($346 per student) for nontargeted bilingual instruction. Since the funds are not targeted for bilingual students, the district does not use a per pupil allocation method. It budgets expenses for the Language Acquisition Office and its programs, which provide most of the district's bilingual services, and for Asian Student Services, an auxiliary program serving Asian bilingual students. Because the state guidelines are so broad, the district has been responsible for developing its own bilingual program. Two key programmatic regulations of the program are a recommended maximum classroom ratio of 60 percent LEP to 40 percent non-LEP students, and careful screening of potential bilingual assistants. The district identifies potential bilingual paraprofessionals and tests their ability to do two-way written translations and their cultural knowledge. A school can hire a half-time assistant for five or more identified bilingual students.

In Oklahoma City, from 1979 to 1988, students attended language centers for bilingual services. In 1988, the district superintendent decided that those instructional settings were not effective. Too much instructional time was wasted on students riding the bus to and from the language centers, and they were still unable to understand their lessons once they returned to the regular classroom. Consequently, the superintendent established a task force charged with eliminating the bilingual centers. He urged schools to adopt in-class programs, and most of the elementary schools (grades kindergarten through four) have complied. Only one primary school continues as a language center where LEP students receive two hours of ESL instruction a day. The fifth-grade LEP students attend their own instructional centers, but the in-class strategy is also employed there. Some Oklahoma City middle schools and all the high schools still rely on language centers, but their transition to an in-class organization is planned.

School 1 in Oklahoma City provides an example of diffuse classroom organization in bilingual education. The school enrolls 550 children; about 240 are Hispanic LEP students from economically deprived backgrounds. Many are recent immigrants from Mexico. Overall, the school is not well funded. According to the staff, it runs out of soap and paper towels, and it is given "substandard" classroom furniture by the district. Teachers often seek outside support to purchase bilingual supplementary texts.

Under the in-class instructional arrangement at this school, a bilingual aide is assigned to classrooms with LEP students. The district has allocated twenty-five bilingual paraprofessionals to School 1 to work with LEP students. They provide individual tutoring for all the bilingual students in a class, but they work more intensively with the less proficient students. They are trained to use the "preview-review" approach. The bilingual assistant previews the lesson in Spanish, instruction is then given in English by the regular teacher, and the aide reviews the lesson in Spanish. The bilingual assistant also teaches Spanish to the entire class. This instructional arrangement is designed to reduce the isolation of LEP students and to maintain their content-area instruction at grade level.

At School 2, a fifth-grade instructional center, all the LEP students are placed in three classes. The school has a total student population of 830, including seventy-five LEP students who are recent immigrants to the United States. The LEP students are a diverse group. For example, one classroom of twenty-five students had twelve Hispanics, one Malaysian, six Vietnamese, two Laotians, one white, one American Indian, and two blacks. The teachers use only English in the classroom. The bilingual paraprofessionals—three Hispanics and two Asians—teach

ESL skills and use both languages for preview-review. According to the teachers in the program, parents are interested in placing their children in these classes because the students leave with "survival English."

In sum, the in-class bilingual organization used in Schools 1 and 2 fits the predicted diffuse structure. Therefore, the organization of bilingual education in Oklahoma City, like the Albuquerque case, supports the hypothesis about untargeted state programs with low levels of funding.

POLICY AND RESEARCH IMPLICATIONS OF STATE SOCIAL EQUITY STRATEGIES

To understand the state role in redressing social inequities, one must take into consideration significant interstate variation in policy formulation and implementation. This chapter suggests that policy decisions made at the macro level are likely to shape classroom organization for special-needs students. Consequently, differences in state policies seem to result in differences in schooling opportunities for the disadvantaged. More specifically, targeting requirements are likely to produce identifiable structures, and the absence of targeting is likely to result in diffuse instructional arrangements. Further, these distinct and diffuse structures can be differentiated in terms of the level of state funding.

The case study findings generally support the central argument that macro–micro linkages actually exist. The four types of structural settings in this framework are supported by findings from most of the cases. First, with highly funded, targeted state programs for LEP students, Illinois' bilingual program contributes to discrete forms of bilingual instruction in two Chicago schools. The two Chicago schools maintained such discrete forms of bilingual instruction as a school within a school and self-contained kindergarten and primary classes. Second, the schools in Lansing met the expected intermittent pattern of targeted programs with limited funds, having pullout ESL and math classes. Third, the Illinois compensatory program (highly funded and untargeted) was a compensatory program in name only. It served as general, supplementary aid to the two Chicago schools, thereby supporting expectations about schoolwide enhancement. Fourth, in Oklahoma City, teachers at School 1 and School 2 relied on bilingual classroom aides because the program was poorly funded and nontargeted. Similarly, the core of Albuquerque's bilingual education program was in-class instruction, even though about one-third of the LEP students also had pullout classes. In short, the case studies provide fairly strong support for this framework about the micro-level outcomes of macro policy strategies.

Significantly, both state policy mechanisms—funding and targeting—need to be considered in combination. A comparison between the structures of bilingual instruction in Lansing and Chicago demonstrates that targeting alone does not determine policy outcomes. With a high level of funding from the state,

Chicago offered school-based bilingual instruction. With limited state funding, Lansing's elementary instruction center in School 2 enrolled LEP students from twenty-six different home schools. Similarly, the vast organizational differences between state-funded bilingual and compensatory education in Chicago schools show that, when considered by itself, the level of funding cannot predict these outcomes either. In the absence of state direction in the use of compensatory funds, Chicago schools allocated the supplemental resources in their own ways.

The importance of state targeting requirements and funding level does not mean that district- and school-level factors are absent in shaping instructional arrangements for the disadvantaged. Quite the contrary, these case studies highlight the relevance of local factors. Three factors are particularly prominent. First, the beliefs of professional staff can influence program organization. In spite of receiving low levels of bilingual funding from the state, the superintendent in Oklahoma City decided that language centers for bilingual students were not effective and had almost succeeded in phasing them out of the elementary schools. Taking the opposite stance, the bilingual teachers at School 1 in Chicago developed their program so that the bilingual students were essentially in a separate school from the mainstream children. Second, the size and stability of the program population in a school can also affect instructional arrangements. There was an insufficient number of LEP students at School 2 in Chicago to staff a bilingual track. School 2 had a self-contained kindergarten and a combined first-, second-, and third-grade classroom but only pullout services for older LEP students. Finally, school governance reform in Albuquerque (school based management) and in Chicago (locally elected school councils) shaped governance for the school as a whole, although in the latter case, it did not affect the implementation of socially oriented programs.[58] Clearly, then, district-level and school factors can affect organizational structures set up by state fiscal policies.

Despite the relevance of local factors, the nature of state strategies plays an important role in structuring student learning opportunities. Consequently, these case study findings may serve as a basis for reconceptualizing state funding strategies and as an impetus to further research. Two implications are particularly important. First, as a policy option, the targeting of a special-needs program can affect the instructional opportunities of disadvantaged children. "Targeting" has been defined as the distribution of specific resources for the benefit of identified and eligible students only. Thus defined, targeting provisions have a recognized impact on instructional arrangement.[59] Moreover, the absence of targeting creates the potential for the absence of a program. My findings in the two Chicago schools underscore this point. The untargeted state compensatory funds did not constitute an instructional "program." Rather, the schools used the funds as general aid to supplement any "educationally beneficial" aspect of their regular programs. In other words, the "compensatory" label associated with these funds was somewhat misleading; the disadvantaged did not necessarily receive more instructional services than their nondisadvantaged peers.

At issue is how to achieve a balance between two goals: reducing organizational fragmentation within a school, and providing additional services to students with special needs. Perhaps state policymakers can consider the latest federal initiatives that would hold Chapter 1 (now Title I) students accountable to national standards that apply to all students in key subject matters. Such an accountability framework would enable us to tell how much progress disadvantaged students have made toward meeting the national curricular standards. As the Clinton administration proposal stated, "Under our proposal for ESEA, Title I, bilingual education, and dozens of other federal programs will become integral to, not separate from, state and community education reforms that center on high standards."[60]

The second implication is that the level of state targeted funding can influence the instruction available to special-needs students. Inadequate resources in Oklahoma City contributed to LEP overcrowding in the three bilingual classes in the fifth-grade center. At least in one class, the number of LEP students far exceeded the district guideline of maintaining 60 percent LEP and 40 percent non-LEP students. Increases in funding generally translated into an extension of services to more eligible students, as suggested in the study of the bilingual program in Illinois. In Chicago's highly funded program, bilingual children were placed in instructional services at their own schools. However, with a poorly funded program, LEP students in Lansing schools were bused to the district's bilingual center for half the school day. Clearly, more state dollars can purchase more (and sometimes better) services for the disadvantaged.

6
Local Politics of Equalizing Class Size

A school board's decision to use its own revenue is shaped predominantly by the number of students assigned to each teacher for instructional purposes.[1] Because educational service is labor intensive, typically 80 percent of a district's budget goes to support personnel. The teaching force costs a district roughly 60 to 70 percent of its total budget. Nationwide, local school districts are hiring teachers at a faster rate than the growth in enrollment. Consequently, pupil-teacher ratios in public schools have decreased persistently over time. In public elementary schools, class size is getting smaller. In 1981, there were 20 pupils for each elementary teacher on average nationwide. The number decreased to 18.8 pupils in 1994 and is expected to fall to 17.6 by the year 2006.[2] Public secondary schools show a similar trend; class size decreased from 16.8 pupils per teacher in 1981 to 14.7 in 1994, and by the year 2006, it is projected to be 14.4 students per teacher.[3] Thus, there is every reason to believe that personnel costs will continue to dominate local educational spending. Given the importance of the teacher-student ratio in local decisions, this chapter examines the political forces that drive teacher allocation policy.

UNDERSTANDING LOCAL ALLOCATIVE PRACTICES

In allocating teachers to schools and classrooms, the local school board generally treats teachers as if they were equal in experience and cost. Local rules on teacher allocation are dominated by one major consideration—that each teacher be given an equal number of students in the instructional unit.[4] Having calculated a more or less equal number of pupils for each regular teacher, the district distributes resources (for example, salaries) accordingly.

In this regard, local allocative rules are distinct from practices adopted at the federal and state levels. For one thing, local allocation does not reinforce equal educational opportunities in ways that are defined in federal and state decisions. In deciding on the use of locally generated resources, school boards treat their students as if they were similar in academic needs. Unlike major federal programs,[5] local revenues are not used to address the needs of the disadvantaged. Rarely do we find local districts using their own property tax revenues to match federal dollars in compensatory education and bilingual programs. Free and reduced-price school lunch programs for low-income children are not supported by local tax dollars. Local schools rely primarily on state funds for special-education programs. As discussed in chapter 2, political pressures at the local level led program administrators to sidestep or resist federal redistributive standards.[6] Thus, local allocative decisions constitute yet another distinctive layer of rules that tend to operate entirely on their own rationale.

Moreover, local allocative decisions differ from the state's fiscal strategy. As chapter 4 argues, state governments have attempted to equalize spending disparity among districts. If local decisions paralleled state equalizing efforts, school boards would take into account socioeconomic differences among neighborhoods within the district. In reality, school boards by and large choose not to address interschool disparities in a collective manner.

An absence of locally funded equity initiatives does not mean that problems do not exist. As William Wilson points out, there was an increase in "underclass" communities in big cities when the economy underwent major restructuring during the 1980s. Racial segregation within urban school systems remains a serious problem, as Gary Orfield's work suggests. Instead of confronting disparities, local decision rules that are "needs neutral" may perpetuate the existing instructional gap between schools with predominantly low achievers and schools that have students with various levels of academic skills.[7]

Clearly, treating teachers and students as if they were alike does not matter much in communities where most teachers and students come from middle- and upper-class backgrounds. The more homogeneous communities in the suburbs often maintain a sound tax base, enjoy a high teacher retention rate, attract a national applicant pool for administrative positions, and receive social support for the preparation of students for college (for example, by more stable two-parent families and safer neighborhoods). In these settings, teachers are less eager to transfer from one school to another due to safety concerns and racial tension. Often, these districts have small enrollments and can concentrate their resources on a single township high school modeled after the college campus. High school seniors can take advantage of nearby colleges for more advanced training. Given the total educational resources both inside and outside of schools, even Chubb and Moe, among the strongest critics of the public school system, concluded that "urban environments are heterogeneous and problem filled in the extreme. . . .

Suburban schools have also been faced by problems—drugs, especially—that are difficult to conquer. Nonetheless, the contrast between urban and suburban settings as environments for schools is striking."[8] Indeed, they observe that suburban schools generally experience a higher level of "social homogeneity" and that they can be characterized as having an "absence of serious problems."[9]

Although local allocative rules tend to have limited effects on educational opportunities in suburban schools, they have broader implications in big-city districts. Clearly, treating teachers as if they were alike may contribute to substantial resource inequity among schools, because experienced (and more costly) teachers tend to stay in schools in stable, middle-class neighborhoods.[10] For example, in the Chicago public schools, a new teacher with a bachelor's degree earned $31,677, whereas an experienced teacher with a bachelor's degree could earn $49,778 (or 57 percent more) in 1996–97.[11] Experienced teachers with master's degrees get $51,972, or 64 percent more than their new colleagues with only bachelor's degrees. One might argue that resource inequity among schools could be ameliorated by changing school attendance boundaries so that each school draws from diverse racial and income groups. Alternatively, the district could eliminate teachers' seniority rights to transfer from school to school. Although pilot experiments exist, systemic reform to equalize resources associated with teaching experience has not been seriously attempted.

Consequently, local decisions on resource allocation can lead to unintended consequences, namely, an uneven distribution of instructional quality and student access to curriculum within urban districts. Embedded in a complex political climate (as discussed in the next section), local allocative policy is not likely to depart from its current emphasis on placement of the regular instructional staff. Alternative allocative practices based on both the needs of disadvantaged students and the experience of teachers are not likely to gain political attention.[12]

POLITICAL PRESSURE FOR EQUALIZING CLASS SIZE

Based on a synthesis of the literature on urban politics, I argue that local allocative rules that focus on pupil-teacher ratios have been facilitated by institutional arrangements and political factors. Among these are bureaucratic decision rules, pluralistic representation, union power, and the declining presence of the middle class in urban districts. In some instances, these factors are interrelated; in other settings, they may operate in isolation from one another. For example, bureaucratic rules may serve as responses to union demands in one district and to minority group protests in another.

Bureaucratic Decision Rules

Studies of urban bureaucracies have challenged the conventional wisdom that local service delivery is shaped by electoral interest. Analysts of routine service provision have found that distribution of a city's resources is determined primarily by bureaucratic rules, which in turn are the result of the nature of the delivery task, demographic shifts, technological advances, certain technical-rational criteria, past policy decisions, and a loosely defined preference for services to be more or less equally allocated at the neighborhood level.[13] Public education, a major local service, seems to fit this pattern of "universalistic" allocation.

The school bureaucracy practices the politics of inclusion rather than exclusion. Consider the historical development of an increasingly professionalized system and its distributive consequences. In his study of three central-city districts from 1870 to 1940, Peterson discussed the importance of the "politics of institutionalization."[14] Although diverse actors and interests contributed to an expanding school system, the real winners were the school system as an organization and its clients. The system gained in prestige, political support, and organizational capacity. But, as Peterson argued, "this self-interest was disciplined by a concomitant concern for the public interest and, in any case, was readily distinguishable from the class interests of corporate elites."[15] These middle-class professionals were just as likely to cooperate with trade-union leaders and working-class groups as with businesses in the popularization of the educational system during this period. The urban school system extended its services from the middle class to the low-income populations, and from the native stocks to various immigrant and racial groups. Indeed, the school bureaucracy, in practicing the politics of inclusion, promoted equal access for diverse racial and ethnic groups.

To cope with a huge and diverse clientele, the school bureaucracy counts students with diverse backgrounds as equals in allocating local resources. In urban districts, per pupil spending and pupil-teacher ratio are closely related to bureaucratic rules. Budgetary allocation to each school is governed by complex formulas, standard organizational procedures, and legal arrangements.[16] Because the bulk of the operating budget goes to teacher salaries, the rules that govern teacher allocation to schools are elaborately defined. Teacher allocation is adjusted for different grade levels, although the needs of disadvantaged students are usually not given additional consideration by the local school board. In the Chicago school code, for example, a teacher is assigned to a class of twenty-eight to thirty kindergarten children in the regular classroom, twenty-eight to thirty students in the primary grades, or thirty-one to thirty-three pupils in the intermediate and upper grades. These allocative rules are the basis for the allocation of teachers and funds to each school. None of these can be altered without extensive negotiations among the major parties, including the school board, the teachers union, and state and federal agencies. The teachers union, particularly, has fought hard to preserve locational choice for tenured members. Even the 1988 school reform legislation in Chicago, when power was given to locally elected parent councils, left these allocative practices unchanged. Consequently, all schools are subject to more or less the same set of universalistic rules when it comes to personnel allocation.

As leadership becomes increasingly unstable in urban school systems, ad-herence to the universalistic rule that treats every classroom the same avoids political controversy, which could be costly to the district. Taking politics out of classroom allocation seems politically sensible in an increasingly politicized school governance context. Tyack and Hansot argued that the tasks for educational leaders have changed three times between 1820 and 1980, as the existing social order was replaced by a new one.[17] Whereas the common-school crusaders of the nineteenth century mobilized support for public schools, the "social engineers" of the early twentieth century sought legitimacy for their expertise, developed the culture of social efficiency, and placed the school "above politics." Superintendents in both periods enjoyed generally long tenure (in some cases over twenty years). Beginning in the 1960s, educational leaders had to reconcile their professional ideology with racial and social conflict. In the current context of political contention, urban school chiefs simply do not have the time and energy to attend to the job they were hired for in the first place—educational improvement. Instead, superintendents have to lobby the state for more aid, develop plans to meet federal mandates, persuade the unions not to strike, and handle their image in the media. In this context, superintendents tend to defer to bureaucratic control over allocative rules.

Political demands and the seemingly intractable tasks of educating the special-needs population have destabilized leadership succession in big-city schools. Turnover of school superintendents has been fairly rapid since the mid-1970s. This unstable leadership succession departs from the historically stable trend. Take Chicago and Boston as examples. In Boston, the average tenure for the twenty superintendents between 1856 and 1987 was six and a half years. In Chicago, the twenty superintendents between 1871 and 1989 held their office for an average of six years. However, superintendents in both systems since the mid-1970s have experienced greater turnover. In Boston, in the fifteen-year period between 1972 and 1987, there were eight superintendents—with an average tenure of less than two years each. Boston experienced a particularly unstable period in 1980 and 1981, when three superintendents left the job, including one who was fired. In a less dramatic manner, Chicago's superintendency changed hands four times between 1975 and 1989, each jobholder averaging three and a half years. Needless to say, as superintendents turned over more rapidly, political contention heightened. Under these politically unstable conditions, the superintendent's office rapidly lost its control over school policy, and interest groups became dominant, as discussed later.

Pluralist Representation

Increases in minority representation in recent years have contributed to an improvement in distributive equity at the local level. Prior to the 1960s, there was wide disparity in resource allocation between black and white schools. Local authorities often withheld local resources for schools that served black children because blacks were not eligible to vote. Many state laws upheld the doctrine of "separate but equal" in public education. Consequently, black schools suffered from classroom overcrowding, shortages of certified teachers, lack of supplies and textbooks, and inadequate school facilities.

Whereas changes in allocative practices tend to be incremental, school governance has been restructured in the post-*Brown* and post–civil rights era. Beginning in the 1960s, big-city school systems began to respond to demands from minority groups by decentralizing some decision-making powers to the community. By the 1980s, parent empowerment gained widespread support from reform interest groups, businesses, and elected officials. Minority groups also gained representation in the district leadership. In the 1980s, many major urban districts were governed by school boards dominated by minority representatives, who hired minorities to fill the position of school superintendent.[18]

Minority representation has improved distributive equity for minority students in two ways. First, minority groups can pressure the school bureaucracy to allocate resources in an equitable manner.[19] As recently as 1986, a coalition of black and Hispanic groups filed suit against the Los Angeles school district for failing to provide equal resources and experienced teachers to predominantly minority schools in inner-city neighborhoods.[20] Five years later, the litigation ended when the state superior court approved a consent decree that required the district to equalize the distribution of experienced teachers among schools and to allocate basic resources and supplies on an equal, per pupil basis.[21] Similar organized actions have occurred in other cities where the school population has undergone major demographic changes.

Demographic changes have given rise to greater racial representation at all levels of the system. For example, in Chicago, all superintendents between the early 1980s and 1995 were black. Moreover, blacks have made significant gains in the teaching force in Chicago. Among secondary school teachers, the black-to-white ratio declined from 1:3.4 in 1965 to 1:1.8 in 1975 and to 1:1.2 in 1990. Among elementary school teachers, the black-to-white ratio narrowed—from 1:1.8 in 1965 to 1:1.3 in 1975. By the 1980s, blacks outnumbered whites in the elementary teaching force—the ratio was 1:0.9 in 1985 and 1:0.8 in 1990. Further, the disparity ratio between Latino and white teachers has been declining over time, although Latino representation in the Chicago schools remains limited. In the secondary teaching force, the Hispanic-white ratio declined from 1:39.8 in 1975 to 1:15.8 in 1990. In the elementary sector, the ratio plunged from 1:22.5 in 1975 to 1:5.9 in 1990. Equally important is an increase in minority representation among Chicago's principals. Between 1970 and 1990, white representation declined from 93 to 56 percent. During the same period, the proportion of black principals increased from 7 to 37 percent. In 1990, Latinos held almost 8 percent of the principalships.

As minority representation affects personnel policy, the hiring of minority teachers may have instructional consequences for disadvantaged pupils. Using data from the Office of Civil Rights in districts with at least 15,000 students and 1 percent black students, Meier, Stewart, and England examined the practice of second-generation discrimination in the classroom following the implementation of school desegregation plans.[22] They found that black representation on the school board contributed to the recruitment of black administrators, who hired more black teachers. Black teachers are crucial in reducing the assignment of black students to classes for the educable mentally retarded. Black representation on the instructional staff also reduces the number of disciplinary actions against black students and increases the latter's participation in classes for the gifted. Another study found that increases in the number of Hispanic teachers tend to reduce dropout rates and increase college attendance for Hispanic students.[23] In other words, minority representation tends to reduce discriminatory practices and facilitate distributive equity in the classroom.

Power of the Teachers Union

Once the states legalized collective bargaining for their public employees beginning in the 1960s, the teachers union became a formidable force in shaping resource allocation. Unions are interested primarily in the economic well-being of their membership. Union organizations have protected the tenure provision, negotiated for annual salary increases, and secured better work rules.[24] To achieve these goals, teachers unions have played an active political role.

During the 1960s, rivalry intensified between the National Education Association (NEA) and the American Federation of Teachers (AFT) as they fought for representational rights. The AFT and its local affiliates succeeded in maintaining a stronghold in big-city districts, enjoying a membership of half a million and retaining sole collective bargaining rights in major cities such as New York, Chicago, Detroit, Cleveland, Philadelphia, and Washington, D.C.[25] The NEA and its local affiliates gained membership in mid- and small-sized districts. The NEA's decisions to move into contract negotiation and to adopt sanctions as a means of resolving administration-teacher disputes during the early 1960s contributed to its growth in subsequent years. For example, sanctions applied to Utah in the mid-1960s led to the beginning of NEA-sponsored work stoppages.[26] The NEA now represents well over 80 percent of all the public school teachers in the nation.

No doubt, teachers unions carry a lot of political weight. They make significant contributions to electoral campaigns at all levels of government. For example, during the 1992 legislative election in Illinois, the Illinois Education Association made the second largest campaign contribution by a single interest group.[27] Union members constitute a formidable voting bloc that approximates an effective political party. Over time, unions have become an autonomous power center that exercises a great deal of influence over resource allocation at the district level. Grimshaw's study of Chicago's teachers union suggested that the union has gone through two phases in its relationship with the city and school administration.[28]

During the formative years, the union largely cooperated with the administration (and the mayor) in return for a legitimate role in the policymaking process.[29] In the second phase, which Grimshaw characterized as "union rule," the union became independent of the local political machine or the reform factions. Instead, it looked to the national union leadership for guidance and engaged in tough bargaining with the administration over better compensation and working conditions. Consequently, Grimshaw argued that policymakers "no longer are able to set policy unless the policy is consistent with the union's objectives."[30]

In the current reform climate, greater attention has been paid to rethinking the role of the union. For example, the Chicago teachers union, known for its adherence to traditional industrial unionism, established the Quest Center to strengthen professional development.[31] In a few urban districts, union and management were able to agree to take over (or reconstitute) one or more of the lowest-performing schools. Drawing on lessons from various districts where unions have become change agents, Kerchner and Caufman proposed a framework for "professional unionism."[32] This new organizing system has three distinct features. First, traditional separation between management and labor is replaced by a mode of shared operation (for example, site decision making). Second, adversarial relationships give way to a strong sense of professional commitment and dedication. Third, the new breed of teachers union is expected to incorporate "the larger interests of teaching as an occupation and education as an institution."[33] If these reform features are adopted, the new breed of teachers union may transform the existing labor-management politics, which, to a large extent, continues to be based on the industrial-relations model developed during the New Deal of the 1930s and 1940s.

However, even with a new kind of management-union relations, unions cannot be expected to give up any protective provisions that define their work rules (such as pupil-teacher ratio) as long as collective bargaining rights exist. My analysis of the 1993–1995 contract agreement between the Chicago teachers union and the school board provides an overview of the union's priorities in a big-city system. The contract agreement contained forty-nine articles that covered 114 pages, with an additional 100 pages of appendix. I identified twelve key issues that fit into three domains: teachers' work conditions (salary and benefits, class size, teacher behavior, and teacher well-being), professionalism (use of time, professional development, accountability, and teacher–principal relations), and teaching practice (student assessment, curriculum, ability grouping, and instructional strategy). Table 6.1 shows the relative emphasis of the three domains (twelve issues), which totaled 1,115 lines in the contract. Of the three domains, teachers' work conditions featured prominently, with 70.5 percent of the total number of lines. Particularly interesting is that class size was ranked second highest and covered 20 percent of all the lines in the analysis. In the section on class size, the contract spelled out in great detail the maximum number of students per teacher in various elementary grades and in different high school classes, such as twenty-

Table 6.1. Analysis of Selected Issues in the Chicago Teachers Union Contract, 1993–1995

	Number of Lines in Contract	Percent of Total
Work conditions	786	70.5
Salary/benefits	272	24.4
Class size	223	20.0
Teacher behavior	214	19.2
Teacher well-being	77	6.9
Professionalism	256	23.0
Use of time	89	8.0
Professional development	71	6.4
Accountability	62	5.6
Teacher–principal relations	34	3.0
Teaching practice	73	6.6
Student assessment	33	3.0
Curriculum/curriculum development	28	2.5
Ability grouping	9	0.8
Instructional strategy	3	0.3
Total lines	1,115	100.1

Source: Based on information in the Agreement between the Board of Education of the City of Chicago and the Chicago Teachers Union Local No. 1 American Federation of Teachers, AFL-CIO, September 1, 1993–August 31, 1995.

eight students in regular, honors, and advanced-placement English and twenty-five students in essential or basic English. There are provisions on class size for special-education students. In contrast, teacher professionalism and teaching practice received relatively less attention in the contract. Issues related to teacher professionalism accounted for 23 percent of the lines. Teaching practice covered only 6.5 percent of the lines in the contract. In short, class size constitutes an important aspect of teachers' work conditions and is easily quantifiable in terms of student count. It is certainly the union's legitimate right to make sure that class size is more or less equal for its members.

Declining Middle-Class Presence

Local allocative practices have been reinforced by the exodus of the middle class from the big-city school system (as distinguished from the city itself). Middle-class taxpayers can be broadly seen as a constituency that is most sensitive to the "benefits-received" principle,[34] whereby they expect to receive an amount of educational services that roughly corresponds to their tax payment. A greater presence of middle-class parents (who generally have a higher turnout rate in elections) would push the district to allocate dollars in their favor. Their out-migration suggests that many middle-class parents have chosen to "exit" instead of to "voice" their response to the perceived decline in urban education. Consequently, the school system does not have to address their benefits-received concerns, thereby disbursing resources evenly to rich and poor schools alike.

By the 1980s, most urban districts had experienced a significant loss of their middle-class clientele. "Consumer" parents who reside in the central city tend to choose nonpublic schools. One indication that central-city public schools may gradually be losing to their nonpublic competitors is that consumers who have choices seem to be less inclined to use public services. Although nonpublic schools account for only about 11 percent of the total school enrollment nationwide, they enroll about 20 percent of the student population in nineteen major central cities.[35] Of central-city residents, the white population has increasingly relied on nonpublic schools. Enrollment in public schools as a percentage of the white school-age population fell from 54 to 45 percent between 1970 and 1980 in nineteen large districts. In contrast, an overwhelming majority of blacks and Hispanics remain in public schools in the nineteen districts.

Chicago and Boston, for example, generally follow this pattern of differential choice between white and minority groups. In Chicago, the percentage of white school-age children who enrolled in the city's public schools fell from 46 to 37 percent between 1970 and 1980. Whereas the city's blacks predominantly attended public schools, over one-fourth of the Hispanic population went to parochial and other private schools. In Boston, the percentage of the white school-age population enrolled in public schools declined from 64 to 49 percent between 1970 and 1980. However, nine out of ten blacks and Hispanics in Boston remained in the city's school system.

Further, the middle-class shift to the nonpublic sector and suburban districts complicates the search for causes of the persistent decline in student performance in big-city schools since the early 1970s. On the one hand, one can argue that middle-class out-migration has contributed to a lowering of student performance in the city. On the other hand, one can make a case that declining test scores have discouraged consumer parents from remaining in urban districts. In any event, today's educational problems are substantially shaped by the interplay between students' social class backgrounds and school location. As Table 6.2 suggests, schools with over 50 percent poor students are performing substantially worse than their counterparts with fewer poor students in the same kind of setting—namely, urban versus nonurban. At the same time, a lower percentage of students in high-poverty schools scored at least at the basic level in the 1994 and 1996 National Assessment of Educational Progress (NAEP) tests. Interestingly, students in high-poverty, nonurban schools scored better in eighth-grade math than students in nonpoor urban schools, suggesting that the former are subject to a less constraining environment.

INSTITUTIONAL EFFECTS OF LOCAL ALLOCATIVE DECISIONS

There is no question that equalizing class size serves important political functions. It depoliticizes allocative procedures by reducing them to a set of computer printouts. The allocative practice institutionalizes the ground rules that govern union–

Table 6.2. Average Percentage of Students Scoring at "Basic" Level or Higher in 1994 and 1996 NAEP Tests

	High-Poverty Schools*	All Other Schools
Fourth-grade reading		
Urban	23	68
Nonurban	46	69
Eighth-grade math		
Urban	33	55
Nonurban	61	70

Source: Compiled from data reported in Education Week, January 8, 1998, p. 58.
*Those in which more than 50 percent of students are eligible for the free and reduced-price school lunch program.

management negotiations. Racial and ethnic succession is not likely to alter the criteria of treating teachers and students alike, because diverse constituency groups fear that other ways of resource allocation may reduce the level of existing services. In short, local decision rules are embedded in the urban political system, where bureaucratic power interacts with diverse interests.

Notwithstanding its political rationale, local allocative practices cumulate several institutional effects that may act at cross-purposes with the goal of improving school performance for all students. In the climate of accountability of the 1990s, local school boards may need to consider broadening their allocative practices. Revision of the existing decision rules may take into consideration the mismatch between school facilities and enrollment changes, inconsistency between staffing patterns and schooling opportunities, the institutional functions of the local school board, and the connection between systemwide policy and site-level school improvement.

Mismatch between School Facilities and Enrollment Changes

Local decisions on equalizing class size may keep a system from taking into account the economies of scale. Making sure that every class and every school are treated equally may hinder cost savings that result from enrollment decline in various neighborhoods.

One indication that urban districts do not operate cost-efficiently is that declining enrollment does not have any effect on the number of schools. In my examination of schools in Chicago and Boston, for example, the number of schools remained relatively stable, despite enrollment decline in both districts. In Boston between 1967 and 1987, when the elementary student population was reduced by half, the number of schools actually increased from thirty-four to forty. The number of secondary schools in Boston also increased from fifty-eight to eighty-one between 1962 and 1982, when enrollment dropped from 38,600 to 33,000. Chicago showed similar patterns. Prior to 1965, enrollment increased faster than the supply of new school buildings. In Chicago, the mean enrollment in both elementary and high schools increased persistently between 1956 and 1965. In elementary schools, the average student population jumped from 786 to 887 during this nine-year period; in high schools, the average student body increased from 1,919 to 2,538. Between 1965 and 1990, when the enrollment in elementary schools declined by over one-fourth, the number of schools increased from 447 to 502. During the same period, when Chicago lost 30 percent of its secondary students, the number of secondary schools jumped from fifty-four to sixty-five. In other words, urban districts do not practice cost containment.

Inconsistency between Staffing Patterns and Schooling Opportunities

Allocative rules that govern the number of teachers do not take into consideration teacher experience, expertise, and salary level. Staffing patterns often lead to substantial differences in schooling opportunity for students. Let us consider a hypothetical situation: There are two schools with an equal number of students and an equal number of teachers. However, the two schools differ significantly in the years of experience of their teaching staffs. School A has ten newly recruited teachers with bachelor's degrees, and School B has ten teachers with master's degrees who have been teaching for fifteen years. If I use the Chicago public schools' 1997 pay schedule, School B will get over $200,000 (or 64 percent) more than School A due to the differential staffing. Such disparities in resource allocation may actually occur in practice, since local decision rules consider only the "body count" and do not challenge the locational choices of experienced teachers. Further, local allocative practices often do not differentiate the "quality" of categories of resources. For example, an equal pupil-teacher ratio in two schools may conceal significant variation in the quality of the teaching staff.[36] Among the teaching staff, those with experience may manage their class time more efficiently than those who have just begun their careers.[37] Compounding this problem is racial segregation at the school and classroom levels, where minority, low-income students are likely to be placed in low-ability tracks.[38]

Restoration of the School Board's Proper Institutional Functions

The decision rule on class size equity does not contribute to an improvement in public confidence in local school board governance. Parents and the taxpaying public are giving greater attention to standards-based curriculum, student performance, teacher quality, and accountability. Class size equity constitutes merely one aspect of favorable schooling conditions. Other aspects of school quality require the local school board to redefine its central mission. Indeed, *The Report of the Twentieth Century Fund Task Force on School Governance* observed that school boards "are facing a serious crisis of legitimacy and relevance."[39] In an op-ed piece that appeared in the *New York Times*, Robert Wagner, Jr., a former president of the New York City Board of Education, warned that "local control of education is out of control." School reform will remain an "illusion," according to Wagner, unless school boards stay away from micro-management and focus more on setting policy.[40] According to a 1988–1990 survey of school board members in 128 districts in sixteen states, even school board members perceived themselves as least effective in "the core elements of governance—leadership, planning and goal setting, involving parents and the community, influence on others, policy oversight, board operations, and board development."[41] For example, the survey showed that boards used inconsistent performance measures to evaluate their superintendents. Clearly, these concerns merit a more systematic reexamination of the role of school boards in the outcome-based accountability climate.

Link between Systemwide Policy and School Practice

Given the pervasiveness of the decision rule on pupil-teacher ratio, local school boards tend to lose sight of their influence over teaching and learning through a variety of policy mechanisms. Even in a loosely coupled organization like a school system, the central school board still maintains crucial functions: selection of the superintendent, disbursment of funds according to various formulas, and evaluation of students. The question is whether board decisions at the districtwide level can create conditions for more productive processes at the school and classroom levels. With the policy impact on schools in mind, a 1987 report issued by the Organization for Economic Cooperation and Development (OECD) suggested several useful questions in assessing board performance, including whether the board sets quality educational goals, provides the necessary means to achieve the goals, monitors the implementation process, and conducts regular appraisals of student performance in the school context.[42]

These concerns about macro-micro linkages call for a more systematic understanding of the nature of resource allocation and utilization in a multilevel, complex organization such as a school system. As Barr and Dreeben suggest, labor in a decentralized school system remains divided and differentiated by tasks across different organizational levels in a hierarchical arrangement.[43] Managerial functions performed at the districtwide level tend to define the fiscal and personnel resources that have a substantial bearing on school and classroom activities. Indeed, how a school operates is directly affected by such systemwide decisions as staff development, assessment standards, administrative promotion, interpretation of and compliance with state and federal mandates, and integration of school and other social services. The top of the system, for example, exercises direct influence over the quality of middle-level administration in charge of curricular development, program operation, and application of state and federal assessment standards. An administrative cadre with strong professional training and aspiration can be both responsive to contingencies at various school sites and responsible to systemwide policy goals, thereby highlighting the importance of recruitment practices developed at the top of the system.

Clearly, the local board needs to sharpen its focus on the connection between districtwide policy decisions and classroom teaching. As shown in Table 6.2, high-poverty schools in urban districts encounter particularly challenging tasks. It is important for urban districts to think strategically about how they can allocate resources in ways that reinforce the purpose of raising student performance. Figure 6.1 considers policy variation between urban and nonurban districts in terms of three conditions that affect the quality of teaching in the classroom. As Figure 6.1 shows, fewer principals in urban than in nonurban districts have control over teacher hiring, although over 70 percent of the former enjoy that authority. In delegating hiring power to principals, local school boards need to ensure that certain professional standards are maintained districtwide. In the absence of districtwide benchmarks on hiring practices, schools are likely to come up with uneven standards. Figure 6.1 also shows that at least 50 percent of the classrooms in both urban and nonurban districts have fewer than twenty-five students each. In other words, class size reduction as a board policy has been fairly popular across districts. Finally, Figure 6.1 suggests the need for local boards to ensure that high school teachers are competent to teach in their assigned subject areas. Over 15 percent of the high school teachers in urban districts lacked even a college minor in their subject areas. By considering the key conditions that affect classroom teaching, school boards can better assess the impact of their allocative decisions.

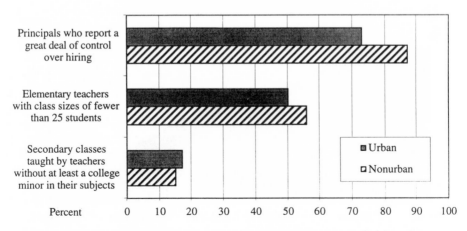

Figure 6.1. Conditions of teaching in urban and nonurban districts. (Compiled from data reported in *Education Week* 17, no. 17, January 8, 1998, pp. 60–61)

RECONSIDERING LOCAL RULES

Local allocative practices can be reconceptualized from at least two seemingly opposing policy concerns: equity and accountability. There are clearly trade-offs between these two views, but they can be placed on a continuum of allocative priority. Finding a proper mix between the two is a challenge for local policy-makers. Analytically, however, it is useful to consider each approach and its implications for reforming local allocative rules.

If policymakers see equity as a local priority, they need to reassess local rules that structure the distribution of resources to schools and classrooms. Specifically, greater attention has to be paid to the educational deprivation of disadvantaged children. Such an effort would require the local school board to revise the local attendance areas to bring about a more diverse student body in each neighborhood school. Allocative reform would also call for a wide range of programs that are not currently available in the city's poorest neighborhoods—elementary school counselors, summer programs, reading specialists, math tutors, and teachers in art and music programs. Local school boards may even consider reducing class size in the most deprived neighborhood schools. As Tennessee's Project STAR (Student-Teacher Achievement Ratio) showed, the minority–white achievement gap was significantly reduced in small classes (with thirteen to seventeen pupils) when compared with regular classes (with twenty-two to twenty-six pupils).[44] In their randomly assigned small classes, students were more actively engaged in learning, and teachers were able to spend more time in direct instruction. These and other kinds of enrichment may ultimately lead to a more equitable distribution of local funds between stable and declining neighborhoods.

From an equity perspective, in the long run, providing disadvantaged students with greater access to better instruction and a better curriculum creates a "social buffer" against the damaging effects of poverty and family disorganization.[45] Obviously, any effort to alter existing practices poses political risks. The few middle-class parents who still send their children to urban schools may be further alienated by a system that gives greater attention to the disadvantaged. Teachers unions will fight off any plan to restrict their members' right to transfer from school to school. Politicians are not likely to endorse any plan that would take resources away from their constituencies. In short, local politics, if unchallenged, will continue to empower the status quo. In maintaining allocative practices that are largely needs neutral, school districts contribute to the process of rule layering. Adding to federal and state guidelines on equal educational opportunity is the locality's definition of fairness as class size equity. As I discussed earlier, local practices, if unaltered, are likely to continue to undermine federal efforts in social targeting.

Alternatively, district-level policymakers may see accountability as a priority. Efforts to connect resource allocation and educational performance standards constitute a promising reform strategy. All racial and income groups clearly want higher academic standards. Will high school graduates acquire adequate skills to compete with their peers in other countries in the global economy? Does the projected labor force shortage mean that employers will have to hire the less skilled in the future? Can the new workforce perform well in a technologically complex world? The public seems uncertain that bureaucratized school organizations can meet these challenges effectively. To be sure, the causes of performance decline are complex, as socioeconomic factors and other cultural barriers continue to constrain teaching and learning. Nevertheless, the public's perception of bureaucratic rules is often reinforced by various accounts of poor student performance on standardized tests in urban areas. For example, the 1997 state report card on New York City showed that 89 percent of all its elementary schools failed to reach the state's expectations for reading performance.[46] These and other kinds of indicators on student achievement are particularly frustrating when the United States is spending a great deal more on education than are other Western countries.[47] Politically, a sharpened policy focus that directs local resources to improve accountability would restore public confidence in public education in the long run, creating the possibility of returning the middle class to urban public schools. Clearly, there is increasing public pressure to reform allocative practices in the climate of outcome-based accountability.

7
Redesigning School Governance and Resource Allocation: Four Alternative Models

Decisions about resources have served important functions in public schools. In the last thirty years, allocative routines have institutionalized intergovernmental grants, promoted equal educational opportunities, sustained functional division among levels of government, and expanded supplemental services in public schools. Politically, the five types of allocative rules I identified are embedded in our federalism. Given its constitutional authority, the state has assumed a primary fiscal role since the early 1980s. The tradition of local control allows the school board to decide on class size and issues of human resources. Organizationally, allocative rules are adaptive to partisan shifts, interest-group pressures, and constitutional challenges. It is no surprise that these rules have enjoyed remarkable stability over time.

A steady progression of decision rules does not mean an absence of policy tension. One institutional effect of rule layering, as I discussed in previous chapters, is that allocative practices developed by different levels of government often work at cross-purposes. Federal funding for socially disadvantaged students is not reinforced by states' allocative practices. For example, less than 10 percent of the state's own revenues are socially targeted, and only about half the states maintain their own compensatory or bilingual education programs. When federal programs are implemented at the local level, districts and schools tend to use the targeted resources for general purposes by shifting funding away from the eligible populations. Further, the state's leveling-up strategy has only a modest impact on reducing the disparity among districts. Despite the states' efforts, the most affluent 5 percent of districts spent 54 percent more than the poorest 5 percent of districts on an average per student basis. Local decisions on resource allocation, in other words, remain fairly autonomous from state and federal direction.

Another institutional effect of rule layering is that existing allocative practices may be at odds with the policy objective of improving teaching and learning, particularly in schools with the lowest academic performance. Indeed, growing public concerns over student performance posed a new challenge to allocative practices during the 1990s. Existing rules create policy fragmentation, as they are grounded in the particular political concerns of different levels of government. Because they were originally designed twenty or thirty years ago, allocative decision rules are not directed primarily at outcome-based performance—the public's preference during the 1990s. The allocative rules that this study identified are likely to misplace incentives and undermine the sanctions needed if organizational changes are to be made to meet the new policy challenge. As I discussed in chapter 2, social targeting in categorical programs, with its emphasis on regulatory compliance, tends to hinder instructional flexibility and curricular coordination. States' strategies to level up spending in poor districts seldom give adequate attention to the notion of performance accountability (see chapter 4). Because of pressure to reduce pupil-teacher ratios in all instructional units, local allocative rules restrict a broader discussion on matching the needs of students with the skills and experience of teachers. As chapter 6 suggests, the kinds of trade-offs associated with a reduction in class size must be considered. For example, one may ask whether more preparation and planning time for teachers is an appropriate trade-off for a larger class size. In other words, previous chapters identified many aspects of policy incongruence between resource allocation and outcome-oriented goals.

These two effects of rule layering—policy fragmentation and lack of focus on academic accountability—call into question the current governance structure's ability to effectively address these challenges. After all, politics embedded in the existing governing process has played a major role in rule layering. To improve policy coherence and raise academic standards, it is useful to reconceptualize the way governance is organized and how the governance redesign can change allocative practices. Clearly, reform efforts in recent years have provided a useful conceptual and empirical base for this discussion. Based on a synthesis of the literature on educational policy and politics, I identified four redesign models that maintain alternative allocative practices. These models are grounded in the concern about raising student performance, yet they differ in terms of the locus of primary decision-making power, which can be placed along a continuum of systemwide restructuring versus school-centered approaches.

As Table 7.1 shows, the two analytical dimensions generate a two-by-two scheme, suggesting four possible kinds of allocative reform. These four redesign models have been implemented to varying extents and thus offer some evidence of their promises and limitations as alternative allocative frameworks. I labeled the two reform models directed at systemwide redesign "intergovernmental coordination" and "integrated governance." These two models recognize that the existing political structures are not likely to change. Consistent with the tradition of state constitutional authority and local control, the two systemwide initiatives clarify the responsibilities in public education among the three levels of govern

Table 7.1. Four Types of Governance Redesign to Reduce Institutional Fragmentation and Raise Academic Standards

	LOCUS OF DECISION MAKING	
Structural Problems Addressed	Systemwide Level	School Centered
Fragmentation and conflict between levels of government	Intergovernmental coordination	Decentralized voice
Fragmentation and conflict among actors and institutions	Integrated governance	Consumer choice

ment. Pressures for improvement are expected to be applied to the formal governmental process. Above all, these systemwide initiatives aim to integrate political and educational accountability. Publicly elected officials at all levels are held accountable for educational performance.

The other two reform models focus on school-centered decision making. To temper direct control from state and district authorities, these decentralized practices attempt to empower the parents and school professionals at the school building level. Whereas the "decentralized voice" reform is designed to promote school autonomy within the public school system, the "consumer choice" model relies on market forces to improve school quality and outcomes. In these arrangements, principals and teachers in each school are accountable for educational performance.

In this chapter, I define the guiding principles of the four reform models, specify how politics shapes these alternative allocative practices, and discuss their promises and limitations for improving schooling opportunities.

SYSTEMWIDE RESTRUCTURING: INTERGOVERNMENTAL COORDINATION

The first type of systemwide reform aims to reduce policy fragmentation across different levels of the government. This type of reform is guided by four political principles:

1. Recognize that political structures are not easily alterable.
2. Specify the division of functions among the three levels of government.
3. Coordinate federal and state resources to help the neediest schools more effectively.
4. Preserve local (district) control over teacher allocation policy.

Clearly, this last rule legitimizes existing local control over teacher allocation, which tends to undermine federal social targeting efforts (as discussed in chapter 6). Nonetheless, to manage intergovernmental complexity in ways that would better serve educational purposes, this reform initiative calls for stronger coordination in grant making, particularly between the federal and state levels. Coordination can improve in several areas, including the purpose of federal and state aid, strategies to stem urban decline, and professional development.

Address Needs in High-Poverty Schools

The educational challenge in high-poverty schools is better coordination in the use of federal and state grants. At issue is the redesign of the current grants system so that resources can better match the educational needs of disadvantaged pupils. In this regard, federal and state aid can provide direct assistance to schools that encounter the kinds of at-risk situations discussed in previous chapters. If policymakers take into consideration different aspects of inequities, they can better define the appropriate roles of the federal and state governments.

To reduce working at cross-purposes, federal and state policy efforts can consider the socioeconomic circumstances of schools. As suggested in Table 7.2, schools encounter two kinds of socioeconomic challenges, each of which forms the basis for governmental resource allocation. Specifically, schools differ in terms of the percentage of students who come from disadvantaged backgrounds, a factor that determines how much a school receives in federal redistributive funding (such as federal Title I dollars). At the same time, schools are located in districts that maintain an uneven fiscal base, a factor that affects how much state aid a district and its schools receive. The interplay of social and fiscal characteristics generates four patterns of schooling circumstances for the disadvantaged. These constraining structures call for a differentiated set of policy responses.

Cell A in Table 7.2 depicts schools that encounter the most constraining conditions, with both a weak local fiscal base and a high concentration of students from low-income and other disadvantaged backgrounds. These schools are likely to be located in the most depressed inner-city neighborhoods, with high unemployment rates and declining local institutions. Consequently, both the federal and the state government may consider prioritizing their resources to address educational problems in these circumstances. Formulas in federal and state programs can be revised to give greater attention to students who enroll in schools under these most constraining environments. For example, state aid formulas can as-

Table 7.2. Setting Priorities in the Allocation of Federal and State Education Funding

Concentration of Socially Disadvantaged Students	DISTRICT FISCAL CAPACITY	
	Weak	Sound
High	(a) High funding priority	(b) Moderate federal funding Low state funding
Low	(c) Low federal funding Moderate state funding	(d) Low funding priority

sign greater weights to students who attend these schools. Indeed, at the federal level, passage of the *Improving America's Schools Act* (P.L. 103-382) in October 1994 was a good (though modest) step in that direction. Although Congress rejected the earlier Clinton proposal for a major funding increase to high-poverty schools, the 1994 act allowed for greater targeting of federal dollars appropriated above the 1995 funding level. Specifically, the additional funds are distributed by one of two formulas.[1] One formula allocates the additional funds to districts with higher percentages or numbers of poor children. Districts are required to have at least 5 percent of students in poverty to be eligible for the additional (or targeted) grants. The other formula is known as the Education Finance Incentive Program, which allocates the additional funds to states that have "higher levels of fiscal effort and within-state equalization." Fiscal effort is measured in terms of the ratio between per student spending and per capita income. The equalization factor is based on the degree of interdistrict disparity in per pupil spending. The inclusion of this factor improves coordination between federal grants and states' efforts to address territorial inequity. However, even if the incentive program is fully implemented, its share of total federal Title I funds remains modest and its impact on spending equalization limited.

My proposed allocative redesign suggests another step in connecting dollars to severe constraints. In addition to rewarding states for their efforts to reduce interdistrict inequity, the federal government can concentrate its social redistributive grants on high-poverty schools located in districts with high tax burdens. A rough estimate of the cost to the federal government in pursuing this policy can be made by considering the cost of providing Title I funds to every student in schools where at least 60 percent of the students are low income. Nationwide, 35 percent of all schools, or 16,744 schools, fall into this category of high poverty. Using the national average of $1,100 for each Title I student in 1993, these schools require about $7 billion in federal supplemental grants, a figure that roughly corresponds to the total federal Title I spending in 1993.[2] From my perspective, if this is what the federal government is able to spend on Title I, then all (or an overwhelming portion) of the fund may have to be concentrated on the poorest one-third of schools in our nation. Given the seemingly intractable nature of poverty, it makes educational sense to target the use of federal dollars.

In contrast, neither the federal government nor the states should provide supplemental resources to schools that enjoy a sound fiscal base and have a relatively low percentage of students with poverty backgrounds (cell D, Table 7.2). These schools clearly benefit from a sound district fiscal capacity. Local revenues can address classroom overcrowding, improve professional development, and operate supplemental services for students with limited English proficiency and those with exceptional learning needs. The few students who are socially disadvantaged are likely to benefit from a socially heterogeneous learning environment. In other words, state aid is not critical to provide the infrastructure in support of teaching and learning in these more affluent districts. Under federal Title I, for example,

35 percent of all the schools (or 16,636 schools) that receive federal funds have less than 35 percent of students from low-income backgrounds. Clearly, federal and state funding can be reallocated to schools that encounter severe constraints, such as those in cell A.

High- and low-revenue districts, even with similar social needs, differ significantly in the kinds of educational opportunities their students experience. One comparative study of districts with varying fiscal capacity found that "the [sampled] schools in high versus low revenue districts have comparable numbers of poor students (34% vs. 37%). . . . Students in the high revenue districts scored higher on standardized achievement tests (at the 70th percentile vs. 58th percentile in the low revenue districts). . . . Principals in the low versus high revenue districts were more likely to perceive moderate to serious problems with student absenteeism (28% vs. 12%), student mobility (51% vs. 39%), student health (25% vs. 15%), and student discipline (34% vs. 18%)."[3] In other words, schools in cell D have both the fiscal base and the social capital to address their educational needs.[4]

A sufficiently differentiated strategy can be applied to schools that fall under "mixed" circumstances. As cell C in Table 7.2 suggests, schools may have a relatively weak fiscal base and enroll a comparatively low percentage of students with poverty backgrounds. In this case, state territorial equity funds can play a prominent role in enhancing the infrastructural support for learning and teaching. However, given the lower demands for special programs, federal social programs may be reduced in these schools. Other schools may enjoy a sound fiscal capacity and enroll a high percentage of disadvantaged students (cell B, Table 7.2). This situation arises when an affluent community practices residential segregation, or when a community experiences a rapid influx of immigrant children with limited English proficiency, or when a community maintains a disproportionate share of exceptional children. Given their special needs, students in these schools would benefit from continual federal support for supplemental services. However, state funding can be shifted from these schools to those that maintain a weak fiscal base.

In short, a strong coordinative framework would rectify the current practice that scatters federal and state funds to districts and schools that do not necessarily need aid to provide supplemental services. Instead, a coordinative grant system could target the most severe constraints on teaching and learning at individual schools. In agreeing to focus their funding on schools with the greatest needs, federal and state policymakers could strengthen the connection between resource allocation and the use of dollars for student learning in the school setting.

Stem Urban Decline

Intergovernmental cooperation is also needed to stem the trend of urban educational decline. Inner-city schools need a proper mix of incentives and sanctions to improve their performance. A promising development is the recent federal effort to restructure the Title I program. The program now focuses on the overall quality of the schools that poor children attend. As a major commission argued, Title I can be substantially improved with a new accountability framework that aims at "producing good schools, not simply good programs."[5] Instead of mandating that schools meet accounting standards, the commission recommended that schools be accountable for student progress in learning. In return, poor schools would be given 20 percent of the Title I money for staff development, curricular enrichment, and organizational improvement. Such a restructuring would reduce the "categorical" nature of Title I, thereby enhancing programmatic coordination among federal, state, and local staff in poor schools. The 1994 reauthorization of Title I lowered the eligibility threshold for schoolwide project to schools with 50 percent low-income students by 1996–97. This change enabled almost half of all Title I schools to participate in schoolwide projects. In big-city districts, the lower threshold meant the inclusion of virtually all Title I schools. During 1995–96, over 8,000 schoolwide programs were in operation out of a total 16,853 eligible school sites. Given this new opportunity to improve urban education, states and districts can facilitate federal reform initiatives by providing technical assistance in planning and evaluation.[6] Teachers unions can support schoolwide programs by allowing for greater flexibility in scheduling, staffing, and other work rule revisions.

Enhance Professional Development

A third area for intergovernmental coordination is professional development. The Goals 2000 legislation added to its initial document the goal that teachers gain access to "programs for the continued improvement of their professional skills." Marshall Smith, the undersecretary of education, summed up the significance of this particular national goal: "If what we're trying to do is to change teaching and learning, isn't the most important thing we can do is try to help teachers get the training they need to be able to work with students in an effective manner?"[7] According to John Jennings, the education counsel for the House Education and Labor Committee, the current congressional concern with professional development is the first such deliberation since the early 1970s.[8] As the debate intensifies, the core issue remains whether Congress should legislate the use of federal dollars for professional development. Not surprisingly, there is a fair amount of disagreement over the appropriate amount of local discretion. For example, a set-aside fund for professional development in Title I schools has been recommended.[9] However, the Clinton administration worries that such a stipulation may undermine its commitment to school autonomy in pursuing Title I schoolwide programs. Regardless of the final legislative outcome regarding local discretion, federal dollars can support a variety of teacher training activities, including the development of a new teacher assessment framework, support for professional networks, and release time.[10]

Politics aside, students can benefit from a coherent teacher development policy. This may include several elements. States can restructure their teacher preservice and in-service programs with a greater emphasis on the new national standards in subject areas. Teachers may be required to be recertified every several years, as is the policy in Massachusetts. The federal government can create monetary incentives (through student fellowships and grants) to attract the best pool of college students to enter the teaching profession. To retain teachers in urban schools, districts can form professional networks around clusters of inner-city schools to strengthen collaboration and support among teachers. In Chicago, one innovative program is Teach for Chicago, which has been in existence for about five years. It is a collaboration among the Chicago public schools, the Chicago teachers union, the Council of Chicago Area Deans of Education, and the Golden Apple Foundation for Excellence in Teaching. Applicants to the program are seeking a career change to teaching and have noneducation degrees with at least a 2.5 grade point average. Out of about 800 to 1,000 applicants, only 100 are selected to participate as interns in the program. The limit of 100 is stipulated by an agreement among the four partners so that the program will not pose a threat to others seeking teaching positions in the district. Interns earn a salary while working full-time in a classroom and receive tuition for university course work that meets certification and master's degree requirements. The university enrolls teacher candidates in an urban schools program and grants them the appropriate degree upon program completion. Interns work closely with experienced teacher-mentors at the school during the program duration (three summers and two school years). After completing the program, graduating interns are required to stay in the Chicago schools for two years. The retention rate was fairly high for the first cohort—87 percent of them planned to remain in the Chicago schools beyond their two-year obligation.

SCHOOL-BASED REFORM: VOICE MODELS

The second type of reform aims to reduce intergovernmental contention by decentralizing decision making to the school sites. Decentralized initiatives are guided by several political principles. They are designed to seek alternative political structures by creating school-site power bases, delegitimize district control over crucial resources, and decentralize decision making to professional and parental bodies at the school site.

Decentralized reforms are directed at reallocating power between the system-wide authority and the schools in the public school system. However, decentralized initiatives often fail to consider powerful quasi-formal actors, such as the teachers union and other organized interests. Decisions made at the school site can be circumscribed by forces such as union agreements. In addition, decentralization may widen the resource gap between schools that have access to external capital (such as parental organizational skills and grants from foundations) and those that receive limited support from nongovernmental sources. Examples of shared decision making can be drawn from Chicago (1989–1995) and abroad.

Norwegian and Swedish Experience

Shared decision making in school policy has different roots and has taken different forms in various national and local settings. In Norway, teacher organizations and other "corporate groups" along a wide political spectrum have pushed for decentralization in educational policy for decades. Decentralization in school appropriations, curriculum, and student assessment has been fully implemented since the 1980s. Since 1986, the national government has lumped its educational subsidies with grants for other social programs in a general block grant, with allocative priorities determined by the local governments. In amending the 1974 Model Plan for the primary schools, reforms in 1985 and 1987 granted teachers greater authority over curricular design, instructional practices, and assessment standards. Consequently, Norwegian teachers have substantial influence over school life, promoting "different and more personalized teaching styles and unique learning approaches."[11]

The political culture of democratic participation in Sweden has facilitated the practice of "democratic discourse" in the public schools.[12] Citizenship education is seen as a major function of the public schools, and pupils participate in "decision-making and the negotiation of the curriculum. Subjects and subject departments are reduced in importance and the need for teachers and pupils to act in working-groups is emphasized."[13] For example, the 1980 national curricular guidelines required equal attendance by pupil and teacher representatives at educational planning meetings organized by the school headmaster. Thus, the notion of school-level management in Sweden seems to be consistent with the notion of political equality in a social democracy.

Local School Councils in Chicago

In the United States, arguably the most extensive effort to make sure that parents are the key decision makers is the Local School Council (LSC) concept in Chicago. The 1988 Chicago reform was guided by the belief that parent and citizen empowerment through LSCs would improve educational performance. The 1988 Chicago School Reform Act was designed to restore public confidence by granting parents substantial "ownership" over schools. The law specifically linked LSCs to better academic outcomes, including a significant reduction in dropout rates and an increase in test scores. To enhance accountability, the central office decentralized policymaking to locally elected parent councils and the principal at each school. The eleven-member councils consist of six elected parents (the majority), two community representatives, two teachers, and the principal. There is also one student member at the high school level. Members of local councils are given substantial authority—they can hire and fire principals (who lost tenure as a result of the 1988 act), allocate lump sums from the state compensatory fund (Chapter 1), and develop school improvement plans. With training and support from business and public-interest groups, local councils have written bylaws, approved school budgets, and reviewed and ratified principals' contracts. According to the most liberal assessment, about one-third of all the elementary schools have LSCs that are in good operational standing after several years of reform.[14]

Not surprisingly, LSCs have a direct impact on principal selection. During the seven years that the LSC model dominated Chicago school governance, selection of principals was often reflective of the racial and ethnic makeup of the LSCs and their neighborhood constituencies.[15] In the first round of contract evaluations, affecting 286 schools in 1990, 38 percent of the principals were replaced. In 1991, when evaluations were conducted in the remaining 207 schools, 37 percent of the principals were replaced. Consequently, the percentage of black principals increased from 37 to 50 percent, and the percentage of Latino principals increased from 7 to 11 percent, between 1989 and 1994. The percentage of white principals decreased from 56 to 39 percent during the five-year period.

Although the LSCs exercised their appointive power fairly visibly throughout the school system, their electoral base shrank during the period of decentralization. Voter turnout declined significantly after the first LSC election in 1989,[16] when 294,213 people voted throughout the system. The 1991 turnout dropped to 161,089. Even lower voter participation occurred in the 1993 election (the last one before the mayor took over the system), when only 131,798 voters were involved. In other words, voter turnout declined by 55 percent over the three LSC elections. Indeed, the decline is even more dramatic when measured in terms of just parents and community residents (without including teachers, staff, and students). For this particular electoral subgroup, there was a 59 percent drop in turnout between 1989 and 1991. Between 1991 and 1993, another 25 percent decline occurred. In short, turnout among parents and community residents plunged by 68 percent in a five-year period.

As voter turnout declined, fewer candidates ran for LSC offices. Between 1989 and 1993, the number of candidates declined from 3.18 to 1.36 per seat.[17] To be sure, the electoral contest was unevenly distributed among schools. Overall, schools that lacked enough candidates for all the LSC offices increased from 3 percent in 1989 to 25 percent in 1991. By 1993, one out of every three schools in Chicago lacked a full slate of candidates.

Turning to the issue of school effectiveness, the experience in Chicago's decentralized council was mixed at best. In 1994, Polsby found no systematic patterns of improvement in any of the major outcome indicators in Chicago schools, including attendance, graduation rates, and achievement.[18] His finding that high schools were further behind national standards than were elementary schools led to the suggestion that the longer students were enrolled in Chicago schools, the less satisfactory their performance. Even the strongest supporters of LSC reform concluded that achievement trends were inconclusive. Whereas the school-by-school trends in standardized test scores in reading showed a fairly sharp decline, math and writing performance did not worsen between 1989 and

1995.[19] These trend-line analyses, however, did not include baseline data in the pre-1989 reform era.

From an institutional perspective, one may argue that the unsatisfactory student outcomes were due to the uneven capacity of the LSCs. However, if the LSCs failed to build up their governing capacity in a seven-year period—a fairly reasonable time frame to expect organizational improvement—one has to question whether the LSC is an effective model to improve schools systemwide. After all, only one-fourth of the elementary teachers perceived a positive impact on the quality of student academic performance.[20] In light of these concerns, a bipartisan legislative coalition adopted a comprehensive reform proposal that created integrated governance in Chicago in July 1995.

SYSTEMWIDE RESTRUCTURING: INTEGRATED GOVERNANCE

The third type of governance reform focuses on district-level capacity to reduce institutional fragmentation and raise academic accountability. This kind of systemwide restructuring is based on four political principles:

1. Recognize that the existing political structures are not easily alterable.
2. Empower the district-level administration to intervene in failing schools.
3. Enable city hall to manage conflicting interests and reduce fragmentary rules.
4. Integrate political accountability and educational performance standards at the systemwide level.

During the 1990s, a new approach to accountability gained prominence in urban districts across the nation. Integrated governance[21] entails three central components: state legislation that focuses on student achievement at the school level as a crucial measure of school performance, state legislation that grants districts or the state educational agency new authority to intervene in failing schools, and district or state willingness to use this authority to improve failing schools. This new governance model tends to reverse the decades-long trend toward shared decision making by integrating power and authority at the district level. In short, integrated governance reform is driven by a focus on student performance and is characterized by district-level capacity and willingness to intervene in failing schools.

Mayoral control over urban school systems constitutes one prominent form of integrated governance. Several mayors have taken control of urban schools or have begun seeking power from state legislatures to do so, including the mayors of Cleveland, Baltimore, and Boston.[22] The best example of integrated governance is Chicago, where mayoral control began in July 1995, and it provides the most detailed information on this new model. As the Chicago experience suggests, political will is critical in creating the necessary conditions for improving teaching and learning in low-performing schools.

Integrated Governance in Chicago

In July 1995, the Chicago School Reform Amendatory Act reversed a seven-year trend toward decentralization of authority over school operations and redesigned the governance arrangement to integrate power and authority. The goal was to reduce competing authorities and coordinate activities in support of systemwide academic improvement. Integrated governance in Chicago is characterized by:

1. Mayoral appointment of board members and top administrators.
2. Elimination of competing sources of authority, such as the School Board Nominating Commission and the School Finance Authority.
3. Empowerment of the Board of Trustees to hold LSCs accountable to systemwide standards (elected parents constitute the majority on LSCs).
4. Creation of the position of chief executive officer (CEO) to oversee the top administrative team, including the chief education officer.

With integrated governance, fewer policy actors compete for decision-making authority. The 1995 law suspended the power of the School Finance Authority, eliminated the School Board Nominating Commission, and diminished the ability of the LSCs to operate independent of board policy. Integrated governance is designed to facilitate policy coherence and improve organizational collaboration among major actors. As a result of the 1995 reform, the board, top administration, and mayor's office are closely linked by appointment decisions emanating from the mayor's office. Finally, integrated governance relies on an administration that enjoys strong managerial authority. The 1995 law expanded the financial powers of the board and enhanced the powers of the CEO to manage the system.

Reducing Institutional and Policy Fragmentation

Although the 1995 legislation left intact some features of the previous decentralized arrangement, it reduced competing institutional authority and recentralized administrative authority. The law decreased the number of school board members from fifteen to five and put the mayor in charge of appointing board members, the board president, and the CEO. Since the board appoints the top administrative officers, these changes facilitated an effective link between the mayor's office and the central office. Under this arrangement, education became part of the mayor's policy agenda and gave the mayor the option to decide how much political capital he is willing to invest in improving the schools.

The new administration in Chicago acted swiftly to demonstrate a commitment to efficient management by adopting a business management model. The management and maintenance of school buildings, for example, were reorganized to stress customer service and contracting out. The board eliminated the Bureau of Facilities Planning in the central office (resulting in the elimination of ten jobs), reduced the number of positions in the Department of Facilities Central Service

Center by half (twenty-six of fifty positions were eliminated), and reduced the citywide administration of facilities from 441 positions to 34. Contracts for these services are now with private firms. To oversee the management and maintenance of school property, the board negotiated contracts with five firms to provide property advisory services for each region. Under this arrangement, the firms advise principals and the Department of Operations on property management and provide custodial, engineering, and construction-related services to the schools. In addition, the board prequalified a number of general construction contractors for schools to select from.

By strengthening the centralized authority of the school system, the 1995 legislation shifted the balance of power between the central office and LSCs. Prior to 1995, the central office competed with LSCs for authority over the educational agenda. LSCs had broad authority, but there was little direct accountability or oversight. For example, state Chapter 1 funds went directly to the schools, but the board remained accountable if the money was misused. Selection of principals by the LSCs was often influenced by the constituencies of the particular neighborhood.

The new administration signaled to the LSCs that they could no longer operate with complete independence and incorporated the LSCs into the overall system by defining standards and responsibilities they must adhere to. This policy established fifteen criteria covering the actions of the principal, staff, LSC, and LSC members. Under the new policy, the board declared that an "educational crisis" existed at Prosser Preparatory Center and Nathan Hale School, and their LSCs were disbanded. The LSC at Prosser was declared nonfunctional, in part because of its failure to approve the school improvement plan or evaluate the principal. At Hale, the LSC was suspended because members had intruded in the day-to-day operations of the school, entered classrooms unannounced and uninvited, and failed "to follow the law regarding their powers and responsibilities," among other violations.

Taken together, these actions significantly improved public confidence in the ability of the board and the central administration to govern the schools, giving the top administration the legitimacy it needed to carry out its educational initiatives.

Improving Financial Management

The 1995 governance redesign enhanced the ability of the central administration to perform financial and management functions efficiently. The 1995 law suspended the budget oversight power of the School Finance Authority, removed the balanced budget requirement, and placed the inspector general under the jurisdiction of the board. In addition, the board was granted new authorities that expanded its financial powers. A number of funded programs (for example, reading improvement, substance abuse prevention, Hispanic programs, gifted education) and categorical funds were collapsed into a general education block grant and an educational services block grant, respectively. Although total revenues available to the board declined by 8 percent in fiscal year 1996 from the previous year, revenues going into the general funds increased by about 2 percent (or $28.5 million). Additionally, the board acquired greater flexibility over the use of pension fund monies and Chapter 1 funds not allocated to the schools. Finally, there were no longer separate tax levies earmarked for specific purposes.

These changes increased board discretion over school revenues, allowing the board to prepare a four-year balanced budget and negotiate a four-year contract, including a raise, with the Chicago teachers union. These actions brought both financial and labor stability to the system. Indeed, by March 1996, Standard and Poor's raised the Chicago public schools' bond rating from BBB⁻ to BBB, and Moody's raised it from Ba to Baa, allowing the board to issue bonds for the construction of new buildings under lower interest rates. By the summer of 1997, the bond ratings were A⁻ from Standard and Poor's and Baa1 from Moody's. The four-year teachers' contract meant that the board could focus on developing and implementing its education agenda.

Providing Sanctions and Support to Low-Performing Schools

The 1995 law incorporated a focus on accountability and academic achievement that compelled the administration to target the lowest-performing schools within the system for intervention. Declaring that an "educational crisis" existed in Chicago, the 1995 legislation directed the Board of Trustees and the CEO to increase the quality of educational services in the system. It enhanced the powers of the CEO to identify poorly performing schools and target them for remediation, probation, intervention, or reconstitution. Prior to 1995, the subdistrict superintendent, not the school board, had the primary responsibility of monitoring school performance and identifying nonperforming schools. In the past, placing a school on remediation or probation required the approval of the subdistrict council, which was made up of parent or community members from each LSC in the subdistrict.

Under the new legislation, the board and central office focused on the lowest-performing schools in the system. In January 1996, the CEO placed twenty-one schools on remediation for failing to meet state standards in the Illinois Goals Assessment Program (IGAP) for three consecutive years. Only six schools had been placed on remediation by the previous administration. At the same time, the board removed two elementary school principals because their schools had failed to improve after a year on remediation. In September 1996, the CEO placed 109 schools (or 20 percent of all the schools) on probation, because 15 percent or less of their students had scored at grade level on nationally normed tests. These schools were being held accountable to their school improvement plans as well as to the goal of improving their students' scores. Since this initiative began, nine schools have been removed from probation, and fifteen have been added. Further, seven high schools were reconstituted. At none of the reconstituted schools were more than 7 percent of the students reading at or above grade level according to test scores. Five of the seven schools had their principals replaced, and 188 of 675 teachers, or 28 percent, were not rehired. These schools will have to improve their test scores or risk being shut down. To help low-performing schools meet district standards, the central office assigned probation managers to provide technical assistance. In addition, schools were given additional dollars to hire external partners from a list of university-based vendors for school improvement and professional development.

Integrated governance also enabled the Chicago school board to end the social promotion of students who failed standardized tests. In 1997, third-, sixth-, eighth-, and ninth-grade students who did not meet specified levels on one of two nationally normed tests (the Iowa Test of Basic Skills [ITBS] or the Test of Academic Proficiency [TAP]) were required to participate in a system-sponsored summer school called the Summer Bridge Program. Teachers in this program were provided with day-by-day lesson plans. Sixty-one percent of eighth graders who participated in the program met the cutoff scores after seven weeks. By the end of the summer, 92 percent of all eighth graders had met the system's new promotion standards. Students were promoted to the next grade if they raised their scores to the cutoff point for their grade; if they did not, they were required to repeat the grade. Repeating students returned to their original schools, unless they were older eighth graders. Half of the repeating eighth graders, who would be fifteen by December 1, attended one of thirteen transition centers that emphasized basic skills.

The board and top administration reorganized the central office to reflect the focus on accountability and established the improvement of IGAP and TAP scores as the primary objective of the system. Some departments within the central office were eliminated or significantly downsized, and the administration created the Office of Accountability, which grew from a staff of fifty in September 1995 to ninety in July 1996. This office monitors the performance of schools, identifies low-performing schools, and intervenes in schools that are not performing well. One administrator said that the mission of the department is "to fix schools . . . so they won't fall below a safety net."

The Office of Accountability has several departments that are in the process of launching various programs to level up schools where test scores are low. The Department of School Quality Review is working with the Illinois State Board of Education to develop a review process to evaluate all schools once every four years. The Department of School Intervention works with schools that are on the state's academic watch list or on probation. These schools receive a one-day visit from School Intervention staff, who recommend corrective actions and pair schools with consultants to provide technical support. In December 1995, the board approved $1,335,500 in contracts to universities and colleges to work with thirty schools on the watch list. During 1996–97, the first year of probation policy, the school board allocated over $11 million to these schools for external partners and support personnel devoted to implementing and overseeing probation. In 1997–98, the central office budget for probation- and reconstitution-associated personnel was close to $8 million.

Despite these additional resources, teachers and principals viewed the university-based external partners with skepticism.[23] They were not convinced that these external actors, who visited their schools infrequently, could significantly improve student performance. In some cases, teachers felt that the external partners offered little meaningful assistance. Teachers, for example, resented planning time being controlled by the external partners and resisted their attempts to evaluate instruction. Teachers in one school actually locked their doors to prevent the external partners from entering. Similarly, principals felt that the external partners lacked a focused plan for school improvement and raised concerns about cost-effectiveness. In other words, variations in the support provided by external partners posed a policy challenge to the district administration. Clearly, the district needs to monitor the quality of the services provided by external partners more closely and to consider whether these contracted services are cost-effective.

Broadening the Political Base of Support

The link between the mayor's office and the board can facilitate political support for the school system. With the redesign of the governance system, Mayor Richard Daley has been more willing to invest political capital in the Chicago schools. To restore public confidence, the new administration has projected an image of efficient, responsive, and "clean" government. The administration also took a number of steps to strengthen the business community's support for the public schools. This support is crucial when appealing to the Illinois legislature, because the business community can lobby in favor of the board's legislative agenda, thereby lending the board credibility.

The mayor's appointments to the Board of Trustees reflect his concern about consolidating business support for the schools. Three of the five board members have extensive experience in the private sector. Moreover, appointments within the central office reflect the mayor's commitment to improving the fiscal conditions and management of the system. The top appointments in the central office made between July 1995 and December 1996 reflected a diversity of expertise: 11 percent from the private sector, 12 percent from nonprofit organizations, 23 percent from city agencies, and 54 percent from within the ranks of the Chicago public schools.

To further enhance business support for the schools and the perception of efficient management, the new administration reorganized the central office according to business principles that stress downsizing and privatization. Within one year of implementing the new system, the number of staff positions in the central administration declined almost 21 percent. The majority of these cuts came from citywide administration and services. The reduction was achieved by awarding contracts to private providers for food services, distribution, and facilities. Other reductions were obtained by consolidating the eleven district offices into six regional offices.

The administration's strategy of focusing on management and budget issues early on can be viewed as a serious effort to establish political credibility. Thus, the administration balanced the budget, developed a five-year capital development plan, and negotiated a four-year teachers' contract. This strategy paid off with improved public confidence in the administration's ability to manage the schools and stabilized relations with the union. Believing that raising test scores is the basis for long-term political support, the mayor, board, and CEO have taken this as their primary strategy. Better test scores, it is hoped, will form the basis for increased state funding and the continuation of centralized governance, with the mayor in control of the schools. This arrangement is likely to shift additional power back to the central office and to further diminish the LSCs' role. Indeed, in August 1996, legislation was adopted that allows the Board of Trustees to develop additional standards and requirements for principals.

Instituting an Ambitious Agenda in Systemwide Restructuring

As integrated governance moved into its fourth year, the CEO and the board initiated a broad reform agenda to sharpen educational accountability. The ambitious plan to improve academic performance has several components, including the design and dissemination of Chicago academic standards in the areas of English language arts, mathematics, biological and physical sciences, and social sciences. Benchmark exams for selected cutoff grades are being developed, with the intention of eventually replacing the ITBS and TAP. Further, all high schools are required to divide students into a junior academy that enrolls ninth and tenth graders and a senior academy that enrolls eleventh and twelfth graders.

Taken as a whole, the use of both sanctions and support by the Chicago school board has brought about steady improvement in student performance since integrated governance began. Student test scores have risen in virtually all grades, and high school dropout rates have declined. Particularly important is the narrowing of the performance gap between high schools on probation or reconstitution and their regular counterparts. If these encouraging trends in student performance continue, integrated governance as articulated in Chicago will become a promising redesign strategy for renewing our urban school systems. Currently, Chicago is the largest urban district where mayoral commitment is highly visible and political capital is used strategically to improve the system. Further research is needed to better understand how this can work in other urban districts and to identify the crucial components of the redesigned system that are transferable.

SCHOOL-BASED REFORM: CONSUMER-DRIVEN MODELS

The fourth type of reform has the potential to introduce fundamental changes in the existing politics of education that would redefine the role of private service providers in public education, eliminate union contracts as a source of political constraint, rely on market competition to drive school improvement, and minimize the legitimate role of public regulatory agencies in resource allocation. Under the consumer-driven arrangement, the public-private boundary is redefined by providing schooling choices to parents. Accountability is no longer determined in the public domain. Rather, parents decide whether their chosen schools meet their preferences and expectations. Dollars follow the students, whose number determines the school's budget. The consumer-centered model creates competition among schools, which may lead to the closure of failing schools. Examples of consumer-driven models include charter schools and the choice experiments in Milwaukee and Cleveland, where only state funds are involved. Skeptics are concerned about resegregration not only by racial and income backgrounds but also by the academic levels of the students.

Although private schools are available in most countries, the public or state school system remains the key provider of educational services. There is, of course, substantial cross-national variation in school enrollment in the private sector. According to a United Nations Educational, Scientific, and Cultural Organization survey,[24] countries with a significant private education sector (as measured by percentage of primary student enrollment in private schools) included Ireland (100 percent), Zimbabwe (87 percent), the Netherlands (69 percent), Belgium (56 percent), Chile (37 percent), Spain (34 percent), Australia (25 percent), and Singapore (24 percent). In contrast, the private sector is modest in Japan (1 percent), Sweden (1 percent), Austria (5 percent), the United Kingdom (5 percent), Greece (6 percent), and Mexico (6 percent). The survey did not differentiate between types of schools (for example, Catholic or independent) within the private sector.

Public versus Catholic High Schools

In the United States, private schools account for slightly over 11 percent of the total school enrollment. Although the public sector continues to dominate educational services, a growing number of empirical studies in the United States have identified bureaucratic power and its regulatory functions at all levels of the school policy organization as key barriers to improving student performance. With the availability of the High School and Beyond (HSB) surveys, researchers are able to compare student performance in the public and nonpublic sectors. These studies engage in a more systematic search for organizational variables that are likely to contribute to student achievements at the school level.

There is a rich body of literature that compares public and Catholic schools. Coleman and Hoffer found that Catholic high schools maintained the highest rates of student progress in verbal and mathematical skills, although student outcomes in science knowledge and civics were comparable to those in the public sector.[25] Students with disadvantaged backgrounds made substantial progress in Catholic schools. Catholic schools also maintained the lowest dropout rates, and their students were more likely to attend four-year colleges. In explaining these successes among students in Catholic schools, Coleman and Hoffer cited the benefits of social integration based on religious identity. They argued that the close social relations among youth, parents, and teachers in parochial schools are likely to generate "social capital," an informal system of value transmission and social support that is largely lacking in public and independent private schools. By participating in a variety of activities that facilitate the child's intellectual development, parents, grandparents, and other adults in the broader social (religious) community provide collective support for educational purposes. In contrast, public schools are embedded in rules and mandates and generally lack a social and normative basis for frequent interaction among youth, families, and teachers. Building on these findings, Bryk, Lee, and Holland identified higher-performing Catholic high schools as having four characteristics: an academic core program for all, a communal (as opposed to a bureaucratic) school organization, site-based professional control, and an inspirational ideology.[26]

Market Competition

Another body of literature focuses on market competition as the driving force behind better student performance. Using the HSB surveys for 1982 and 1984 and the Administrator and Teacher Survey data for 1984, Chubb and Moe found that the more market-oriented nonpublic schools were far more likely to produce what they described as effective organizations.[27] These high-performing schools (mostly nonpublic) can be distinguished from low-performing schools (mostly urban public): "Their goals are clearer and more academically ambitious, their principals are stronger educational leaders, their teachers are more professional and harmonious, their course work is more academically rigorous, and their classrooms are more orderly and less bureaucratic."[28] Consequently, Chubb and Moe suggested parental choice as a way of eliminating the constraining effects of interest-group politics and governmental regulation.

Chubb and Moe's recommendation to transform public education into a marketplace has been controversial. Opposition to choice has been based on concerns about equal educational opportunities and self-selection. Choice programs are likely to "skim off" better students and take other resources out of neighborhood schools. Local residents may perceive that the conversion of their neighborhood school to a choice program deprives them of direct access to a community-based service institution. Questions have been raised about the implementation of a systemwide choice plan, with regard to distribution of school information to all parents, transportation costs, and compliance with civil rights provisions. In short, viable choice programs have to take into consideration the values and practices that the public is already accustomed to. Otherwise, choice may come into conflict with other prevailing popular expectations, thereby jeopardizing any potential benefits of consumer choice.

Charter Schools

The case for school choice to promote better student performance seems to be partially supported by studies on the relatively small number of "magnet schools" in the United States—public schools with specialty academic programs that admit students (often selectively) from throughout the system.[29] The growing literature on charter schools and contracting out also suggests their potential for school improvement. Although two-thirds of the states now have charter school legislation, there has been no serious legislative attempt to replace the urban district with a system of charter (or contract) schools.[30] Nonetheless, there is no question that the charter school movement is growing rapidly across the nation.[31] Although they are labeled as public schools, charter schools are distinctive in several major aspects. The school's charter or contract explicitly spells out the conditions and expectations for outcome-based performance. The authorizing agency can be the local school board or other legal entities (such as universities). Once established, charter schools enjoy substantial autonomy in setting teacher salaries and work conditions, although they are bound by state regulations regarding safety, health, dismissal, and civil rights. School funding follows students to the charter schools, which operate on multiyear renewable contracts.

The literature on charter schools suggests that they serve several educational purposes. Charter schools can either replace or substantially restructure failing schools in the public sector. These schools can become learning centers for dropouts and other students at risk. Further, experimental models can be implemented under the charter arrangement in the absence of bureaucratic and union contract constraints. These schools clearly enjoy the flexibility to design their curricula in ways that more effectively address their students' needs. The nation's first charter school, for example, began a year-round academic program for thirty-five inner-city high school dropouts in St. Paul in 1992. As a founding teacher put it, "We can change the curriculum to meet these needs as soon as we see them. Anywhere else it would take a year to change. It is much better than anything we have known in the traditional setting."[32] In some cases, charter schools can revitalize community support for public education. For example, to prevent their school from closing when enrollment declined, a community of parents and teachers in rural District 2142 in Minnesota formed a charter school. As the school superintendent observed, "[I]t has mobilized a community that was very complacent and had allowed their school system to erode. This brought them together and they worked very, very hard to save their school."[33] Because charter schools are recent innovations, most of the information on their effects on student achievement is self-reported. As expected, these preliminary results are largely positive.[34] More reliable assessment is expected to emerge in the next few years.

Milwaukee's Choice Experiment

Additional support for choice has come from an evaluation of the small-scale choice experiment for low-income students in Milwaukee. Assessment of the Milwaukee pilot program has been controversial, however, fueled by charges and countercharges between two teams of researchers. On one side is the Witte team at the University of Wisconsin. Witte showed that the choice program encountered many implementation problems during its first year.[35] Reviewing the program's fourth-year data, Witte, Thorn, Pritchard, and Claibourn concluded that "in terms of achievement test scores . . . students perform approximately the same as students [in the Milwaukee public schools]."[36] The report also recognized that the choice students maintained higher attendance rates and that their parents were highly satisfied with the selected schools.

On the other side of the debate is the Peterson team at Harvard University. Peterson and Noyes found that students made significant gains by their third and fourth years of enrollment in the choice program.[37] In comparing student applicants who were not selected with students who were admitted to the choice program, Peterson's research team found that the latter scored, on average, 5 percentile points higher in math in year three and more than 11 points higher in year four. In reading, choice participants scored nearly 5 percentile points higher than their comparison group after four years. These positive patterns led Peterson and Noyes to conclude, "If duplicated nationwide, [choice programs] would reduce the current difference between white and minority test score performance by at least one third and perhaps by more than one half."[38] Encouraged by the results in Milwaukee, Peterson is leading similar evaluation research on the state-funded choice program in Cleveland and on the privately funded scholarship programs in New York City and Dayton. The policy challenge is whether student gains in pilot choice projects, such as the one in Milwaukee, can be sustained when they are scaled up to the systemwide level. In this regard, the British experience can be useful.

Choice within a National System: Lessons from England

In assessing the first three years of implementation of the 1988 Education Reform Act (ERA), which affected 33,000 British public schools, Chubb and Moe claimed that school autonomy was producing positive results.[39] Although ERA standardized student assessment and the national curriculum for all "state-maintained" schools, the 1988 reform gave parents and governing boards of individual schools the choice to "opt out" of the existing bureaucratic system, "taking students, money, and all relevant decision-making power with them."[40] During the first three years of the reform, about 100 schools opted out, and another 140 were in the process of becoming "grant-maintained" schools. Although opted-out schools represented only a tiny fraction of all schools in the United Kingdom, Chubb and Moe believed that "if enough schools were to follow this path, the existing system would collapse and a very new and different one would take its place—a system whose hallmark is . . . school autonomy."[41]

One of Chubb and Moe's most important observations was that choice in England did not discriminate against pupils with disadvantaged backgrounds. Instead, according to the authors, the opted-out schools were drawing students from "all ability levels" and were catering to the educational interests of their clients, who were seen as "ordinary people by class-based standards."[42] This observation of choice without stratification has been challenged by several studies. Whitty pointed out that many of the first schools that opted out were already highly selective in their student admissions.[43] These schools had gained academic reputations and maintained the traditional sixth form. In Birmingham, the largest local education authority (LEA) in England, six of the city's eight most selective grammar schools opted out of the state-maintained system. In their study of admissions practices in the London area, Pennell and West warned against the tendency toward polarization in student selection.[44] They found that school autonomy in London tends to reward "those parents who are able and prepared to negotiate the complexities [of the system] compared with those who are less willing or less able to do so."[45] In other words, more systematic research on the dynamics of choice, access, and diversity is needed.

In England, student performance is driven by a complex mix of three policy components: parental choice, site-based management, and national standards. Individual schools are managed by local governing bodies, which consist of the head teacher, parents, community representatives, teachers, and "co-opted members" who offer needed specialties to the particular school setting. The schools are in control of most of the total educational budget.[46] In some cases, schools receive 90 percent of the funds. Because the size of the school budget is determined by the number of pupils, schools have to make efforts to maintain a stable enrollment. Within each community area, parents can select from a wide range of "free" schools, including grant-maintained (government funded but not regulated), LEA (government-maintained), and Church of England and Catholic schools, and "expensive" private schools. Head teachers are keenly aware of the need to compete for enrollments. Each year, student performance on national tests is widely publicized by the media.

Equally interesting is the role of the central office (or the LEA). Although LEAs are responsible for statutory services (such as special education), they are dependent on "purchasing decisions" made by individual schools. Schools can use their funds to "buy back" professional training, special education, and other services that they see as useful.[47] Otherwise, schools can look for alternatives or private vendors.

To conclude, the U.K. experience suggests that choice can include religious schools, and that choice and national standards can go hand in hand to improve student achievement. After all, international comparisons rank U.K. students higher than their U.S. counterparts in mathematics and science.

Public education continues to be shaped by layers of allocative rules that can be traced back to particular political concerns at different levels of government some thirty years ago. In this book, I have examined the institutional effects of rule layering in terms of policy fragmentation and a disconnection to teaching and learning in the classroom. These institutional effects are fairly widespread in public educational systems across the nation. Given the enormous cumulative power of the status quo, one cannot expect to see a comprehensive overhaul in the existing allocative rules. Nonetheless, over the last ten years, a growing number of states, districts, and schools have experimented with new designs that allow them to move away from existing allocative practices. Based on a synthesis of the literature on policy redesign, I have examined four types of reform models that aim to allocate resources more effectively to improve teaching and learning.

A key challenge is to decide on the policy tasks that the redesign strategies are expected to address. In this book, I have focused on the tasks of reducing institutional fragmentation and raising academic standards for all students. Clearly, with 15,000 districts and fifty states, there are numerous possible routes to accomplish these goals. Our marketplace of ideas will not cease to produce policy experimentation and to challenge existing practices, thereby producing institutional diversity in the way we allocate resources in public schools.

In this final chapter, I have identified the range of institutional possibilities in the context of governance diversity. In my view, governance redesign involves both systemwide and school-site levels. From an intergovernmental perspective, policymakers at the federal and state levels can collaborate on the use of resources to improve teaching quality and promote schooling opportunities for the disadvantaged. For those who are concerned about not having enough "voice" for the school community, we can learn from experiments that involve a variety of power-sharing arrangements—the Swedish model of democratic education, teacher control in Norway, and parental empowerment in Chicago. Those who are concerned about fragmentation and standards ought to consider the recent developments in a mode of accountability that I label "integrated governance." Unlike the traditional bureaucratic model that commands excessive regulations, integrated governance, as exemplified in Chicago since 1995, uses both sanctions and support to improve student outcomes, policy coherence, and accountability. This model suggests that an integration of political will and educational accountability is feasible in big-city systems. Finally, there are those who are frustrated with the limited choices available to parents, particularly in inner-city, low-income neighborhoods. As concerns about service quality are translated into a search for alternatives, different strands of parental choice are gaining support both in the United States and abroad. In sum, diversity in governing structures—not only within the public sector but also between public and private schools—will offer competing ways of allocating resources to improve schooling quality and promote educational opportunities.

Notes

1. POLITICS OF ALLOCATING RESOURCES IN SCHOOLS

1. National Commission on Excellence in Education, *A Nation at Risk* (Washington, D.C.: U.S. Government Printing Office, 1983), p. 1.

2. "Quality Counts: A Report Card on the Condition of Public Education in the 50 States," supplement to *Education Week,* January 22, 1997, p. 3. Substantial interstate variation existed. Vermont adopted the most comprehensive set of standards, whereas Wyoming and Iowa were given failing grades in student assessment.

3. On decision rules, see Frank Levy, Arnold Meltsner, and Aaron Wildavsky, *Urban Outcomes* (Berkeley: University of California Press, 1974); Terry Nichols Clark, ed., *Urban Innovation: Creative Strategies for Turbulent Times* (Thousand Oaks, Calif.: Sage, 1994).

4. Eric Hanushek, *Making Schools Work* (Washington, D.C.: Brookings Institution, 1994), p. xv.

5. Ibid., p. xviii.

6. Ibid., p. 64.

7. John Chubb and Terry Moe, *Politics, Markets, and America's Schools* (Washington, D.C.: Brookings Institution, 1990); Terry Moe, "Private Vouchers: Politics and Evidence," paper presented at the conference on Education in Cities: What Works and What Doesn't, sponsored by Temple University Laboratory for Student Success and the Johnson Foundation, Racine, Wis., November 1998.

8. Hanushek, *Making Schools Work,* p. 153.

9. Ibid., p. 55.

10. Ibid., p. xxiv.

11. Ibid., p. 151.

12. See Paul E. Peterson, Barry G. Rabe, and Kenneth K. Wong, *When Federalism Works* (Washington, D.C.: Brookings Institution, 1986).

13. Alice Rivlin, *Reviving the American Dream* (Washington, D.C.: Brookings Institution, 1992).

14. Ibid., p. 118.

15. Paul E. Peterson, *The Price of Federalism* (Washington, D.C.: Brookings Institution, 1995).

16. Ibid., p. 191.

17. Ibid., p. 194.

18. Kenneth K. Wong, "Can the Big-City School System Be Governed?" in *Transforming Schools: Rhetoric and Reality,* ed. Peter Cookson and Barbara Schneider (New York: Garland, 1995), pp. 457–88.

19. Ibid.

20. Charles Benson, *The Cheerful Prospect: A Statement on the Future of Public Education* (Boston: Houghton Mifflin, 1965); Arthur Wise, *Rich Schools, Poor Schools: The Promise of Equal Educational Opportunity* (Chicago: University of Chicago Press, 1972); F. Harrison and E. McLoone, *Profiles in School Report: A Decennial Overview* (Washington, D.C.: U.S. Government Printing Office, 1965).

21. Wise, *Rich Schools, Poor Schools,* p. 124.

22. Jonathan Kozol, *Savage Inequalities* (New York: Crown, 1991), pp. 54.

23. Ibid., p. 225.

24. Rebecca Barr and Robert Dreeben, *How Schools Work* (Chicago: University of Chicago Press, 1983).

25. Linda Darling-Hammond, "Teacher Quality and Equality," in *Access to Knowledge: An Agenda for Our Nation's Schools,* ed. John Goodlad and P. Keating (New York: College Entrance Examination Board, 1990), pp. 237–58.

26. Arthur Wise, Linda Darling-Hammond, and B. Berry, *Effective Teacher Selection: From Recruitment to Retention* (Santa Monica, Calif.: Rand Corporation, 1987).

27. Jeannie Oakes, *Keeping Track: How Schools Structure Inequality* (New Haven, Conn.: Yale University Press, 1985); also see Jeannie Oakes, "Can Tracking Research Inform Practice?" *Educational Researcher* 21, no. 4 (1992): 12–21.

28. Betty Malen and Rodney Ogawa, "Professional-Patron Influence on Site-based Governance Councils: A Confounding Case Study," *Educational Evaluation and Policy Analysis* 10, no. 4 (1988): 251–70; Daniel Brown, *Decentralization and School-based Management* (London: Falmer Press, 1990); William Clune and P. White, *School-based Management: Institutional Variation, Implementation, and Issues for Further Research* (New Brunswick, N.J.: Center for Policy Research in Education, 1988).

29. Consortium on Chicago School Research, *A View from the Elementary Schools: The State of Reform in Chicago* (Chicago: Consortium on Chicago School Research, 1993).

30. Chubb and Moe, *Politics, Markets, and America's Schools.*

31. Marshall S. Smith and Jennifer A. O'Day, "Systemic School Reform," in *The Politics of Curriculum and Testing,* ed. Susan Fuhrman and Betty Malen (Bristol, Pa.: Falmer Press, 1991), pp. 233–67.

32. See Hanushek, *Making Schools Work;* Richard Murnane, "Interpreting the Evidence on 'Does Money Matter?'" *Harvard Journal on Legislation* 28 (1991): 457–564; Larry Hedges, Richard Laine, and Robert Greenwald, "Does Money Matter? A Meta-analysis of Studies of the Effects of Differential School Inputs on Student Outcomes," *Educational Researcher* 23, no. 3 (April 1994): 5–14.

33. Murnane, "Interpreting the Evidence."

34. Barr and Dreeben, *How Schools Work.*

35. Jay Scribner and Donald Layton, eds., *The Study of Educational Politics* (London: Falmer Press, 1995).

2. POLITICS OF SOCIAL TARGETING AT THE FEDERAL LEVEL

1. Paul E. Peterson, Barry G. Rabe, and Kenneth K. Wong, *When Federalism Works* (Washington, D.C.: Brookings Institution, 1986).

2. Theodore Lowi, "American Business and Public Policy, Case Studies and Political Theory," *World Politics* 16, no 4 (July 1964): 677–715; Randall Ripley and Grace Franklin, *Congress, the Bureaucracy, and Public Policy* (Homewood, Ill.: Dorsey Press, 1984).

3. Michael Reagan and John Sanzone, *The New Federalism,* 2d ed. (New York: Oxford University Press, 1981); Wallace Oates, *Fiscal Federalism* (New York: Harcourt Brace Jovanovich, 1972); Paul E. Peterson, *City Limits* (Chicago: University of Chicago Press, 1981); Kenneth K. Wong, *City Choices: Education and Housing* (Albany: State University of New York Press, 1990).

4. Gary Orfield, *Must We Bus?* (Washington, D.C.: Brookings Institution, 1978); Frank J. Munger and Richard F. Fenno, *National Politics and Federal Aid to Education* (Syracuse, N.Y.: Syracuse University Press, 1962); James L. Sundquist, *Politics and Policy* (Washington, D.C.: Brookings Institution, 1968); Lowi, "American Business and Public Policy"; Ripley and Franklin, *Congress, the Bureaucracy, and Public Policy;* Thomas E. Cavanagh and James L. Sundquist, "The New Two-Party System," in *The New Direction in American Politics,* ed. John Chubb and Paul E. Peterson (Washington, D.C.: Brookings Institution, 1985), pp. 33–67.

5. Sundquist, *Politics and Policy.*

6. David R. Mayhew, *Congress: The Electoral Connection* (New Haven, Conn.: Yale University Press, 1974); Cavanagh and Sundquist, "The New Two-Party System."

7. Orfield, *Must We Bus?;* Peterson, Rabe, and Wong, *When Federalism Works.*

8. Theodore Lowi, *The End of Liberalism,* 2d ed. (New York: W. W. Norton, 1979).

9. Orfield, *Must We Bus?*

10. Thomas Anton, *American Federalism and Public Policy: How the System Works* (New York: Random House, 1989).

11. Mary Ann Millsap, Brenda Turnbull, Marc Moss, Nancy Brigham, Beth Gamse, and Ellen Marks, *The Chapter 1 Implementation Study: Interim Report* (Washington, D.C.: U.S. Department of Education, 1992).

12. Peterson, Rabe, and Wong, *When Federalism Works,* pp. 110–12.

13. Gary Orfield, "Race, Income and Educational Inequality: Students and Schools at Risk in the 1980s," in *School Success for Students at Risk,* by Council of Chief State School Officers (Orlando, Fla.: Harcourt Brace Jovanovich, 1988).

14. Kenneth K. Wong, "City Implementation of Federal Antipoverty Programs: Proposing a Framework," *Urban Resources* 5, no. 2 (1989): 27–31.

15. See Peterson, Rabe, and Wong, *When Federalism Works.*

16. Millsap et al., *Chapter 1 Implementation Study.*

17. David L. Clark and Terry A. Astuto, "The Significance and Permanence of Changes in Federal Education Policy," *Educational Researcher* 15 (1986): 4–13.

18. U.S. General Accounting Office, *Magnet Schools: Information on the Grant Award Process* (Washington, D.C.: U.S. General Accounting Office, 1987).

19. Michael Knapp and R. A. Cooperstein, "Early Research on the Federal Education Block Grant: Themes and Unanswered Questions," *Educational Evaluation and Policy Analysis* 8, no. 2 (1986): 121–37.

20. Martin E. Orland and S. Tillander, "Redistribution and the Education Block Grant: An Analysis of State Chapter 2 Allocation Formulas," *Educational Evaluation and Policy Analysis* 9, no. 3 (1987): 245–57.

21. Commission on Chapter 1, *Making Schools Work for Children in Poverty* (Washington, D.C.: Council for Chief State School Officers, 1992).

22. David S. Cloud, "Shakeup Time," *Congressional Quarterly: Committee Guide,* March 25, 1995, p. 9.

23. Gerald Sroufe, "Politics of Education at the Federal Level," in *The Study of Educational Politics,* ed. Jay Scribner and Donald Layton (London: Falmer Press, 1995), p. 83.

24. Lori Nitschke, "Alternate Routes Considered for D.C. Spending Bill," *Congressional Quarterly Weekly Report,* March 2, 1996, p. 549.

25. *New York Times Magazine,* January 28, 1996, p. 54.

26. Ibid., p. 40.

27. Charles O. Jones, "Bill Clinton and the GOP Congress," *Brookings Review* 13 (spring 1995): 30–33.

28. Jerome Murphy, "Title I of ESEA: The Politics of Implementing Federal Education Reform," *Harvard Educational Review* 41 (February 1971): 35–63; James S. Coleman, Sara D. Kelley, and John A. Moore, *Trends in School Desegregation, 1968–73* (Washington, D.C.: Urban Institute, 1975); Jeffrey Pressman and Aaron Wildavsky, *Implementation* (Berkeley: University of California Press, 1973); Ruby Martin and Phyllis McClure, *Title I of ESEA: Is It Helping Poor Children?* (Washington, D.C.: Washington Research Project of the Southern Center for Studies in Public Policy and the NAACP Legal Defense of Education Fund, 1969); David Kirp and Donald N. Jensen, *School Days, Rule Days* (Philadelphia: Falmer Press, 1985).

29. Peterson, Rabe, and Wong, *When Federalism Works;* Allan Odden and David Marsh, "State Education Reform Implementation: A Framework for Analysis," in *The Politics of Reforming School Administration,* ed. Jane Hannaway and Robert Crowson (London: Falmer Press, 1989), pp. 41–59; Richard Jung and Michael Kirst, "Beyond Mutual Adaptation, into the Bully Pulpit: Recent Research on the Federal Role in Education," *Educational Administration Quarterly* 22 (summer 1986): 80–109; Judith Singer and John Butler, "The Education of All Handicapped Children Act: Schools as Agents of School Reform," *Harvard Educational Review* 2 (1987): 125–52.

30. Peterson, Rabe, and Wong, *When Federalism Works.*

31. Ibid.; Michael Kirst and Richard Jung, "The Utility of a Longitudinal Approach in Assessing Implementation: A Thirteen-Year View of Title I, ESEA," in *Studying Implementation: Methodological and Administrative Issues,* ed. Walter Williams (New York: Chatham House, 1982).

32. Martin and McClure, *Title I of ESEA.*

33. See Milbrey McLaughlin, "The Rand Change Agent Study Revisited: Macro Perspective and Realities," *Educational Researcher* 19, no. 9 (1990): 11–16.

34. Wong, *City Choices,* p. 135.

35. On linking site-level variables to the design of macro policy, see M. McLaughlin, "Learning from Experience: Lessons from Policy Implementation," *Educational Evaluation and Policy Analysis* 9, no. 2 (1987): 171–78; R. Elmore, "Backward Mapping: Implementation Research and Policy Decisions," *Political Science Quarterly* 94, no. 4 (1980): 601–16; M. McLaughlin and P. Berman, *Federal Program Supporting Educational*

Change, vol. 8, *Implementing and Sustaining Innovation* (Santa Monica, Calif.: Rand Corporation, 1978).

36. Millsap et al., *Chapter 1 Implementation Study.*

37. Ibid., pp. 2–44.

38. See William Julius Wilson, *The Truly Disadvantaged: The Inner City, the Underclass, and Public Policy* (Chicago: University of Chicago Press, 1987).

39. Mary Kennedy, Richard Jung, and Martin Orland, *Poverty, Achievement and the Distribution of Compensatory Education Services* (Washington, D.C.: U.S. Department of Education, 1986), p. 107.

40. U.S. General Accounting Office, *Remedial Education: Modifying Chapter 1 Formula Would Target More Funds to Those Most in Need* (Washington, D.C.: U.S. General Accounting Office, 1992).

41. Kennedy, Jung, and Orland, *Poverty, Achievement and Distribution.*

42. *Congressional Quarterly Weekly,* January 15, 1994, pp. 70–73.

43. Ibid., p. 71.

44. Marshall S. Smith, "Selecting Students and Services for Chapter 1," in *Federal Aid to the Disadvantaged: What Future for Chapter 1?* ed. Dennis Doyle and Bruce Cooper (London: Falmer Press, 1988), p. 130.

45. Michael Kirst, "The Federal Role and Chapter 1: Rethinking Some Basic Assumptions," in Doyle and Cooper, *Federal Aid to the Disadvantaged,* p. 110.

46. Commission on Chapter 1, *Making Schools Work.* Also see Thomas Timar, "Program Design and Assessment Strategies in Chapter 1," in *Rethinking Policy for At-Risk Students,* ed. Kenneth K. Wong and Margaret C. Wang (Berkeley, Calif.: McCutchan, 1994).

47. See Camilla A. Heid, "The Dilemma of Chapter 1 Program Improvement," *Educational Evaluation and Policy Analysis* 13, no. 4 (1991): 394–98.

48. Carolyn Herrington and Martin Orland, "Politics and Federal Aid to Urban School Systems: The Case of Chapter One," in *The Politics of Urban Education in the United States,* ed. James G. Cibulka, Rodney J. Reed, and Kenneth K. Wong (London: Falmer Press, 1992). pp. 167–79.

49. Mary Rose C. de Baca, Cecilia Rinaldi, Shelley Billig, and Beatriz Martinez Kinnison, "Santo Domingo School: A Rural Schoolwide Project Success," *Educational Evaluation and Policy Analysis* 13, no. 4 (1991): 363–68.

50. Millsap et al., *Chapter 1 Implementation Study.*

51. Sam Stringfield, Shelley Billig, and Alan Davis, "Chapter 1 Program Improvement: Cause for Cautious Optimism and a Call for Much More Research," *Educational Evaluation and Policy Analysis* 13, no. 4 (1991): 399–406.

52. Millsap et al., *Chapter 1 Implementation Study.*

53. Ibid.

54. Commission on Chapter 1, *Making Schools Work.*

55. Kenneth K. Wong, Gail L. Sunderman, and Jaekyung Lee, *When Federal Chapter 1 Works to Improve Student Learning in Inner City Schools: Preliminary Findings on Schoolwide Projects in Minneapolis* (Philadelphia: National Center on Education in the Inner Cities, Temple University, 1994).

56. Margaret C. Wang and Kenneth K. Wong, eds. *Implementing School Reform: Practice and Policy Imperatives* (Philadelphia: Temple University Center for Research in Human Development and Education, 1997).

57. Robert Slavin, Nancy L. Karweit, and Nancy A. Madden, eds., *Effective Programs for Students at Risk* (London: Allyn and Bacon, 1989).

58. Peter Scheirer, "Metropolitan Chicago Public Schools: Concerto for Grades, Schools and Students in F Major," draft paper, Metropolitan Opportunity Project, University of Chicago, 1989.

59. John Witte and Daniel Walsh, "Metropolitan Milwaukee District Performance Assessment Report," staff report no. 4 to the Commission on the Quality of Education in the Metropolitan Milwaukee Public Schools, 1985.

60. Gary Orfield and Sean Reardon, "Separate and Unequal Schools: Political Change and the Shrinking Agenda of Urban School Reform," paper presented at the annual meeting of the American Political Science Association, Chicago, 1992.

61. U.S. General Accounting Office, *Compensatory Education: Most Chapter 1 Funds in Eight Districts Used for Classroom Services* (Washington, D.C.: U.S. General Accounting Office, 1992).

62. See Robert Dreeben and Rebecca Barr, "The Formation and Instruction of Ability Groups," *American Journal of Education* 97, no. 1 (1988): 34–64.

3. MAPPING INTERSTATE VARIATION IN STATE AID TO SCHOOLS

1. U.S. General Accounting Office, *Intergovernmental Relations: Changing Patterns in State–Local Finances* (Washington, D.C.: U.S. General Accounting Office, 1992).

2. See Kenneth K. Wong, "Fiscal Support for Education in American States: The 'Parity-to-Dominance' View Examined," *American Journal of Education* 97, no. 4 (1989): 329–57.

3. See discussions in Richard Nathan and Fred Doolittle, *Reagan and the States* (Princeton, N.J.: Princeton University Press, 1987); John Chubb, "Effective Schools and the Problems of the Poor," in *Federal Aid to the Disadvantaged,* ed. Denis Doyle and Bruce Cooper (London: Falmer Press, 1988); Susan Fuhrman, "Increased State Capacity and Aid to the Disadvantaged," in Doyle and Cooper, *Federal Aid to the Disadvantaged.*

4. See Paul E. Peterson, Barry G. Rabe, and Kenneth K. Wong, *When Federalism Works* (Washington, D.C.: Brookings Institution, 1986).

5. Michael Kirst, "The Federal Role and Chapter 1: Rethinking Some Basic Assumptions," in Doyle and Cooper, *Federal Aid to the Disadvantaged;* Richard Murnane and Frank Levy, "Education and Training," in *Setting Domestic Priorities,* ed. Henry Aaron and Charles Schultze (Washington, D.C.: Brookings Institution, 1992), pp. 185–222.

6. Stephen Gold, "State Aid for Local Schools: Trends and Prospects," in *Public Schools: Issues in Budgeting and Financial Management,* ed. John Augenblick (New Brunswick, N.J.: Transaction, 1985).

7. Wong, "Fiscal Support for Education."

8. J. R. Aronson and J. Hilley, *Financing State and Local Governments,* 4th ed. (Washington, D.C.: Brookings Institution, 1986); Paul E. Peterson, *City Limits* (Chicago: University of Chicago Press, 1981); Kenneth K. Wong, *City Choices: Education and Housing* (Albany: State University of New York Press, 1990).

9. Aronson and Hilley, *Financing State and Local Governments,* chap. 6.

10. Ibid.

11. Michael Reagan and John Sanzone, *The New Federalism,* 2d ed. (New York: Oxford University Press, 1981).

12. Allan Odden, "School Finance Reform: An Example of Redistributive Policy at the State Level," paper presented for the School Finance Project, National Institute of Education, Washington, D.C., 1981.

13. Walter Garms, James G. Guthrie, and Lawrence C. Pierce, *School Finance* (Englewood Cliffs, N.J.: Prentice Hall, 1978), p. 354.

14. David Long, "Rodriguez: The State Courts Respond," *Phi Delta Kappan* 64 (March 1983): 10; Garms, Guthrie, and Pierce, *School Finance,* p. 354.

15. *Serrano v. Priest,* 96 Cal. Rptr. 601, 437, P.2d 1241 (1971).

16. Ibid., at 611–12.

17. Betsy Levin et al., *Paying for Public Schools: Issues of School Finance in California* (Washington, D.C.: Urban Institute, 1972). Michael Kirst and S. Somers, "California Educational Interest Groups: Collective Action as a Logical Response to Proposition 13," *Education and Urban Society* 13, no. 2 (1981): 235–56.

18. *San Antonio Independent School District v. Rodriguez,* 36 L. Ed. 2d 16, 93 S. Ct. 1278 (1973).

19. J. Callahan and W. Wilken, "The Federal Interest in Financing Schooling: A View from the States," in *The Federal Interest in Financing Schooling,* ed. Michael Timpane (Cambridge, Mass.: Ballinger, 1978), pp. 21–46.

20. Patricia Brown and Richard Elmore, "Analyzing the Impact of School Finance Reform," in *The Changing Politics of School Finance,* ed. Nelda Cambron-McCabe and Allan Odden (Cambridge, Mass.: Ballinger, 1982).

21. Ibid.; Joel Berke, Margaret Goertz, and Richard Coley, *Politicians, Judges, and City Schools: Reforming School Finance in New York* (New York: Russell Sage Foundation, 1984).

22. Stephen D. Gold, David M. Smith, Stephen B. Lawton, and Andrea C. Hyary, eds., *Public School Finance Programs of the United States and Canada 1990–91* (Albany, N.Y.: American Education Finance Association and the Center for the Study of the States, Nelson A. Rockefeller Institute of Government, 1992).

23. Jack Leppert, Larry Huxel, Walter Garms, and Heber Fuller, "Pupil Weighting Programs in School Finance Reform," in *School Finance Reform: A Legislator's Handbook,* ed. Joseph Callahan and William Wilken (Washington, D.C.: National Conferences of State Legislators, 1976), pp. 12–26.

24. Daniel Mullins and Phillip Joyce, *Tax and Expenditure Limitations and State and Local Fiscal Structures* (Bloomington: Center for Urban Policy and Environment, School of Public and Environmental Affairs, Indiana University, December 1995).

25. Philip Piele and John Hall, *Budget, Bonds, and Ballots* (Lexington, Mass.: Lexington, 1973).

26. Levin et al., *Paying for Public Schools.*

27. Phi Delta Kappa, *Gallup Polls of Attitudes toward Education 1969–1984: A Topical Summary* (Bloomington, Ind.: Phi Delta Kappa, 1984).

28. M. Williams, "Earthquakes or Tremors? Tax and Expenditure Limitations and School Finance," in Cambron-McCabe and Odden, *The Changing Politics of School Finance;* Advisory Commission on Intergovernmental Relations (ACIR), *Significant Features of Fiscal Federalism* (Washington, D.C.: ACIR, 1980); Stephen Gold, "State Aid for Local Schools," in *State and Local Fiscal Relations in the Early 1980s* (Washington, D.C.: Urban Institute, 1983).

29. Technically speaking, a state assumes a dominance status as long as its share exceeds the local contribution. For example, state dominance can be reached when the state

contributes 47 percent, the locality provides 46 percent, and the federal share is 7 percent of total school revenues. I use 50 percent as the benchmark because the figure offers an unambiguous way of substantiating the concept of dominance.

30. Frederick Wirt, "School Policy Culture and State Decentralization," in *The Politics of Education,* ed. Jay D. Scribner (Chicago: University of Chicago Press, 1977), pp. 164–87.

31. Daniel Elazar, *American Federalism: A View from the States,* 2d ed. (New York: Crowell, 1972); Wirt, "School Policy Culture and State Decentralization."

32. Susan Fuhrman, " New Hampshire," in *Shaping Education Policy in the States,* ed. Susan Fuhrman and Alan Rosenthal (Washington, D.C.: Institute for Educational Leadership, 1981).

33. Wirt, "School Policy Culture and State Decentralization."

34. Alan Rosenthal and Susan Fuhrman, *Legislative Education Leadership in the States* (Washington, D.C.: Institute for Educational Leadership, 1981).

35. Odden, "School Finance Reform."

36. Stephen Gold, *The State Fiscal Agenda for the 1990s* (Denver: National Conference of State Legislatures, 1990).

37. T. van Geel, "The Courts and School Finance Reform: An Expected Utility Model," in Cambron-McCabe and Odden, *The Changing Politics of School Finance.*

38. D. Massell and M. Kirst, "State Policymaking for Educational Excellence: School Reform in California" in *The Fiscal, Legal, and Political Aspects of State Reform of Elementary and Secondary Education,* ed. V. D. Mueller and M. McKeown (Cambridge, Mass.: Ballinger, 1986).

39. Thomas Timar, "Urban Politics and State School Finance in the 1980s," in *The Politics of Urban Education in the United States,* ed. James Cibulka, Rodney Reed, and Kenneth Wong (London: Falmer Press, 1992), pp. 105–21.

40. Ibid.

41. *Governing,* February 1993.

42. On sectoral interests, see Terry N. Clark and Lorna Ferguson, *City Money: Political Processes, Fiscal Strain, and Retrenchment* (New York: Columbia University Press, 1983).

43. *Edgewood Independent School District v. Kirby,* 777 S.W. 391 (1989).

44. *Education Week,* October 3, 1990.

45. Jeffrey Mirel, *The Rise and Fall of an Urban School System: Detroit, 1907–81* (Ann Arbor: University of Michigan Press, 1993).

46. *New York Times,* March 21, 1993.

47. Advisory Commission on Intergovernmental Relations, *Significant Features of Fiscal Federalism,* vol. 2 (Washington, D.C.: ACIR, 1992), p. 275, table R-2.

48. *Chicago Fed Letter,* May (no. 81), Federal Reserve Bank of Chicago, 1994.

4. POLITICS OF LEVELING UP SPENDING AT THE STATE LEVEL

1. *San Antonio Independent School District v. Rodriguez,* 36 L. Ed. 2d 16, 93 S. Ct. 1278 (1973).

2. Charles Benson, "State Government Contributions to the Public Schools," in *Public Schools: Issues in Budgeting and Financial Management,* ed. John Augenblick (New Brunswick, N.J.: Transaction, 1985), pp. 11–23.

3. James Guthrie, Walter Garms, and Lawrence Pierce, *School Finance and Education Policy,* 2d ed. (Englewood Cliffs, N.J.: Prentice Hall, 1988); Vincent G. Munley, *The Structure of State Aid to Elementary and Secondary Education* (Washington, D.C.: Advisory Commission on Intergovernmental Relations, 1990); Richard Salmon, Christina M. Dawson, Stephen Lawton, and Thomas Johns, eds. *Public School Finance Programs in the United States and Canada: 1986–87* (Blacksburg, Va.: American Education Finance Association and Virginia Polytechnic and State University, 1987); and Stephen D. Gold, David M. Smith, Stephen B. Lawton, and Andrea C. Hyary, eds., *Public School Finance Programs of the United States and Canada 1990–1991* (Albany, N.Y.: American Education Finance Association and Center for the Study of the States, Nelson A. Rockefeller Institute of Government, 1992).

4. George Strayer and Robert Haig, *Financing of Education in the State of New York* (New York: Macmillan, 1923).

5. Charles Benson, *The Economics of Public Education* (New York: Houghton Mifflin, 1961).

6. This concept was developed by John Coons, William Clune, and Stephen Sugarman in *Private Wealth and Public Education* (Cambridge: Harvard University Press, 1970).

7. Deborah Verstegen and Kent McGuire, *School Finance at a Glance* (Denver: Education Commission of the States, 1988).

8. Arthur Wise, *Rich Schools, Poor Schools: The Promise of Equal Educational Opportunity* (Chicago: University of Chicago Press, 1972); James N. Fox, "School Finance and the Economics of Education: An Essay Review of Major Works," *Educational Evaluation and Policy Analysis* 11 (1989): 69–83.

9. Patricia Brown and Richard Elmore, "Analyzing the Impact of School Finance Reform," in *The Changing Politics of School Finance,* ed. Nelda Cambron-McCabe and Allan Odden (Cambridge, Mass.: Ballinger, 1982).

10. Mary Fulton, "School Finance System Changes," Education Commission of the States, www.ecs.org, November 1998.

11. Michael Kirst, "Review of Dilemmas in School Finance," *American Journal of Education* 88, no. 4 (August 1980): 502–5.

12. Susan Fuhrman, *State Education Politics: The Case of School Finance Reform* (Denver: Education Commission of the States, 1979).

13. Allan Odden, "School Finance Reform: An Example of Redistributive Policy at the State Level," paper presented for the School Finance Project, National Institute of Education, Washington, D.C., 1981.

14. Phi Delta Kappa, *Gallup Polls of Attitudes toward Education 1969–1984: A Topical Summary* (Bloomington, Ind.: Phi Delta Kappa, 1984).

15. Jack Citrin, "Introduction: The Legacy of Proposition 13," in *California and the American Tax Revolt,* ed. Terry Schwadron (Berkeley and Los Angeles: University of California Press, 1984).

16. Stephen Carroll and Rolla Park, *The Search for Equity in School Finance* (Cambridge, Mass.: Ballinger, 1983).

17. Citrin, "Introduction: The Legacy of Proposition 13," p. 58.

18. Helen Ladd and Julie Wilson, "Proposition 2½: Explaining the Vote," in *Research in Urban Policy,* vol. 1, ed. Terry N. Clark (Greenwich, Conn.: JAI Press, 1985), pp. 199–243.

19. Ibid., p. 217.

20. See Citrin, "Introduction: The Legacy of Proposition 13"; Paul Courant, Edward Gramlich, and Daniel Rubinfeld, "Why Voters Support Tax Limitation Amendments: The Michigan Case," *National Tax Journal* 32 (1980): 1–21; Ladd and Wilson, "Proposition 2½."

21. Citrin, "Introduction: The Legacy of Proposition 13," p. 29.

22. See A. Lipson and M. Lavin, *Political Responses to Proposition 13 in California* (Santa Monica, Calif.: Rand Corporation, 1980).

23. Robert Palaich, James Kloss, and Mary Williams, *Tax and Expenditure Limitation Referenda* (Denver: Education Commission of the States, 1980), p. 53.

24. Ibid.

25. Ibid.

26. I conducted this analysis using the information reported in "Changing Course: A 50-state Survey of Reform Measures," *Education Week,* February 6, 1985, pp. 11–30.

27. Catherine Marshall, Douglas Mitchell, and Frederick Wirt, "The Context of State-Local Policy Formation," *Educational Evaluation and Policy Analysis* 8, no. 4 (winter 1986): 347–78. Also see E. H. Wahlke, W. Buchanon, and L. C. Ferguson, *The Legislative System: Explorations in Legislative Behavior* (New York: John Wiley and Sons, 1962); and Kenneth K. Wong, "Policymaking in the American States: Typology, Process and Institutions," *Policy Studies Review* 8, no. 3 (spring 1989): 527–48.

28. Kenneth K. Wong, "Fiscal Support for Education in American States: The 'Parity-to-Dominance' View Examined," *American Journal of Education* 97, no. 4 (1989): 329–57.

29. Joel Berke, Margaret Goertz, and Richard Coley, *Politicians, Judges, and City Schools: Reforming School Finance in New York* (New York: Russell Sage Foundation, 1984).

30. Alan Rosenthal and Susan Fuhrman, *Legislative Education Leadership in the States* (Washington, D.C.: Institute for Education Leadership, 1981).

31. Wong, "Policymaking in the American States."

32. Joseph Cronin, "Financing Urban Schools," in Cambron-McCabe and Odden, *The Changing Politics of School Finance.*

33. Berke, Goertz, and Coley, *Politicians, Judges, and City Schools.*

34. *Education Week,* April 18, 1990.

35. *Rose v. The Council for Better Education, Inc.,* No. 88-SC-804-TG, S.Ct. Ky., 8 June 1989, modified 28 September 1989.

36. *Education Week,* March 7, 1990.

37. *New York Times,* June 10, 1990.

38. Jacob Adams, Jr. "School Finance Policy and Students' Opportunities to Learn: Kentucky's Experience," *The Future of Children* 7, no. 3 (winter 1997): 79–95.

39. *Edgewood Independent School District v. Kirby,* 777 S.W. ed 391 (1989).

40. *Education Week,* October 3, 1990, p. 1.

41. *Education Week,* October 3, 1990, p. 17.

42. Carey Goldberg, "Vermont's School Tax Splits the 'Haves' and 'Have Nots,'" *New York Times,* December 19, 1997, pp. A1, A16.

43. W. Riddle, *Expenditures in Public School Districts: Why Do They Differ?* (Washington, D.C.: Congressional Research Service, 1990).

44. W. Taylor and D. Piche, *A Report on Shortchanging Children: The Impact of Fiscal Inequity on the Education of Students at Risk* (Washington, D.C.: U.S. Government Printing Office, 1991).

45. U.S. General Accounting Office, *School Finance: State Efforts to Reduce Funding Gaps between Poor and Wealthy Districts* (Washington, D.C.: U.S. Government Printing Office, 1997).

46. See R. Goertz and Margaret Goertz, "The Quality Education Act of 1990: New Jersey Responds to *Abbott v. Burke*," *Journal of Education Finance* 16, no. 1 (1990): 104–14; Harvey Brazer and Teresa McCarty, "Municipal Overburden: An Empirical Analysis," *Economics of Education Review* 5 (1986): 353–61.

47. U.S. General Accounting Office, *School Finance*.

48. Charles Benson, "Definitions of Equity in School Finance in Texas, New Jersey, and Kentucky," *Harvard Journal on Legislation* 28 (1991): 401–21; G. Levine, "Meeting the Third Wave: Legislative Approaches to Recent Judicial School Finance Rulings," *Harvard Journal on Legislation* 28 (1991): 507–42.

49. Julie Underwood, "School Finance Adequacy as Vertical Equity," *University of Michigan Journal of Law Reform* 28, no. 3 (spring 1995): 493–519.

50. Taylor and Piche, *Report on Shortchanging Children*.

51. William Hartman, "District Spending Disparities: What Do the Dollars Buy?" *Journal of Education Finance* 13 (1988): 436–59.

52. Taylor and Piche, *Report on Shortchanging Children*.

53. *Abbott v. Burke,* S. Ct. N. J., A-63 (1990).

54. Taylor and Piche, *Report on Shortchanging Children*.

55. *Rose v. Council for Better Education,* No. 88-SC-804-TG, S. Ct. Ky. (1990).

56. *Education Week,* August 1, 1990.

57. *Education Week,* November 21, 1990.

58. See *New York Times,* July 14, 1994, p. A12.

59. See *New York Times* editorial, July 14, 1994. Also see Fulton, "School Finance System Changes."

60. Riddle, *Expenditures in Public School Districts*.

61. Gary Orfield and Sean Reardon, "Separate and Unequal Schools: Political Change and the Shrinking Agenda of Urban School Reform," paper presented at the annual meeting of the American Political Science Association, Chicago, 1992; Johnathan Kozol, *Savage Inequalities* (New York: Crown, 1991).

5. THE EMERGING STATE ROLE IN SOCIAL TARGETING

1. 20 U.S.C. 1401 (1975).

2. Jack Leppert, Larry Huxel, Walter Garms, and Heber Fuller, "Pupil Weighting Programs in School Finance Reform," in *School Finance Reform: A Legislator's Handbook,* ed. Joseph Callahan and William Wilken (Washington, D.C.: National Conference of State Legislators, 1976), pp. 12–26.

3. These are Georgia, Illinois, Massachusetts, Minnesota, Missouri, Nebraska, New York, Ohio, Oklahoma, South Carolina, Texas, Utah, and Vermont. See Deborah Verstegen and Kent McGuire, *School Finance at a Glance* (Denver: Education Commission of the States, 1988).

4. These are California, Colorado, Connecticut, Delaware, Florida, Louisiana, Maryland, Michigan, New Jersey, North Carolina, Oregon, Pennsylvania, Rhode Island, Virginia, and Washington.

5. These are Alaska, Arizona, Massachusetts, New Mexico, Oklahoma, and Texas.

6. These are California, Colorado, Connecticut, Georgia, Illinois, Kansas, Louisiana, Michigan, Minnesota, New Jersey, New York, Rhode Island, Utah, Washington, and Wisconsin.

7. A. M. Milne and Jay Moskowitz, "Implications of State Programs: The Case of Special Needs Pupils," *Education and Urban Society* 15, no. 4 (1983): 500–524.

8. Mary Moore, Margaret Goertz, and Terry Hartle, "Interaction of Federal and State Programs," *Education and Urban Society* 15, no. 4 (1983): 452–78.

9. Janice Funkhouser and Mary Moore, *Summary of State Compensatory Education Programs* (Washington D.C.: Decision Resources Corporation, 1985).

10. David Osborne and Ted Gaebler, *Reinventing Government* (Reading, Mass.: Addison-Wesley, 1992).

11. Paul E. Peterson, Barry G. Rabe, and Kenneth K. Wong, *When Federalism Works* (Washington, D.C.: Brookings Institution, 1986).

12. Gary Orfield, *Public School Desegregation in the United States, 1968–1980* (Washington, D.C.: Joint Center for Political Studies, 1983).

13. Joseph Cronin, "Financing Urban Schools," in *The Changing Politics of School Finance,* ed. Nelda Cambron-McCabe and Allan Odden (Cambridge, Mass.: Ballinger, 1982).

14. National Association of State Directors of Special Education, Inc., *A Description of State Funding Procedures for Special Education in the Public Schools* (Washington, D.C.: NASDSE, 1982).

15. National Commission on Excellence in Education, *A Nation at Risk* (Washington, D.C.: U.S. Government Printing Office, 1983).

16. Michael Knapp and R. Cooperstein, "Early Research on the Federal Education Block Grant: Themes and Unanswered Questions," *Educational Evaluation and Policy Analysis* 8, no. 2 (1986): 121–37; Susan Fuhrman, "State-Level Politics and School Financing," in Cambron-McCabe and Odden, *The Changing Politics of School Finance.*

17. Jerome Murphy, "Progress and Problems: The Paradox of State Reform," in *Policymaking in Education,* ed. Ann Lieberman and Milbrey McLaughlin (Chicago: University of Chicago Press, 1982), p. 204.

18. Maynard Reynolds, "A Brief History of Categorical School Programs, 1945–1993," in *Rethinking Policy for At-Risk Students,* ed. Kenneth K. Wong and Margaret C. Wang (Berkeley: McCutchan, 1994), p. 15.

19. Chicago Urban League, *Access and Outreach: A Directory of Organizations Serving Women and Minorities in the Chicago Area* (Chicago: Chicago Urban League, n.d.).

20. J. David Greenstone and Paul E. Peterson, *Race and Authority in Urban Politics* (Chicago: University of Chicago Press, 1976). Also see Rufus P. Browning, Dale Rogers Marshall, and David H. Tabb, *Protest Is Not Enough* (Berkeley: University of California Press, 1984); and Kenneth K. Wong, *City Choices: Education and Housing* (Albany: State University of New York Press, 1990).

21. Kenneth J. Meier and Robert England, "Black Representation and Educational Policy: Are They Related?" *American Political Science Review* 78 (June 1984): 392–403.

22. Thomas Anton, *American Federalism and Public Policy: How the System Works* (New York: Random House, 1989).

23. James N. Fox, "School Finance and the Economics of Education: An Essay Review of Major Works," *Educational Evaluation and Policy Analysis* 11 (spring 1989): 69–83.

24. Joel Berke, Margaret Goertz, and Richard Coley, *Politicians, Judges, and City Schools: Reforming School Finance in New York* (New York: Russell Sage Foundation, 1984).

25. Harvey Brazer and Teresa McCarty, "Municipal Overburden: An Empirical Analysis," *Economics of Education Review* 5 (1986): 353–61.

26. Milbrey McLaughlin and James Catterall, "Notes on the New Politics of Education," *Education and Urban Society* 16 (May 1984): 375–81.

27. L. Dean Webb, "The Role of Special Interest Groups in the Shaping of State Educational Policy Relative to School Finance: A Case Study," *Journal of Education Finance* 7 (fall 1981): 168–88.

28. S. Ct. N.J., A-63, June 5, 1990.

29. Quoted in *Education Week,* October 10, 1990, p. 13.

30. *Education Week,* August 1, 1990, p. 34.

31. *Education Week,* October 10, 1990, p. 13

32. Ibid., p. 15.

33. Peterson, Rabe, and Wong, *When Federalism Works.*

34. Deborah Verstegen and Kent McGuire, *School Finance at a Glance* (Denver: Education Commission for the States, 1988).

35. Margaret Goertz, *Chapter 1 Study* (Princeton, N.J.: Educational Testing Service, 1993); Milne and Moskowitz, "Implications of State Programs."

36. D. L. Franklin and G. Alan Hickrod, "School Finance Equity: The Courts Intervene. A National Perspective," *Policy Briefs* 6 and 7 (Oak Brook, Ill.: North Central Regional Educational Laboratory, 1990).

37. Susan Flinspach, "State Commitment to Equal Educational Opportunities for Special-Needs Children," *Administrator's Notebook* 34, no. 9 (Chicago: Midwest Administration Center, University of Chicago, 1990).

38. See the review by Michael Kirst, "A New School Finance for a New Era of Fiscal Constraint," in *School Finance Reform: A Legislator's Handbook,* ed. Allan Odden and L. Dean Webb (Cambridge, Mass.: Ballinger, 1983), pp. 1–10.

39. S. Carroll, *Words + Numbers: The CT Summer Incentive Program: An Evaluation of Three years—FY86, FY87, FY88,* sponsored by the Connecticut State Department of Education, 1987.

40. Georgia State Department of Education, *State Compensatory Education Annual Report, 1982–83* (Atlanta: Georgia State Department of Education, 1983).

41. J. Rachal and L. G. Hoffman, "The Relationship between Service Schedule, Additional Services, and Student Gain in a Statewide Grade 2 Compensatory Education Program," paper presented at the annual meeting of the American Educational Research Association, New Orleans, 1984.

42. South Carolina Department of Education, *What Is the Penny Buying for South Carolina? Assessment of the Third Year of the South Carolina Education Improvement Act of 1984* (Columbia: South Carolina Department of Education, 1987); South Carolina Department of Education, *Evaluation of the 1987–88 EIA Remedial and Compensatory Program* (Columbia: South Carolina Department of Education, 1989).

43. M. E. Defino and V. Jenkins, *State Compensatory Education: Final Technical Report, 1984–85* (Austin, Tex.: Austin Independent School District, 1985).

44. J. Baker, "Five-Year Assessment of the State Compensatory Education Program in the Dade County Public Schools, Miami, Florida," paper presented at the annual meeting of the American Educational Research Association, San Francisco, 1986.

45. New York City Board of Education, *Chapter 1/P.S.E.N. Remedial Reading and Mathematics Program 1985–86 End of the Year Report* (Brooklyn: New York City Board of Education, 1987).

46. K. Yagi, *State Disadvantaged Child Project: Evaluation Report, 1983–84* (Portland, Oreg.: Portland Public Schools, 1985).

47. R. N. Claus and B. E. Quimper, *State Bilingual and ECIA Chapter 1 Migrant Process Evaluation Report: 1987–88* (Saginaw, Mich.: Saginaw Public Schools, 1988); R. N. Claus and B. E. Quimper, *State Bilingual and ECIA Chapter 1 Migrant Process Evaluation Report: 1988–89* (Saginaw, Mich.: Saginaw Public Schools, 1989).

48. Funkhouser and Moore, *Summary of State Compensatory Education Programs*.

49. Lorraine M. McDonnell and Milbrey W. McLaughlin, *Education and the Role of the States* (Santa Monica, Calif.: Rand Corporation, 1982).

50. Susan Fuhrman, "Increased State Capacity and Aid to the Disadvantaged," in *Policy Options for the Future of Compensatory Education,* ERIC Doc. No. ED 298 204 (1987).

51. Verstegen and McGuire, *School Finance at a Glance.*

52. Flinspach, "State Commitment to Equal Educational Opportunities."

53. Roe L. Johns and E. Morphet, *The Economics and Financing of Education: A System Approach* (Englewood Cliffs, N.J.: Prentice Hall, 1975); J. F. Murphy and W. Hack, "Expenditure and Revenue Problems in Central City School Districts: Problems for the 1980s," *Urban Review* 15, no. 4 (1983): 229–44.

54. Launor F. Carter, "The Sustaining Effects Study of Compensatory and Elementary Education," *Educational Researcher* (August/September 1984): 4–13; Brian Rowan and Larry Guthrie, "The Quality of Chapter 1 Instruction: Results from a Study of Twenty-four Schools," in *Effective Programs for Students at Risk,* ed. Robert Slavin, Nancy L. Karweit, and Nancy A. Madden (London: Allyn and Bacon, 1989).

55. C. B. Paulston, *Bilingual Education: Theories and Issues* (Rowley, Mass: Newbury House Publishers, 1980).

56. Robert Dreeben and Rebecca Barr, "The Formation and Instruction of Ability Groups," *American Journal of Education* 97, no. 1 (1988): 34–64; Jeannie Oakes, *Keeping Track: How Schools Structure Inequality* (New Haven, Conn.: Yale University Press, 1985).

57. Verstegen and McGuire, *School Finance at a Glance.*

58. Kenneth K. Wong, "Linking Governance Reform to Schooling Opportunities for the Disadvantaged," *Educational Administration Quarterly* 30, no. 2 (May 1994): 153–77.

59. On the "supplement, not supplant" controversy in federal compensatory education, see Gene V. Glass and M. L. Smith, *Meta-analysis of Research on the Relationship of Class Size and Achievement* (San Francisco: Far West Laboratory for Educational Research and Development, 1978).

60. U.S. Department of Education, *Prospects: The Congressionally Mandated Study of Educational Growth and Opportunity: The Interim Report* (Washington, D.C.: U.S. Department of Education, 1993), p. 3.

6. LOCAL POLITICS OF EQUALIZING CLASS SIZE

1. I use the terms "class size" and "pupil-teacher ratios" interchangeably. For a more detailed examination of measurement issues and these concepts, see Eugene Lewit and Linda Schuurmann Baker, "Class Size," in *The Future of Children* 7, no. 3 (winter 1997): 112–21. As Jeremy Finn reminds us, the debate over the proper number of students for each teacher and the financial means to support that decision is as old as the Babylonian Talmud. This sixth-century document stipulated that "the number of pupils assigned to each teacher is 25. If there are 50, we appoint two teachers. If there are 40, we appoint an assistant, at the expense of the town." See Jeremy Finn, *Class Size: What Does Research Tell Us?* (Philadelphia: Temple University Laboratory for Student Success, 1997).

2. National Center for Education Statistics, *Projections of Education Statistics to 2006* (Washington, D.C.: U.S. Department of Education, 1996), pp. 566–67.

3. Ibid.

4. Jesse Burkhead, *Input and Output in Large-City High Schools* (Syracuse, N.Y.: Syracuse University, 1967); Paul E. Peterson, *City Limits* (Chicago: University of Chicago Press, 1981); H. Thomas James, James A. Kelly, and Walter Garms, *Determinants of Educational Expenditures in Large Cities in the United States* (Palo Alto, Calif.: Stanford University, 1966); Martin Katzman, *The Political Economy of Urban Schools* (Cambridge: Harvard University Press, 1971); Kenneth K. Wong, "The Politics of Urban Education as a Field of Study: An Interpretive Analysis," in *The Politics of Urban Education in the United States,* ed. James G. Cibulka, Rodney J. Reed, and Kenneth K. Wong (London: Falmer Press, 1992), pp. 3–26.

5. See Table 2.1.

6. See Paul E. Peterson, Barry G. Rabe, and Kenneth K. Wong, *When Federalism Works* (Washington, D.C.: Brookings Institution, 1986); also see Kenneth K. Wong, *City Choices: Education and Housing* (Albany: State University of New York Press, 1990).

7. William Julius Wilson, *The Truly Disadvantaged: The Inner City, the Underclass, and Public Policy* (Chicago: University of Chicago Press, 1987); Gary Orfield, Susan Eaton, and the Harvard Project on School Desegregation, *Dismantling Desegregation* (New York: New Press, 1996).

8. John Chubb and Terry Moe, *Politics, Markets, and America's Schools* (Washington, D.C.: Brookings Institution, 1990), pp. 64–65.

9. Ibid., p. 62.

10. Arthur Wise, Linda Darling-Hammond, and B. Berry, *Effective Teacher Selection: From Recruitment to Retention* (Santa Monica, Calif.: Rand Corporation, 1987).

11. Illinois State Board of Education, *Illinois Teacher Salary Study* (Springfield: State Board of Education, 1997).

12. David Tyack and Elizabeth Hansot, *Managers of Virtue* (New York: Basic Books, 1982).

13. Robert Lineberry, *Equality and Urban Policy* (Beverly Hills, Calif.: Sage, 1977); Frank Levy, Arnold Meltsner, and Aaron Wildavsky, *Urban Outcomes* (Berkeley: University of California Press, 1974); Kenneth Mladenka, "The Urban Bureaucracy and the Chicago Political Machine: Who Gets What and the Limits to Political Control," *American Political Science Review* 74 (1980): 991–98.

14. Paul E. Peterson, *The Politics of School Reform 1870–1940* (Chicago: University of Chicago Press, 1985).

15. Ibid., p. 207.

16. Paul E. Peterson, *School Politics Chicago Style* (Chicago: University of Chicago Press, 1976), chap. 5; Tyack and Hansot, *Managers of Virtue.*

17. Tyack and Hansot, *Managers of Virtue.*

18. Barbara Jackson and James Cibulka, "Leadership Turnover and Business Mobilization: The Changing Political Ecology of Urban School Systems," in Cibulka, Reed, and Wong, *The Politics of Urban Education in the United States,* pp. 71–86.

19. David Rogers, *110 Livingston Street* (New York: Random House, 1968); Diane Ravitch, *The Great School Wars* (New York: Basic Books, 1974).

20. *Rodriguez v. Los Angeles Unified School District,* Supreme Court of California, S041703 (1994).

21. *Education Week,* September 9, 1992.

22. Kenneth Meier, Joseph Stewart, and Robert England, *Race, Class, and Education* (Madison: University of Wisconsin Press, 1989).

23. Luis Ricardo Fraga, Kenneth J. Meier, and Robert E. England, "Hispanic Americans and Educational Policy: Limits to Equal Access," *Journal of Politics* 48 (1986): 850–76.

24. Marjorie Murphy, *Blackboard Unions: The AFT and the NEA 1900–1980* (Ithaca, N.Y.: Cornell University Press, 1990).

25. Lorraine McDonnell and Anthony Pascal, *Organized Teachers in American Schools* (Santa Monica, Calif.: Rand Corporation, 1979).

26. Edgar Fuller and Jim B. Pearson, eds., *Education in the States* (Washington, D.C.: National Education Association, 1969), p. 673.

27. Kent Redfield, *Cash Clout: Political Money in Illinois Legislative Elections* (Springfield: University of Illinois at Springfield, 1995), p. 58.

28. William Grimshaw, *Union Rule in the Schools* (Lexington, Mass.: D. C. Health, 1979).

29. Stephen Cole also found that union recognition was a key objective in the 1960 teachers' strike in New York City. See Cole, *The Unionization of Teachers: A Case Study of the United Federation of Teachers* (New York: Praeger, 1969).

30. Grimshaw, *Union Rule in the Schools,* p. 150.

31. See William Ayers, "Chicago: A Restless Sea of Social Forces," in *A Union of Professionals: Labor Relations and Educational Reform,* ed. Charles Kerchner and Julia Koppich (New York: Teachers College Press, 1993).

32. Charles Kerchner and Krista Caufman, "Building the Airplane While It's Rolling Down the Runway," in Kerchner and Koppich, *A Union of Professionals.*

33. Ibid., p. 19.

34. Peterson, *City Limits.*

35. Kenneth K. Wong, "Can the Big-City School System Be Governed?" in *Transforming Schools: Rhetoric and Reality,* ed. Peter Cookson and Barbara Schneider (New York: Garland, 1995), pp. 457–88.

36. Linda Darling-Hammond, "Inequality and Access to Knowledge," in *The Handbook of Multicultural Education,* ed. James Banks (New York: Macmillan, in press).

37. Wise, Darling-Hammond, and Berry, *Effective Teacher Selection;* Ronald Ferguson, "Paying for Public Education: New Evidence on How and Why Money Matters," *Harvard Journal on Legislation* 28 (1991): 465–98.

38. Jeannie Oakes, *Keeping Track: How Schools Structure Inequality* (New Haven, Conn.: Yale University Press, 1985); Jeannie Oakes, "Can Tracking Research Inform Practice?" *Educational Researcher* 21, no. 4 (1992): 12–21.

39. Twentieth Century Fund, *Facing the Challenge: The Report of the Twentieth Century Fund Task Force on School Governance* (New York: Twentieth Century Fund Press, 1992), p. 1.

40. Robert Wagner, Jr., "Can School Board Be Saved?" *New York Times,* April 30, 1992, p. A23.

41. Jacqueline Danzberger, Michael Kirst, and Michael Usdan, *Governing Public Schools: New Times, New Requirements* (Washington, D.C.: Institute for Educational Leadership, 1992), p. 56.

42. Organization for Economic Cooperation and Development, *Quality of Schooling: A Clarifying Report* (Restricted Secretariat Report, 1987), p. 13.

43. Rebecca Barr and Robert Dreeben, *How Schools Work* (Chicago: University of Chicago Press, 1983), p. 12.

44. Finn, *Class Size.* Also see Frederick Mosteller, "The Tennessee Study of Class Size in the Early School Grades," *The Future of Children* 5, no. 2 (1995): 113–37; Gene V. Glass and M. L. Smith, *Meta-analysis of Research on the Relationship of Class Size and Achievement* (San Francisco: Far West Laboratory for Educational Research and Development, 1978); Jeremy Finn and Charles M. Achilles, "Answers and Questions about Class Size: A Statewide Experiment," *American Educational Research Journal* 27 (1990): 557–77.

45. Wilson, *The Truly Disadvantaged.*

46. Diane Ravitch and Joseph Viteritti, eds., *New Schools for a New Century* (New Haven, Conn.: Yale University Press, 1997).

47. Organization for Economic Cooperation and Development, *Education at a Glance: OECD Indicators* (Paris: OECD, 1997).

7. REDESIGNING SCHOOL GOVERNANCE AND RESOURCE ALLOCATION: FOUR ALTERNATIVE MODELS

1. See U.S. Department of Education, *Improving America's Schools Act of 1994, Public Law 103-382: The Reauthorization of the Elementary and Secondary Education Act of 1965 and Related Programs* (Washington, D.C.: U.S. Department of Education, 1994).

2. Mary Ann Millsap, Marc Moss, and Beth Gamse, *The Chapter 1 Implementation Study: Final Report, Chapter 1 in Public Schools* (Washington, D.C.: U.S. Department of Education, 1993); Iris C. Rotberg and James J. Harvey, *Federal Policy Options for Improving the Education of Low-Income Students,* vol. 1, *Findings and Recommendations* (Santa Monica, Calif.: Rand Corporation, 1993).

3. Jay Chambers, Thomas Parrish, Margaret Goertz, Camille Marder, and Christine Padilla, *Translating Dollars into Services: Chapter 1 Resources in the Context of State and Local Resources for Education* (Washington, D.C.: U.S. Department of Education, 1993), p. x.

4. A good indicator is the significant differences in teachers' pay between big-city districts and the suburbs. In New York City, the median salary for full-time teachers was $43,014 in 1993–94. The median pay was $63,576 in Suffolk County, $62,316 in West-

chester County, $71,102 in Great Neck, Long Island, $70,000 in Scarsdale, and $70,500 in Bronxville. See Raymond Hernandez, "Wealthier Suburbs Are Joining Revolt on School Outlays," *New York Times,* January 18, 1995, pp. A1, B9.

5. Commission on Chapter 1, *Making Schools Work for Children in Poverty* (Washington, D.C.: Council of Chief State School Officers, 1992), p. 7.

6. Kenneth Wong, Gail Sunderman, and Jaekyung Lee, "Redesigning the Federal Compensatory Education Program: Lessons from the Implementation of Title I Schoolwide Projects," in *Implementing School Reform: Practice and Policy Imperatives,* ed. Magaret C. Wang and Kenneth K. Wong (Philadelphia: Temple University Center for Research in Human Development and Education, 1997) pp. 59–84.

7. Quoted in Ann Bradley, "Teacher Training a Key Focus for Administration," *Education Week,* July 13, 1994, pp. 1, 20.

8. Ibid.

9. Commission on Chapter 1, *Making Schools Work.*

10. Ibid.

11. V. D. Rust and K. Blakemore, "Educational Reform in Norway and in England and Wales: A Corporatist Interpretation," *Comparative Education Review* 34, no. 4 (1990): 512.

12. S. Ball, "Costing Democracy: Schooling, Equality and Democracy in Sweden," in *Education in Search of a Future,* ed. H. Lauder and P. Brown (London: Falmer Press, 1988).

13. Ibid., p. 80.

14. Consortium on Chicago School Research, *A View from the Elementary Schools: The State of Reform in Chicago* (Chicago: Consortium on Chicago School Research, 1993).

15. Kenneth K. Wong and M. Moulton, "Developing Institutional Performance Indicators for Chicago Schools: Conceptual and Methodological Issues Considered," in *Advances in Educational Policy,* vol. 2, *Rethinking School Reform in Chicago,* ed. Kenneth K. Wong (Greenwich, Conn.: JAI Press, 1996), pp. 57–92.

16. Ibid.

17. Ibid.

18. Reported in H. Walberg and R. Niemiec, "Can the Chicago Reforms Work?" *Education Week,* May 22, 1996, p. 39.

19. T. Bryk, D. Kerbow, and S. Rollow, "Chicago School Reform," in *New Schools for a New Century,* ed. Diane Ravitch and Joseph Viteritti (New Haven, Conn.: Yale University Press, 1997), pp. 164–200.

20. P. Sebring, T. Bryk, and J. Easton, *Charting Reform: Chicago Teachers Take Stock* (Chicago: Consortium on Chicago School Research, 1995).

21. Kenneth K. Wong, Robert Dreeben, Jr., Laurence E. Lynn, and Gail L. Sunderman, *Integrated Governance as a Reform Strategy in the Chicago Public Schools* (Chicago: Department of Education and Irving B. Harris Graduate School of Public Policy Studies, University of Chicago, 1997).

22. On the new breed of mayors and their involvement in education, see Kenneth Wong, Pushpam Jain, and Terry Clark, "Mayoral Leadership in the 1990s and Beyond: Fiscally Responsible and Outcome Oriented," paper presented at the annual meeting of the Association for Public Policy Analysis and Management, Washington, D.C., November 1997.

23. Kenneth Wong, *Transforming Urban School Systems: Integrated Governance in Chicago and Birmingham (UK)* (Chicago: Gleacher Center, University of Chicago, 1998).

24. United Nations Educational, Scientific, and Cultural Organization, *World Education Report 1991* (Paris: UNESCO, 1991).

25. J. Coleman and T. Hoffer, *Public and Private High Schools: The Impact of Communities* (New York: Basic Books, 1987).

26. A. Bryk, V. Lee, and P. Holland, *Catholic Schools and the Common Good* (Cambridge: Harvard University Press, 1993).

27. J. Chubb and T. Moe, *Politics, Markets, and America's Schools* (Washington, D.C.: Brookings Institution, 1990).

28. Ibid., p. 99.

29. See M. A. Raywid, "Family Choice Arrangements in Public Schools: A Review of Literature," *Review in Educational Research* 55, no. 4 (1985): 435–67; Kenneth K. Wong, "The Politics of Urban Education as a Field of Study: An Interpretive Analysis," in *The Politics of Urban Education in the United States,* ed. James G. Cibulka, Rodney J. Reed, and Kenneth K. Wong (London: Falmer Press, 1992), pp. 3–26.

30. P. Hill, "Contracting in Public Education," in Ravitch and Viteritti, *New Schools for a New Century,* pp. 61–85.

31. L. Bierlein, "The Charter School Movement, " in Ravitch and Viteritti, *New Schools for a New Century,* pp. 37–60.

32. Quoted in C. Sautter, *Charter Schools: A New Breed of Public Schools* (Oak Brook, Ill.: North Central Regional Educational Laboratory, 1993), p. 3.

33. Ibid., p. 14.

34. See Bierlein, "Charter School Movement."

35. J. Witte, *First Year Report: Milwaukee Parental Choice Program* (Madison: La Follette Institute of Public Affairs, University of Wisconsin–Madison, 1991).

36. J. Witte, C. Thorn, K. Pritchard, and M. Claibourn, *Fourth Year Report: Milwaukee Parental Choice Program* (Madison: University of Wisconsin, 1994), p. 28.

37. P. E. Peterson and C. Noyes, "School Choice in Milwaukee," in Ravitch and Viteritti, *New Schools for a New Century,* pp. 123–46.

38. Ibid., p. 145.

39. J. Chubb and T. Moe, *A Lesson in School Reform from Great Britain* (Washington, D.C.: Brookings Institution, 1992).

40. Chubb and Moe, *Politics, Markets, and America's Schools,* p. 28.

41. Ibid.

42. Ibid., p. 40.

43. G. Whitty, "Creating Quasi-Markets in Education," *Review of Research in Education* 22 (1997): 3–47.

44. H. Pennell and A. West, *Changing Schools: Secondary Schools' Admissions Policies in Inner London in 1995* (London: London School of Economics and Political Science, 1995).

45. Ibid., p. 14.

46. Allison Bullock and Hewel Thomas, *Schools at the Centre?* (London and New York: Routledge, 1997).

47. Wong, *Transforming Urban School Systems.*

Selected Bibliography

Adams, Jacob, Jr. "School Finance Policy and Students' Opportunities to Learn: Kentucky's Experience." *The Future of Children* 7, no. 3 (winter 1997): 79–95.

Advisory Commission on Intergovernmental Relations (ACIR). *Significant Features of Fiscal Federalism.* Washington, D.C.: ACIR, 1980.

———. *Significant Features of Fiscal Federalism.* Vol. 2. Washington, D.C.: ACIR, 1992.

Anton, Thomas. *American Federalism and Public Policy: How the System Works.* New York: Random House, 1989.

Aronson, J. R., and J. Hilley. *Financing State and Local Governments,* 4th ed. Washington, D.C.: Brookings Institution, 1986.

Ayers, William. "Chicago: A Restless Sea of Social Forces." In *A Union of Professionals: Labor Relations and Educational Reform,* ed. Charles Kerchner and Julia Koppich. New York: Teachers College Press, 1993.

Baker, J. "Five-Year Assessment of the State Compensatory Education Program in the Dade County Public Schools, Miami, Florida." Paper presented at the annual meeting of the American Educational Research Association, San Francisco, 1986.

Ball, S. "Costing Democracy: Schooling, Equality and Democracy in Sweden." In *Education in Search of a Future,* ed. H. Lauder and P. Brown. London: Falmer Press, 1988.

Barr, Rebecca, and Robert Dreeben. *How Schools Work.* Chicago: University of Chicago Press, 1983.

Benson, Charles. *The Cheerful Prospect: A Statement on the Future of Public Education.* Boston: Houghton Mifflin, 1965.

———. "Definitions of Equity in School Finance in Texas, New Jersey, and Kentucky." *Harvard Journal on Legislation* 28 (1991): 401–21.

———. *The Economics of Public Education.* New York: Houghton Mifflin, 1961.

———. "State Government Contributions to the Public Schools." In *Public Schools: Issues in Budgeting and Financial Management,* ed. John Augenblick. New Brunswick, N.J.: Transaction, 1985.

Berke, Joel, Margaret Goertz, and Richard Coley. *Politicians, Judges, and City Schools: Reforming School Finance in New York.* New York: Russell Sage Foundation, 1984.

Bierlin, L. "The Charter School Movement." In *New Schools for a New Century,* ed. Diane Ravitch and Joseph Viteritti. New Haven, Conn.: Yale University Press, 1997.

Bradley, Ann. "Teacher Training a Key Focus for Administration." *Education Week,* July 13, 1994.

Brazer, Harvey, and Teresa McCarty. "Municipal Overburden: An Empirical Analysis." *Economics of Education Review* 5 (1986): 353–61.

Brown, Daniel. *Decentralization and School-based Management.* London: Falmer Press, 1990.

Brown, Patricia, and Richard Elmore. "Analyzing the Impact of School Finance Reform." In *The Changing Politics of School Finance,* ed. Nelda Cambron-McCabe and Allan Odden. Cambridge, Mass.: Ballinger, 1982.

Browning, Rufus P., Dale Rogers Marshall, and David H. Tabb. *Protest Is Not Enough.* Berkeley: University of California Press, 1984.

Bryk, A., V. Lee, and P. Holland. *Catholic Schools and the Common Good.* Cambridge: Harvard University Press, 1993.

Bryk, T., D. Kerbow, and S. Rollow. "Chicago School Reform." In *New Schools for a New Century,* ed. Diane Ravitch and Joseph Viteritti. New Haven, Conn.: Yale University Press, 1997.

Bullock, Allison, and Hewel Thomas. *Schools at the Centre?* London and New York: Routledge, 1997.

Burkhead, Jesse. *Input and Output in Large-City High Schools.* Syracuse, N.Y.: Syracuse University, 1967.

Burtless, Gary, ed. *Does Money Matter? The Effect of School Resources on Student Achievement and Adult Success.* Washington, D.C.: Brookings Institution, 1996.

Callahan, Joseph, and William Wilken. "The Federal Interest in Financing Schooling: A View from the States." In *The Federal Interest in Financing Schooling,* ed. Michael Timpane. Cambridge, Mass.: Ballinger, 1978.

———, eds. *School Finance Reform: A Legislator's Handbook.* Washington, D.C.: National Conference of State Legislators, 1976.

Carroll, Stephen, and Rolla Park. *The Search for Equity in School Finance.* Cambridge, Mass.: Ballinger, 1983.

Carter, Launor F. "The Sustaining Effects Study of Compensatory and Elementary Education." *Educational Researcher* (August/September 1984): 4–13.

Cavanagh, Thomas E., and James L. Sundquist. "The New Two-Party System." In *The New Direction in American Politics,* ed. John Chubb and Paul E. Peterson. Washington, D.C.: Brookings Institution, 1985.

Chambers, Jay, Thomas Parrish, Margaret Goertz, Camille Marder, and Christine Padilla. *Translating Dollars into Services: Chapter 1 Resources in the Context of State and Local Resources for Education.* Washington, D.C.: U.S. Department of Education, 1993.

Chicago Urban League. *Access and Outreach: A Directory of Organizations Serving Women and Minorities in the Chicago Area.* Chicago: Chicago Urban League, n.d.

Chubb, John. "Effective Schools and the Problems of the Poor." In *Federal Aid to the Disadvantaged,* ed. Denis Doyle and Bruce Cooper. London: Falmer Press, 1988.

Chubb, John, and Terry Moe. *A Lesson in School Reform from Great Britain.* Washington, D.C.: Brookings Institution, 1992.

———. *Politics, Markets, and America's Schools.* Washington, D.C.: Brookings Institution, 1990.

Cibulka, James G., Rodney J. Reed, and Kenneth K. Wong, eds. *The Politics of Urban Education in the United States.* London: Falmer Press, 1992.

Citrin, Jack. "Introduction: The Legacy of Proposition 13." In *California and the American Tax Revolt*, ed. Terry Schwadron. Berkeley and Los Angeles: University of California Press, 1984.

Clark, David L., and Terry A. Astuto. "The Significance and Permanence of Changes in Federal Education Policy." *Educational Researcher* 15 (1986): 4–13.

Clark, Terry Nichols, ed. *Urban Innovation: Creative Strategies for Turbulent Times.* Thousand Oaks, Calif.: Sage, 1994.

Clark, Terry Nichols, and Lorna Crowley Ferguson. *City Money: Political Processes, Fiscal Strain, and Retrenchment.* New York: Columbia University Press, 1983.

Claus, R. N., and B. E. Quimper. *State Bilingual and ECIA Chapter 1 Migrant Process Evaluation Report: 1987–88.* Saginaw, Mich.: Saginaw Public Schools, 1988.

———. *State Bilingual and ECIA Chapter 1 Migrant Process Evaluation Report: 1988–89.* Saginaw, Mich.: Saginaw Public Schools, 1989.

Cloud, David S. "Shakeup Time." *Congressional Quarterly: Committee Guide,* March 25, 1995.

Clune, William, and P. White. *School-based Management: Institutional Variation, Implementation, and Issues for Further Research.* New Brunswick, N.J.: Center for Policy Research in Education, 1988.

Cole, Stephen. *The Unionization of Teachers: A Case Study of the United Federation of Teachers.* New York: Praeger, 1969.

Coleman, J., and T. Hoffer. *Public and Private High Schools: The Impact of Communities.* New York: Basic Books, 1987.

Coleman, James S., Sara D. Kelly, and John A. Moore. *Trends in School Desegregation, 1968–73.* Washington, D.C.: Urban Institute, 1975.

Commission on Chapter 1. *Making Schools Work for Children in Poverty.* Washington D.C.: Council of Chief State School Officers, 1992.

Consortium on Chicago School Research. *A View from the Elementary Schools: The State of Refrom in Chicago.* Chicago: Consortium on Chicago School Research, 1993.

Coons, John, William Clune, and Stephen Sugarman. *Private Wealth and Public Education.* Cambridge: Harvard University Press, 1970.

Courant, Paul, Edward Gramlich, and Daniel Rubinfeld. "Why Voters Support Tax Limitation Amendments: The Michigan Case." *National Tax Journal* 32 (1980): 1–21.

Cronin, Joseph. "Financing Urban Schools." In *The Changing Politics of School Finance,* ed. Nelda Cambron-McCabe and Allan Odden. Cambridge, Mass.: Ballinger, 1982.

Danzberger, Jacqueline, Michael Kirst, and Michael Usdan. *Governing Public Schools: New Times, New Requirements.* Washington, D.C.: Institute for Educational Leadership, 1992.

Darling-Hammond, Linda. "Inequality and Access to Knowledge." In *The Handbook of Multicultural Education,* ed. James Banks. New York: Macmillan, in press.

———. "Teacher Quality and Equality." In *Access to Knowledge: An Agenda for Our Nation's Schools,* ed. John Goodlad and P. Keating. New York: College Entrance Examination Board, 1990.

de Baca, Mary Rose C., Cecilia Rinaldi, Shelley Billig, and Beatriz Martinez Kinnison. "Santo Domingo School: A Rural Schoolwide Project Success." *Educational Evaluation and Policy Analysis* 13, no. 4 (1991): 363–68.

Defino, M. E., and V. Jenkins. *State Compensatory Education: Final Technical Report, 1984–85.* Austin, Tex.: Austin Independent School District, 1985.

Dreeben, Robert. *The Nature of Teaching.* Glenview, Ill.: Scott, Foresman and Company, 1970.

Dreeben, Robert, and Rebecca Barr. "The Formation and Instruction of Ability Groups." *American Journal of Education* 97, no. 1 (1988): 34–64.

Educational Testing Service. *The State of Inequality.* Princeton, N.J.: Educational Testing Service, 1991.

Elazar, Daniel. *American Federalism: A View from the States,* 2d ed. New York: Crowell, 1972.

Elmore, R. "Backward Mapping: Implementation Research and Policy Decisions." *Political Science Quarterly* 94, no. 4 (1980): 601–16.

Ferguson, Ronald. "Paying for Public Education: New Evidence on How and Why Money Matters." *Harvard Journal on Legislation* 28 (1991): 465–98.

Finn, Jeremy. *Class Size: What Does Research Tell us?* Philadelphia: Temple University Laboratory for Student Success, 1997.

Finn, Jeremy, and Charles M. Achilles. "Answers and Questions about Class Size: A Statewide Experiment." *American Educational Research Journal* 27 (1990): 557–77.

Flinspach, Susan. "State Commitment to Equal Educational Opportunities for Special-Needs Children." *Administrator's Notebook* 34, no. 9 (Chicago: Midwest Administration Center, University of Chicago, 1990).

Fox, James N. "School Finance and the Economics of Education: An Essay Review of Major Works." *Educational Evaluation and Policy Analysis* 11 (spring 1989): 69–83.

Fraga, Luis Ricardo, Kenneth J. Meier, and Robert E. England. "Hispanic Americans and Educational Policy: Limits to Equal Access." *Journal of Politics* 48 (1986): 850–76.

Franklin, D. L., and G. Alan Hickrod. "School Finance Equity: The Courts Intervene. A National Perspective." *Policy Briefs* 6 and 7 (Oak Brook, Ill.: North Central Regional Educational Laboratory, 1990).

Fuhrman, Susan. "Increased State Capacity and Aid to the Disadvantaged." In *Federal Aid to the Disadvantaged,* ed. Denis Doyle and Bruce Cooper. London: Falmer Press, 1988.

———. "Increased State Capacity and Aid to the Disadvantaged." In *Policy Options for the Future of Compensatory Education.* ERIC Doc. No. ED 298 204. 1987.

———. "New Hampshire." In *Shaping Education Policy in the States,* ed. Susan Fuhrman and Alan Rosenthal. Washington, D.C.: Institute for Educational Leadership, 1981.

———. *State Education Politics: The Case of School Finance Reform.* Denver: Education Commission of the States, 1979.

———. "State-level Politics and School Financing." In *The Changing Politics of School Finance,* ed. Nelda Cambron-McCabe and Allan Odden. Cambridge, Mass.: Ballinger, 1982.

Fulton, Mary. "School Finance System Changes." Education Commission of the States, www.ecs.org, November 1998.

Funkhouser, Janice, and Mary Moore. *Summary of State Compensatory Education Programs.* Washington, D.C.: Decision Resources Corporation, 1985.

Garms, Walter, James G. Guthrie, and Lawrence C. Pierce. *School Finance.* Englewood Cliffs, N.J.: Prentice Hall, 1978.

Georgia State Department of Education. *State Compensatory Education Annual Report, 1982–83.* Atlanta: Georgia State Department of Education, 1983.

Glass, Gene V., and M. L. Smith. *Meta-analysis of Research on the Relationship of Class Size and Achievement.* San Francisco: Far West Laboratory for Educational Research and Development, 1978.

Goertz, Margaret. *Chapter 1 Study.* Princeton, N.J.: Educational Testing Service, 1993.

Goertz, R., and Margaret Goertz. "The Quality Education Act of 1990: New Jersey Responds to *Abbott v. Burke.*" *Journal of Education Finance* 16, no. 1 (1990): 104–14.

Gold, Stephen. "State Aid for Local Schools: Trends and Propsects." In *Public Schools: Issues in Budgeting and Financial Management,* ed. John Augenblick. New Brunswick, N.J.: Transaction, 1985.

———. *State and Local Fiscal Relations in the Early 1980s.* Washington, D.C.: Urban Institute, 1983.

———. *The State Fiscal Agenda for the 1990s.* Denver: National Conference of State Legislatures, 1990.

Gold, Stephen D., David M. Smith, Stephen B. Lawton, and Andrea C. Hyary, eds. *Public School Finance Programs of the United States and Canada 1990–91.* Albany, N.Y.: American Education Finance Association and Center for the Study of the States, Nelson A. Rockefeller Institute of Government, 1992.

Goldberg, Carey. "Vermont's School Tax Splits the 'Haves' and 'Have Nots.'" *New York Times,* December 19, 1997.

Greenstone, David, and Paul E. Peterson. *Race and Authority in Urban Politics.* Chicago: University of Chicago Press, 1976.

Grimshaw, William. *Union Rule in the Schools.* Lexington, Mass.: D. C. Heath, 1979.

Guthrie, James, Walter Garms, and Lawrence Pierce. *School Finance and Education Policy,* 2d ed. Englewood Cliffs, N.J.: Prentice Hall, 1988.

Hanushek, Eric. *Making Schools Work.* Washington, D.C.: Brookings Institution, 1994.

Harrison, F., and E. McLoone. *Profiles in School Report: A Decennial Overview.* Washington, D.C.: U.S. Government Printing Office, 1965.

Hartman, William. "District Spending Disparities: What Do the Dollars Buy?" *Journal of Education Finance* 13 (1988): 436–59.

Hedges, Larry, Richard Laine, and Robert Greenwald. "Does Money Matter? A Meta-analysis of Studies of the Effects of Differential School Inputs on Student Outcomes." *Educational Researcher* 23, no. 3 (April 1994): 5–14.

Heid, Camilla A. "The Dilemma of Chapter 1 Program Improvement." *Educational Evaluation and Policy Analysis* 13, no. 4 (1991): 394–98.

Hernandez, Raymond. "Wealthier Suburbs Are Joining Revolt on School Outlays." *New York Times,* January 18, 1995.

Herrington, Carolyn, and Martin Orland. "Politics and Federal Aid to Urban School Systems: The Case of Chapter One." In *The Politics of Urban Education in the United States,* ed. James G. Cibulka, Rodney J. Reed, and Kenneth K. Wong. London: Falmer Press, 1992.

Hill, P. "Contracting in Public Education." In *New Schools for a New Century,* ed. Diane Ravitch and Joseph Viteritti. New Haven, Conn.: Yale University Press, 1997.

Hill, Paul T., Lawrence C. Pierce, and James W. Guthrie. *Reinventing Public Education.* Chicago and London: University of Chicago Press, 1997.

Hirschman, Albert. *Exit, Voice, and Loyalty.* Cambridge: Harvard University Press, 1971.

Illinois State Board of Education. *Illinois Teacher Salary Study.* Springfield: State Board of Education, 1997.

Jackson, Barbara, and James Cibulka. "Leadership Turnover and Business Mobilization: The Changing Political Ecology of Urban School Systems." In *The Politics of Urban Education in the United States,* ed. James G. Cibulka, Rodney J. Reed, and Kenneth K. Wong. London: Falmer Press, 1992.

James, H. Thomas, James A. Kelly, and Walter Garms. *Determinants of Educational Expenditures in Large Cities in the United States.* Palo Alto, Calif.: Stanford University, 1966.

Johns, Roe L., and E. Morphet. *The Economics and Financing of Education: A System Approach.* Englewood Cliffs, N.J.: Prentice Hall, 1975.

Jones, Charles O. "Bill Clinton and the GOP Congress." *Brookings Review* 13 (spring 1995): 30–33.

Jung, Richard, and Michael Kirst. "Beyond Mutual Adaptation, into the Bully Pulpit: Recent Research on the Federal Role in Education." *Educational Administration Quarterly* 22 (summer 1986): 80–109.

Katzman, Martin. *The Political Economy of Urban Schools.* Cambridge: Harvard University Press, 1971.

Kennedy, Mary, Richard Jung, and Martin Orland. *Poverty, Achievement and the Distribution of Compensatory Education Services.* Washington, D.C.: U.S. Department of Education, 1986.

Kerchner, Charles, and Krista Caufman. "Building the Airplane While It's Rolling Down the Runway." In *A Union of Professionals: Labor Relations and Educational Reform,* ed. Charles Kerchner and Julia Koppich. New York: Teachers College Press, 1993.

Kincaid, John. "A Proposal to Strengthen Federalism." *Journal of State Government* 62 (1989): 36–45.

Kirp, David, and Donald N. Jensen. *School Days, Rule Days.* Philadelphia: Falmer Press, 1985.

Kirst, Michael. "The Federal Role and Chapter 1: Rethinking Some Basic Assumptions." In *Federal Aid to the Disadvantaged: What Future for Chapter 1?* ed. Dennis Doyle and Bruce Cooper. London: Falmer Press, 1988.

———. "A New School Finance for a New Era of Fiscal Constraint." In *School Finance Reform: A Legislator's Handbook,* ed. Allan Odden and L. Dean Webb. Cambridge, Mass.: Ballinger, 1983.

———. "Review of Dilemmas in School Finance." *American Journal of Education* 88, no. 4 (August 1980): 502–5.

Kirst, Michael, and Richard Jung. "The Utility of a Longitudinal Approach in Assessing Implementation: A Thirteen-Year View of Title I, ESEA." In *Studying Implementation: Methodological and Administrative Issues,* ed. Walter Williams. New York: Chatham House, 1982.

Kirst, Michael, and S. Somers. "California Educational Interest Groups: Collective Action as a Logical Response to Proposition 13." *Education and Urban Society* 13, no. 2 (1981): 235–56.

Knapp, Michael, and R. A. Cooperstein. "Early Research on the Federal Education Block Grant: Themes and Unanswered Questions." *Educational Evaluation and Policy Analysis* 8, no. 2 (1986): 121–37.

Kozol, Johnathan. *Savage Inequalities.* New York: Crown, 1991.

Ladd, Helen, and Julie Wilson. "Proposition 2½: Explaining the Vote." In *Research in Urban Policy,* ed. Terry N. Clark. Greenwich, Conn.: JAI Press, 1985.

Leppert, Jack, Larry Huxel, Walter Garms, and Heber Fuller. "Pupil Weighting Programs in School Finance Reform." In *School Finance Reform: A Legislator's Handbook,* ed. Joseph Callahan and William Wilken. Washington, D.C.: National Conference of State Legislators, 1976.

Levin, Betsy, et al. *Paying for Public Schools: Issues of School Finance in California.* Washington, D.C.: Urban Institute, 1972.

Levine, G. "Meeting the Third Wave: Legislative Approaches to Recent Judicial School Finance Rulings." *Harvard Journal on Legislation* 28 (1991): 507–42.

Levy, Frank, Arnold Meltsner, and Aaron Wildavsky. *Urban Outcomes.* Berkeley: University of California Press, 1974.

Lewit, Eugene, and Linda Schuurmann Baker. "Class Size." *The Future of Children* 7, no. 3 (winter 1997): 112–21.

Lineberry, Robert. *Equality and Urban Policy.* Beverly Hills, Calif.: Sage, 1977.

Lipson, A., and M. Lavin. *Political Responses to Proposition 13 in California.* Santa Monica, Calif.: Rand Corporation, 1980.

Long, David. "*Rodriguez:* The State Courts Respond." *Phi Delta Kappan* 64 (March 1983): 481–84.

Lortie, Dan C. *Schoolteacher: A Sociological Study.* Chicago and London: University of Chicago Press, 1975.

Lowi, Theodore. "American Business and Public Policy, Case Studies and Political Theory." *World Politics* 16, no. 4 (July 1964): 677–715.

———. *The End of Liberalism,* 2d ed. New York: W. W. Norton, 1979.

Malen, Betty, and Rodney Ogawa. "Professional-Patron Influence on Site-based Governance Councils: A Confounding Case Study." *Educational Evaluation and Policy Analysis* 10, no. 4 (1988): 251–70.

Marshall, Catherine, Douglas Mitchell, and Frederick Wirt. "The Context of State-Local Policy Formation." *Educational Evaluation and Policy Analysis* 8, no. 4 (winter 1986): 347–78.

Martin, Ruby, and Phyllis McClure. *Title I of ESEA: Is It Helping Poor Children?* Washington, D.C.: Washington Research Project of the Southern Center for Studies in Public Policy and the NAACP Legal Defense of Education Fund, 1969.

Massell, D., and M. Kirst. "State Policymaking for Educational Excellence: School Reform in California." In *The Fiscal, Legal, and Political Aspects of State Reform of Elementary and Secondary Education,* ed. V. D. Mueller and M. McKeown. Cambridge, Mass.: Ballinger, 1986.

Mayhew, David R. *Congress: The Electoral Connection.* New Haven, Conn.: Yale University Press, 1974.

McDonnell, Lorraine M., and Milbrey W. McLaughlin. *Education and the Role of the States.* Santa Monica, Calif.: Rand Corporation, 1982.

McDonnell, Lorraine, and Anthony Pascal. *Organized Teachers in American Schools.* Santa Monica, Calif.: Rand Corporation, 1979.

McLaughlin, Milbrey. "Learning from Experience: Lessons from Policy Implementation." *Educational Evaluation and Policy Analysis* 9, no. 2 (1987): 171–78.

———. "The Rand Change Agent Study Revisited: Macro Perspective and Realities." *Educational Researcher* 19, no. 9 (1990): 11–16.

McLaughlin, M., and P. Berman. *Federal Program Supporting Educational Change.* Vol. 8. *Implementing and Sustaining Innovation.* Santa Monica, Calif.: Rand Corporation, 1978.

McLaughlin, Milbrey, and James Catterall. "Notes on the New Politics of Education." *Education and Urban Society* 16 (May 1984): 375–81.

Meier, Kenneth J., and Robert England. "Black Representation and Educational Policy: Are They Related?" *American Political Science Review* 78 (June 1984): 392–403.

Meier, Kenneth, Joseph Stewart, and Robert England. *Race, Class, and Education.* Madison: University of Wisconsin Press, 1989.

Millsap, Mary Ann, Brenda Turnbull, Marc Moss, Nancy Brigham, Beth Gamse, and Ellen Marks. *The Chapter 1 Implementation Study: Interim Report.* Washington, D.C.: U.S. Department of Education, 1992.

Millsap, Mary Ann, Marc Moss, and Beth Gamse. *The Chapter 1 Implementation Study: Final Report, Chapter 1 in Public Schools.* Washington, D.C.: U.S. Department of Education, 1993.

Milne, A. M., and Jay Moskowitz. "Implications of State Programs: The Case of Special Needs Pupils." *Education and Urban Society* 15, no. 4 (1983): 500–524.

Mirel, Jeffrey. *The Rise and Fall of an Urban School System: Detroit, 1907–81.* Ann Arbor: University of Michigan Press, 1993.

Mladenka, Kenneth. "The Urban Bureaucracy and the Chicago Political Machine: Who Gets What and the Limits to Political Control." *American Political Science Review* 74 (1980): 991–98.

Moe, Terry. "Private Vouchers: Politics and Evidence." Paper presented at the conference on Education in Cities: What Works and What Doesn't, sponsored by Temple University Laboratory for Student Success and the Johnson Foundation, Racine, Wis., November 1998.

Moore, Mary, Margaret Goertz, and Terry Hartle. "Interaction of Federal and State Programs." *Education and Urban Society* 15, no. 4 (1983): 452–78.

Mosteller, Frederick. "The Tennessee Study of Class Size in the Early School Grades." *The Future of Children* 5, no. 2 (1995): 113–37.

Mullins, Daniel, and Phillip Joyce. *Tax and Expenditure Limitations and State and Local Fiscal Structures.* Bloomington: Center for Urban Policy and Environment, School of Public and Environmental Affairs, Indiana University, December 1995.

Munger, Frank J., and Richard F. Fenno. *National Politics and Federal Aid to Education.* Syracuse, N.Y.: Syracuse University Press, 1962.

Munley, Vincent G. *The Structure of State Aid to Elementary and Secondary Education.* Washington, D.C.: Advisory Commission on Intergovernmental Relations, 1990.

Murnane, Richard. "Interpreting the Evidence on 'Does Money Matter?'" *Harvard Journal on Legislation* 28 (1991): 457–564.

Murnane, Richard, and Frank Levy. "Education and Training." In *Setting Domestic Priorities,* ed. Henry Aaron and Charles Schultze. Washington, D.C.: Brookings Institution, 1992.

Murphy, Jerome. "Progress and Problems: The Paradox of State Reform." In *Policy-making in Education,* ed. Ann Lieberman and Milbrey McLaughlin. Chicago: University of Chicago Press, 1982.

———. "Title I of ESEA: The Politics of Implementing Federal Education Reform." *Harvard Educational Review* 41 (February 1971): 35–63.

Murphy, J. F., and W. Hack. "Expenditure and Revenue Problems in Central City School Districts: Problems for the 1980s." *Urban Review* 15, no. 4 (1983): 229–44.

Murphy, Marjorie. *Blackboard Unions: The AFT and the NEA 1900–1980.* Ithaca, N.Y.: Cornell University Press, 1990.

Nathan, Richard, and Fred Doolittle. *Reagan and the States.* Princeton, N.J.: Princeton University Press, 1987.

National Association of State Directors of Special Education, Inc. *A Description of State Funding Procedures for Special Education in the Public Schools.* Washington, D.C.: NASDSE, 1982.

National Center for Education Statistics. *Projections of Education Statistics to 2006.* Washington, D.C.: U.S. Department of Education, 1996.

National Commission on Excellence in Education. *A Nation at Risk.* Washington, D.C.: U.S. Government Printing Office, 1983.

New York City Board of Education. *Chapter 1/P.S.E.N. Remedial Reading and Mathematics Program 1985–86 End of the Year Report.* Brooklyn: New York City Board of Education, 1987.

Nitschke, Lori. "Alternate Routes Considered for D.C. Spending Bill." *Congressional Quarterly Weekly Report,* March 2, 1996.

Oakes, Jeannie. "Can Tracking Research Inform Practice?" *Educational Researcher* 21, no. 4 (1992): 12–21.

———. *Keeping Track: How Schools Structure Inequality.* New Haven, Conn.: Yale University Press, 1985.

Oates, Wallace. *Fiscal Federalism.* New York: Harcourt Brace Jovanovich, 1972.

Odden, Allan. "School Finance Reform: An Example of Redistributive Policy at the State Level." Paper presented for the School Finance Project, National Institute of Education, Washington, D.C., 1981.

Odden, Allan, and David Marsh. "State Education Reform Implementation: A Framework for Analysis." In *The Politics of Reforming School Administration,* ed. Jane Hannaway and Robert Crowson. London: Falmer Press, 1989.

Orfield, Gary. *Must We Bus?* Washington, D.C.: Brookings Institution, 1978.

———. *Public School Desegregation in the United States, 1968–1980.* Washington, D.C.: Joint Center for Political Studies, 1983.

———. "Race, Income and Educational Inequality: Students and Schools at Risk in the 1980s." In *School Success for Students at Risk,* by Council of Chief State School Officers. Orlando, Fla.: Harcourt Brace Jovanovich, 1988.

Orfield, Gary, Susan Eaton, and the Harvard Project on School Desegregation. *Dismantling Desegregation.* New York: New Press, 1996.

Orfield, Gary, and Sean Reardon. "Separate and Unequal Schools: Political Change and the Shrinking Agenda of Urban School Reform." Paper presented at the annual meeting of the American Political Science Association, Chicago, 1992.

Organization for Economic Cooperation and Development. *Education at a Glance: OECD Indicators.* Paris: OECD, 1997.

———. *Quality of Schooling: A Clarifying Report.* Restricted Secretariat Report. 1987.

Orland, Martin E., and S. Tillander. "Redistribution and the Education Block Grant: An Analysis of State Chapter 2 Allocation Formulas." *Educational Evaluation and Policy Analysis* 9, no. 3 (1987): 245–57.

Osborne, David, and Ted Gaebler. *Reinventing Government.* Reading, Mass.: Addison-Wesley, 1992.

Palaich, Robert, James Kloss, and Mary Williams. *Tax and Expenditure Limitation Referenda.* Denver: Education Commission of the States, 1980.

Paulston, C. B. *Bilingual Education: Theories and Issues.* Rowley, Mass.: Newbury House Publishers, 1980.

Pennell, H., and A. West. *Changing Schools: Secondary Schools' Admissions Policies in Inner London in 1995.* London: London School of Economics and Political Science, 1995.

Peterson, Paul E. *City Limits.* Chicago: University of Chicago Press, 1981.

——. *The Politics of School Reform 1870–1940.* Chicago: University of Chicago Press, 1985.

——. *The Price of Federalism.* Washington, D.C.: Brookings Institution, 1995.

——. *School Politics Chicago Style.* Chicago: University of Chicago Press, 1976.

Peterson, P. E., and C. Noyes. "School Choice in Milwaukee." In *New Schools for a New Century,* ed. Diane Ravitch and Joseph Viteritti. New Haven, Conn.: Yale University Press, 1997.

Peterson, Paul E. , Barry G. Rabe, and Kenneth K. Wong. *When Federalism Works.* Washington, D.C.: Brookings Institution, 1986.

Phi Delta Kappa. *Gallup Polls of Attitudes toward Education 1969–1984: A Topical Summary.* Bloomington, Ind.: Phi Delta Kappa, 1984.

Picus, Lawrence O., and James L. Wattenbarger, eds. *Where Does the Money Go? Resource Allocation in Elementary and Secondary Schools.* Thousand Oaks, Calif.: Corwin Press, 1996.

Piele, Philip, and John Hall. *Budget, Bonds, and Ballots.* Lexington, Mass.: Lexington, 1973.

Pressman, Jeffrey, and Aaron Wildavsky. *Implementation.* Berkeley: University of California Press, 1973.

"Quality Counts: A Report Card on the Condition of Public Education in the 50 States." Supplement to *Education Week,* January 22, 1997.

Rachal, J., and L. G. Hoffman. "The Relationship between Service Schedule, Additional Services, and Student Gain in a Statewide Grade 2 Compensatory Education Program." Paper presented at the annual meeting of the American Educational Research Association, New Orleans, 1984.

Ravitch, Diane. *The Great School Wars.* New York: Basic Books, 1974.

Ravitch, Diane, and Joseph Viteritti, eds. *New Schools for a New Century.* New Haven, Conn.: Yale University Press, 1997.

Raywid, M. A. "Family Choice Arrangements in Public Schools: A Review of Literature." *Review in Educational Research* 55, no. 4 (1985): 435–67.

Reagan, Michael, and John Sanzone. *The New Federalism,* 2d ed. New York: Oxford University Press, 1981.

Redfield, Kent. *Cash Clout: Political Money in Illinois Legislative Elections.* Springfield: University of Illinois at Springfield, 1995.

Reynolds, Maynard. "A Brief History of Categorical School Programs, 1945–1993." In *Rethinking Policy for At-Risk Students,* ed. Kenneth K. Wong and Margaret C. Wang. Berkeley, Calif.: McCutchan, 1994.

Riddle, W. *Expenditures in Public School Districts: Why Do They Differ?* Washington, D. C.: Congressional Research Service, 1990.

Ripley, Randall, and Grace Franklin. *Congress, the Bureaucracy, and Public Policy.* Homewood, Ill.: Dorsey Press, 1984.

Rivlin, Alice. *Reviving the American Dream.* Washington, D.C.: Brookings Institution, 1992.

Rogers, David. *110 Livingston Street.* New York: Random House, 1968.

Rosenthal, Alan, and Susan Fuhrman. *Legislative Education Leadership in the States.* Washington, D.C.: Institute for Educational Leadership, 1981.

Rotberg, Iris C., and James J. Harvey. *Federal Policy Options for Improving the Education of Low-Income Students.* Vol. 1. *Findings and Recommendations.* Santa Monica, Calif.: Rand Corporation, 1993.

Rowan, Brian, and Larry Guthrie. "The Quality of Chapter 1 Instruction: Results from a Study of Twenty-four Schools." In *Effective Programs for Students at Risk,* ed. Robert Slavin, Nancy L. Karweit, and Nancy A. Madden. London: Allyn and Bacon, 1989.

Rust, V. D., and K. Blakemore. "Educational Reform in Norway and in England and Wales: A Corporatist Interpretation." *Comparative Education Review* 34, no. 4. (1990): 500–522.

Salmon, Richard, Christina M. Dawson, Stephen Lawton, and Thomas Johns, eds. *Public School Finance Programs in the United States and Canada: 1986–87.* Blacksburg, Va.: American Education Finance Association and Virginia Polytechnic and State University, 1987.

Sauter, C. *Charter Schools: A New Breed of Public Schools.* Oak Brook, Ill.: North Central Regional Educational Laboratory, 1993.

Scheirer, Peter. "Metropolitan Chicago Public Schools: Concerto for Grades, Schools and Students in F Major." Draft paper, Metropolitan Opportunity Project, University of Chicago, 1989.

Scribner, Jay, and Donald Layton, eds. *The Study of Educational Politics.* London: Falmer Press, 1995.

Sebring, P., T. Bryk, and J. Easton. *Charting Reform: Chicago Teachers Take Stock.* Chicago: Consortium on Chicago School Research, 1995.

Singer, Judith, and John Butler. "The Education of all Handicapped Children Act: Schools as Agents of School Reform." *Harvard Educational Review* 2 (1987): 125–52.

Slavin, Robert, Nancy L. Karweit, and Nancy A. Madden, eds. *Effective Programs for Students at Risk.* London: Allyn and Bacon, 1989.

Smith, Marshall S. "Selecting Students and Services for Chapter 1." In *Federal Aid to the Disadvantaged: What Future for Chapter 1?* ed. Dennis Doyle and Bruce Cooper. London: Falmer Press, 1988.

Smith, Marshall S., and Jennifer A. O'Day. "Systematic School Reform." In *The Politics of Curriculum and Testing,* ed. Susan Fuhrman and Betty Malen. Bristol, Pa.: Falmer Press, 1991.

South Carolina Department of Education. *Evaluation of the 1987–88 EIA Remedial and Compensatory Program.* Columbia: South Carolina Department of Education, 1989.

———. *What Is the Penny Buying for South Carolina? Assessment of the Third Year of the South Carolina Education Improvement Act of 1984.* Columbia: South Carolina Department of Education, 1987.

Sroufe, Gerald. "Politics of Education at the Federal Level." In *The Study of Educational Politics,* ed. Jay Scribner and Donald Layton. London: Falmer Press, 1995.

Strayer, George, and Robert Haig. *Financing of Education in the State of New York.* New York: Macmillan, 1923.

Stringfield, Sam, Shelly Billig, and Alan Davis. "Chapter 1 Program Improvement: Cause for Cautious Optimism and a Call for Much More Research." *Educational Evaluation and Policy Analysis* 13, no. 4 (1991): 399–406.

Sundquist, James L. *Politics and Policy,* Washington, D.C.: Brookings Institution, 1968.

Taylor, W., and D. Piche. *A Report on Shortchanging Children: The Impact of Fiscal Inequity on the Education of Students at Risk.* Washington, D.C.: U.S. Government Printing Office, 1991.

Timar, Thomas. "Program Design and Assessment Strategies in Chapter 1." In *Rethinking Policy for At-Risk Students,* ed. Kenneth K. Wong and Margaret C. Wang. Berkeley, Calif.: McCutchan, 1994.

———. "Urban Politics and State School Finance in the 1980s." In *The Politics of Urban Education in the United States,* ed. James G. Cibulka, Rodney J. Reed, and Kenneth K. Wong. London: Falmer Press, 1992.

Twentieth Century Fund. *Facing the Challenge: The Report of the Twentieth Century Fund Task Force on School Governance.* New York: Twentieth Century Fund Press, 1992.

Tyack, David, and Elizabeth Hansot. *Managers of Virtue.* New York: Basic Books, 1982.

Underwood, Julie. "School Finance Adequacy as Vertical Equity." *University of Michigan Journal of Law Reform* 28, no. 3 (spring 1995): 493–519.

United Nations Educational, Scientific, and Cultural Organization. *World Education Report 1991.* Paris: UNESCO, 1991.

U.S. Department of Education. *Improving America's Schools Act of 1994, Public Law 103-382: The Reauthorization of the Elementary and Secondary Education Act of 1965 and Related Programs.* Washington, D.C.: U.S. Department of Education, 1994.

———. *Prospects: The Congressionally Mandated Study of Educational Growth and Opportunity: The Interim Report.* Washington, D.C.: U.S. Department of Education, 1993.

U.S. General Accounting Office. *Compensatory Education: Most Chapter 1 Funds in Eight Districts Used for Classroom Services.* Washington, D.C.: U.S. General Accounting Office, 1992.

———. *Intergovernmental Relations: Changing Patterns in State-Local Finances.* Washington, D.C.: U.S. General Accounting Office, 1992.

———. *Magnet Schools: Information on the Grant Award Process.* Washington, D.C.: U.S. General Accounting Office, 1987.

———. *Remedial Education: Modifying Chapter 1 Formula Would Target More Funds to Those Most in Need.* Washington, D.C.: U.S. General Accounting Office, 1992.

———. *School Finance: State Efforts to Reduce Funding Gaps between Poor and Wealthy Districts.* Washington, D.C.: U.S. Government Printing Office, 1997.

van Geel, T. "The Courts and School Finance Reform: An Expected Utility Model." In *The Changing Politics of School Finance,* ed. Nelda Cambron-McCabe and Allan Odden. Cambridge, Mass.: Ballinger, 1982.

Verstegen, Deborah, and Kent McGuire. *School Finance at a Glance.* Denver: Education Commission of the States, 1988.

Wagner, Robert, Jr. "Can School Board Be Saved?" *New York Times,* April 30, 1992.

Wahlke, E. H., W. Buchanon, and L. C. Ferguson. *The Legislative System: Explorations in Legislative Behavior.* New York: John Wiley and Sons, 1962.

Walberg, H., and R. Niemiec. "Can the Chicago Reforms Work?" *Education Week,* May 22, 1996.

Wang, Margaret C., and Kenneth K. Wong, eds. *Implementing School Reform: Practice and Policy Imperatives.* Philadelphia: Temple University Center for Research in Human Development and Education, 1997.

Webb, L Dean. "The Role of Special Interest Groups in the Shaping of State Educational Policy Relative to School Finance: A Case Study." *Journal of Education Finance* 7 (fall 1981): 168–88.

Whitty, G. "Creating Quasi-Markets in Education." *Review of Research in Education* 22 (1997): 3–47.

Williams, M. "Earthquakes or Tremors? Tax and Expenditure Limitations and School Finance." In *The Changing Politics of School Finance,* ed. Nelda Cambron-McCabe and Allan Odden. Cambridge, Mass.: Ballinger, 1982.

Wilson, William Julius. *The Truly Disadvantaged: The Inner City, the Underclass, and Public Policy.* Chicago: University of Chicago Press, 1987.

Wirt, Frederick. "School Policy Culture and State Decentralization." In *The Politics of Education,* ed. Jay D. Scribner. Chicago: University of Chicago Press, 1977.

Wise, Arthur. *Rich Schools, Poor Schools: The Promise of Equal Educational Opportunity.* Chicago: University of Chicago Press, 1972.

Wise, Arthur, Linda Darling-Hammond, and B. Berry. *Effective Teacher Selection: From Recruitment to Retention.* Santa Monica, Calif.: Rand Corporation, 1987.

Witte, J. *First Year Report: Milwaukee Parental Choice Program.* Madison: La Follette Institute of Public Affairs, University of Wisconsin–Madison, 1991.

Witte, J., C. Thorn, K. Pritchard, and M. Claibourn. *Fourth Year Report: Milwaukee Parental Choice Program.* Madison: University of Wisconsin, 1994.

Witte, John, and Daniel Walsh. "Metropolitan Milwaukee District Performance Assessment Report." Staff report no. 4 to the Commission on the Quality of Education in the Metropolitan Milwaukee Public Schools, 1985.

Wong, Kenneth K. "Can the Big-City School System Be Governed?" In *Transforming Schools: Rhetoric and Reality,* ed. Peter Cookson and Barbara Schneider. New York: Garland, 1995.

———. *City Choices: Education and Housing.* Albany: State University of New York Press, 1990.

———. "City Implementation of Federal Antipoverty Programs: Proposing a Framework." *Urban Resources* 5, no. 2 (1989): 27–31.

———. "Fiscal Support for Education in American States: The 'Parity-to-Dominance' View Examined." *American Journal of Education* 97, no. 4 (1989): 329–57.

———. "Governance Structure, Resource Allocation, and Equity Policy." *Review of Research in Education* 20 (1994): 257–89.

———. "Linking Governance Reform to Schooling Opportunities for the Disadvantaged." *Educational Administration Quarterly* 30, no. 2 (May 1994): 153–77.

———. "Policymaking in the American States: Typology, Process and Institutions." *Policy Studies Review* 8, no. 3 (spring 1989): 527–48.

———. "The Politics of Urban Education as a Field of Study: An Interpretive Analysis."

In *The Politics of Urban Education in the United States,* ed. James G. Cibulka, Rodney J. Reed, and Kenneth K. Wong. London: Falmer Press, 1992.

————. *Transforming Urban School Systems: Integrated Governance in Chicago and Birmingham (UK).* Chicago: Gleacher Center, University of Chicago, 1998.

Wong, Kenneth K. , Robert Dreeben, Jr., Laurence E. Lynn, and Gail L. Sunderman. *Integrated Governance as a Reform Strategy in the Chicago Public Schools.* Chicago: Department of Education and Irving B. Harris Graduate School of Public Policy Studies, University of Chicago, 1997.

Wong, Kenneth, Pushpam Jain, and Terry Clark. "Mayoral Leadership in the 1990s and Beyond: Fiscally Responsible and Outcome Oriented." Paper presented at the annual meeting of the Association for Public Policy Analysis and Management, Washington, D.C., November 1997.

Wong, Kenneth K., and M. Moulton. "Developing Institutional Performance Indicators for Chicago Schools: Conceptual and Methodological Issues Considered." In *Advances in Educational Policy.* Vol. 2. *Rethinking School Reform in Chicago,* ed. Kenneth K. Wong. Greenwich, Conn.: JAI Press, 1996.

Wong, Kenneth, Gail Sunderman, and Jaekyung Lee. "Redesigning the Federal Compensatory Education Program: Lessons from the Implementation of Title I Schoolwide Projects." In *Implementing School Reform: Practice and Policy Imperatives,* ed. Margaret C. Wang and Kenneth K. Wong. Philadelphia: Temple University Center for Research in Human Development and Education, 1997.

————. *When Federal Chapter 1 Works to Improve Student Learning in Inner City Schools: Preliminary Findings on Schoolwide Projects in Minneapolis.* Philadelphia: National Center on Education in the Inner Cities, Temple University, 1994.

Wong, Kenneth K., and Margaret C. Wang, eds. *Rethinking Policy for At-Risk Students.* Berkeley, Calif.: McCutchan, 1994.

Yagi, K. *State Disadvantaged Child Project: Evaluation Report, 1983–84.* Portland, Oreg.: Portland Public Schools, 1985.

Index